EPISTEMOLOGY

SOURCES IN CONTEMPORARY PHILOSOPHY

FRANK A. TILLMAN, CONSULTING EDITOR

HARPER & ROW, PUBLISHERS

NEW YORK
EVANSTON
LONDON

EPISTEMOLOGY

New Essays in the Theory of Knowledge

Edited

by

AVRUM STROLL

University of California,
San Diego

CONTENTS

Editor's Introduction   vii

Introduction: Avrum Stroll   1

1. Knowledge   8
   David Rynin: Knowledge, Sensation, and Certainty   8
   Arthur C. Danto: On Knowing That We Know   32
   E. J. Lemmon: If I Know, Do I Know That I Know?   54

2. The Other Minds Problem   83
   Terry Forrest: P-Predicates   83
   Isabel C. Hungerland: My Pains and Yours   107
   Norman Malcolm: The Privacy of Experience   129

3. Saying, Believing, Statements   159
   Henry A. Alexander, Jr.: Comments on Saying and
       Believing   159
   Avrum Stroll: Statements   179

4. Reasons, Causes, Actions   204
   David Pears: Are Reasons for Actions Causes?   204
   A. I. Melden: Philosophy and the Understanding of
       Human Fact   229

Index   251

EDITOR'S INTRODUCTION

No volume by a single scholar can recreate the incessant dialectic of contemporary philosophic inquiry; hence we are offering a series that is a collaboration of many hands. The present series is intended to provide students, teachers, and interested nonprofessionals with collections of essays in every major problem area of contemporary philosophy. Each volume is devoted to a single set of interconnected issues; each issue is currently the subject of intense philosophic discussion. The editors have been uncompromising in their attempt to bring together essays of great clarity and high technical excellence. Most of the essays were written during the last ten years, some newly written for this series; a number have already become contemporary classics. Each collection is large enough to display a cumulative diversity of viewpoint and detail.

In making relatively inaccessible essays available, this series will enable teachers of philosophy to find strategic or supplementary materials for a wide range of courses. To the student it offers the luxury of possessing essays formerly buried in bound journals or closeted in library reserves;. To readers other than teachers and students, the series offers an opportunity to explore contemporary philosophy at first hand. To all readers, it offers original formulations of new ideas and fresh insight into topics of ancient ancestry.

FRANK A. TILLMAN

EPISTEMOLOGY

INTRODUCTION

AVRUM STROLL

As the title indicates, this is a collection of essays in the theory of knowledge, a subject as ancient as philosophy itself. It is not only a new collection, but the essays themselves are new. By saying they are "new," I do not only mean that they have never before appeared in print—although that is in fact true, and in this sense of the term they are examples of the the most recent work of some of the best philosophers in the English-speaking world today. But the word "new" was also chosen for another reason; to suggest that these essays are new in conception; that they are modern examples of the original, exciting, and inventive work which makes contemporary philosophy an absorbing and compelling discipline to those of us who practice it professionally.

Philosophy is, perhaps, unique among the academic disciplines of the twentieth century in constantly returning to old themes, to a relatively small group of issues which its devotees seem compulsively to subject to continuing scrutiny and refinement. And this is why, to the outsider, it appears as if there is no progress in philosophy, no real advance over what went on in the past. There is, I must admit, some substance in such a charge. It is true that philosophers seem, more than other professional thinkers, to walk and rewalk the same pathways. Yet the main thrust of such a charge is essentially misleading. There are good reasons why philosophers do what they do. First is the

1

fact that these questions are fundamental, touching us at the deepest levels of what we can know and do. No matter how he starts out, the philosopher quickly finds himself impelled to work at these deeper levels, to cut beneath the surface inquiries and the superficial answers to them, and to examine the sources that give rise to them. What he finds at these deeper levels, in multiform guises to be sure, are the traditional questions about "the true, the good, and the beautiful," as the phrase goes. Such questions seem to thrust themselves upon him, to demand answers from anyone who, by systematic reflection, wishes to gain real insight into the fundamental features of the world in which he lives.

What is interesting about such questions is how difficult to formulate they are, and, even when formulated, how susceptible to infinite study and to inexhaustible illumination. Like all benthic creatures, the philosopher dwells where the waters are muddy, where vision is obscured, and where the light is faint; and this is why, in an obsessive quest for illumination, he returns again and again to the same fundamental considerations, turning them this way and that in the mind's eye, examining them from this perspective and that, in an effort to achieve a perspicuous view of the matters which the answers to these questions are designed to provide. Advance in philosophy is thus not so much a matter of shifting from one set of issues to another, wrapping them up definitively as it were, as it is a matter of dealing with a basic set of issues in an increasingly sophisticated and illuminating way.

These remarks are singularly applicable to contemporary philosophy, and especially to epistemology, or the theory of knowledge. In this domain of the subject, the basic questions are: "What is knowledge?" and "If this (according to some definition or characterization) is knowledge, how is it possible for us to have knowledge of X?" (where "X" may be replaced by such phrases as "the external world," "the mind of another," and so on. Such questions have been asked by philosophers since time immemorial, and they are still asked; for they take us to the heart of one of the great issues in philosophy; the combat with Skepticism. Here the issue is to resolve those threats to any systematic attempt to give a clear and cogent account of what it is to know anything. That this should be a difficult matter may be surprising to some, since it seems obvious that we do have knowledge, and plenty of it; and yet when one attempts to define, characterize, or describe this, which we seem obviously to have, such efforts invariably open us to the deadly assaults of the skeptical doubter. What makes the Skeptic such a redoubtable foe (no pun intended) is that, at his best, he does not take any stand or put forth any view; his technique rather is to undermine the positions which systematic thinkers themselves advance, usually by working with assumptions and principles which they themselves espouse. Even if, in the end, the Skeptic can be vanquished or circumvented (and it is not obvious that he can be), it is clear that he cannot be ignored. Hence there is the need constantly to re-examine the defenses against him and to provide a theoretical foundation which is immune to his eroding moves. In part, the need to emphasize the same old questions, so characteristic of philosophy, is to be explained as the need to give an accurate, true account of things as they really are, and this turns out to be a more difficult task than one might have supposed. In particular, it requires enormous sophistication and the use of new techniques to say in a simple, readily understandable way how things are. It is characteristic of modern philosophy to have developed such techniques; and in the development and application of such procedures lie the possibilities of genuinely creative work, as well as the possibilities of conceptual advance.

In my judgment, the present volume is an excellent illustration of how new insights can emerge from such persistent, sophisticated inquiries into perennial problems. The ten contributors, left free to choose their own subjects, have focussed their attention upon a narrow range of questions—questions which are fundamental in the sense described above. They deal with such issues as: "What is knowledge?" "What is a person?" "How can we know that another is in pain?" "What is it to say something true about the world (e.g., to make a statement) ?" and so forth. Yet each of the essayists deals with his particular concern in his own way, and from his own perspective. Such inquiries result in a transformation of the familiar questions, to a shift in the light which exposes them, and to the depiction of features which others have not noticed. It is by such devices that "progress" takes place in this subject.

Let me now turn from these general remarks to somewhat more explicit comments on the main contents of each of the papers. Three of them deal, broadly speaking, with the question "What is knowledge?" In "Knowledge, Sensation and Certainty," David Rynin attacks this question directly, defending the view that we have knowledge (1) when what we claim to know is true, (2) that we believe that it is, and (3) that we can give adequate evidence that it is. Each of these conditions is in turn explained and defended. The main burden of his paper is to confute those views that identify knowledge with sensation, or knowledge with certainty. There is a considerable overlap between the matters discussed by Rynin and those discussed by Arthur Danto in "On Knowing That We Know," and by E. J. Lemmon in "If I Know, Do I Know That I Know?" Both of these writers offer ingenious arguments to show that it is possible to know something without knowing that one knows that something. Professor Danto's argument begins with the widely accepted assumption that whatever analysis one finally offers for "m know that s," such an analysis must satisfy the condition that "m understands that s." But, he argues, if this is so, then the following considerations may be advanced in support of the thesis that it is possible to know something without knowing that one knows that something. Let s be the sentence "m knows that t," and let us substitute this expression for the variable "s" in the matrix, "m knows that s," thus transforming this into "m knows that m knows that t." But now, he states, it is quite obvious that "m knows that m knows that t" must satisfy a truth condition in excess of the truth conditions for "m knows that t." For the latter to be true, it is required that m understand t, while for the former to be true, it is required in addition that m understand the sentence "m knows that t." But the latter requires no such thing, for it is possible that men might know a great deal, and yet not know that they know these things because they do not understand what knowledge is, or what "know that" means. Professor Lemmon undertakes to develop an analysis of "know" which differs from that offered by Professor Rynin. He claims that "I know that *p*," if and only if "I have learned (found out) that *p*, and have not forgotten that *p*." On the basis of this analysis, which he defends by appeals both to ordinary usage and by testing it against counter examples, he shows that it is not analytic that if *A* knows that *p*, then *A* knows that *A* knows that *p*. His conclusion is similar to that of Danto, but he arrives at this goal by the use of strikingly different techniques and by a radically different route.

The papers by Norman Malcolm, "The Privacy of Experience," Isabel C. Hungerland, "My Pains and Yours," and Terry Forrest, "*P*-Predicates," each deal, roughly speaking, with sophisticated versions of the Other Minds Problem. Each of these writers proffers what amounts to a different "solution" to this classical conundrum. The full impact of each of these papers is difficult to capture in a brief summary, but each is an impressive example of the way in which modern techniques of analysis can be brought to bear on a difficult and resistant problem. Mr. Forrest argues that the supposed asymmetry between my mind and the mind of another stems from assumptions which turn out to be untenable, if not positively incoherent, when exposed to detailed analysis, while Mrs. Hungerland suggests that the concept of being in pain not only refers to an inner feeling and to an outward manifestation, but that these two aspects are so related that no "logical wedge" can be driven between them. Her general point is that the notion of a wholly inner (private) feeling called "pain" is empty, and the notion of "pain-behavior" which is not manifesting behavior is equally empty. The position she thus advances turns out to be an intermediate position between crude behaviorism, on the one hand, and the doctrine of the privacy of the mind on the other. Professor Malcolm convincingly develops the thesis that there is no sense of the expression "same pain" such that it is impossible for two people to have the same pain, and via this account shows that the underlying model which leads to the Other Minds Problem is essentially "a mountain of confusion."

Professor Henry Alexander's paper, "Comments on Saying and Believing," is a powerful attack, utilizing the latest techniques of ordinary language philosophy, on the position (now widely held) that when A asserts that p, A believes that p. Through a series of detailed examples he shows how such claims misdescribe the facts, that in no sense is this claim generally true; and then goes on to diagnose the factors which impel philosophers to tell us that anyone who states that p, implies that he believes it. In my judgment, this paper goes further toward solving the difficulties attending the recent discussions of "presupposing" and "contextual implication" than any that has hitherto appeared in the literature. In "Statements," using somewhat similar techniques, Avrum Stroll attempts to show how two common philosophical views about the nature of statements—those identifying them with sentences or utterances, and those holding them to be nonlinguistic, mysterious entities—arise from adherence to a conceptual model ("the vehicle-content" model) which is highly compelling, but which turns out to be misleading in a variety of ways. In particular, such a model produces a disposition in philosophers to give distorted descriptions of statements. At the end of his paper, he suggests alternative ways of characterizing statements which illuminate them more accurately and which minimize the tendency to give such distorted accounts.

The final two articles in the volume, "Are Reasons For Actions Causes?" by David Pears, and "Philosophy and The Understanding of Human Fact," by A. I. Melden, show the close connection between epistemological considerations and moral problems. Mr. Pears discusses the commonly received, contemporary view that reasons for actions are not causes. Those who assert that reasons for action are causes maintain that when an action is performed for a reason it is caused by the agent's desire and information, and is such that if the agent were to give his reason in full what he said would entail that it was caused by that desire and that information. After refining this thesis until it becomes acceptably clear for appraisal, Pears discusses three arguments which are now commonly advanced against it; and these in turn he reformulates in order to appraise them. His conclusion, after a meticulous examination of the various steps they involve, is that none of them is cogent, and accordingly that they do not destroy the thesis that reasons for actions are causes. This paper is unquestionably an important contribution to our ultimate understanding of whether human actions can be brought under scientific descriptions, and thus directly bears upon the question of the truth or falsity of some form of materialism. Professor Melden also touches on this theme, taking a different position. His paper primarily deals with the question whether, and in what way, the philosopher can be concerned with understanding the world in which we live. He challenges, in a very persuasive way, the common view that philosophy, insofar as it engages in conceptual clarification, is "merely engaged in a kind of intellectual sanitation in order to prepare the way for cultivation by others of the inquiry into those facts that really interest us." His contention is that the work of the philosopher, insofar as it is successful in achieving conceptual clarification as such, not only sharpens but "enriches his sense of the way things are." He illustrates this point with regard to the concept of a human action, arguing—as against Pears—that reasons for action are not causes, and that part of what a philosopher can understand about the world is such facts as these.

In this brief survey I have not brought out the considerable overlap in particular themes which these essays exhibit, nor have I indicated the depth of concern they reveal about the importance and the difficulty of the problems under investigation. Even though the methods employed by the various writers differ from one another, in some cases markedly so, all of them are invested with seriousness of purpose and intensity of vision. In my judgment they make a remarkable collection. But to feel the full impact of these comments the reader must turn to the essays themselves; and this I now invite you to do.

KNOWLEDGE

KNOWLEDGE, SENSATION, AND CERTAINTY

DAVID RYNIN

It is some years now since Plato undertook to show (with some success, I believe) that knowledge is not sensation. And few will be found to disagree with him openly and in so many words; but it seems to me that the tacit assumption that knowledge is indeed sensation underlies many views that regularly show themselves in epistemological discussions. Even where the identity is not assumed, serious errors arise, I believe, because of a mistaken notion of the role that sensation does play in knowing, for that it does usually play an important role can hardly be denied, at least when one considers knowledge of nature as contrasted with conceptual knowledge as this is exhibited in, say, logic and mathematics.

Closely connected with the above-mentioned error is the view that knowledge implies certainty. For concerning what is given in sensation we are thought to be in some sense certain, it is indubitable, and hence if knowledge implies certainty it might be supplied in sensation. The assumption of the intimate connection of sensation with certainty is revealed with exceptional clarity in the so-called problem of the knowledge of other minds, or, as it might better be expressed if one goes by the literature, *knowledge of other pains*. Here, as we all know, the difficulty seems to be that as we cannot sense other people's pains, we have no grounds for claiming that we know

This paper was originally written to be read before the *Graduate Students Philosophy Club*, University of California, Berkeley.

that they have them, for we might be mistaken. We can, it is sometimes granted, know that others *behave* as if they were in pain, but lacking direct access to their sensations or feelings we lack that certainty required for *knowledge* that they have them. The implication seems clear: if we could sense their pains as we can our own, we could be certain that they have them and the problem of the knowledge of other minds would be solved; or if not solved then at any rate deprived of its special character that makes it so morbidly fascinating to many.

Although above I spoke in the usual manner of errors and mistakes, I disapprove of such language, which I consider on the whole question-begging, so allow me to state my position more clearly. It seems evident that few, if any, words, especially those central to philosophical discussions, are possessed of one and only one meaning, if this be determined by actual usage. And if someone strongly desires to use the term "knowledge," or any of its forms or variants, with the sense of "sensation," I would not try to prevent it. For there is, indeed, one well-known sense of the term which appears to come rather close to this, namely, so-called "knowledge by acquaintance." Having once met a man face to face, it would not be wholly wrong to say, "Yes, I know him." But this is a very thin sense indeed. And even here, the term "him" would normally be held to refer to more than to the immediately given, to the sense data which I report when affirming my knowledge of him. The enduring, endlessly complex spatiotemporal history which constitutes the man I claim to know transcends in almost all respects the practically infinitesimal aspect the sensing of which constitutes the grounds for my claim that I know him. Even if we identify the sensa had by me, when I supposedly met him, as in some way a part of him, which is to say the least a dubious sense of "part," it is an assumption that the whole of which they are considered a part actually exists in the manner, whatever it be, implied when I speak of him, i.e., of the animal in question. In any case, the sense in which it might be held that I am certain of having the sensa at the moment of having is not applicable to my claim that I know him, for clearly *he* is not *given* in the sense that the sensa said to be of him are given. I could, that is even when having them, be mistaken in supposing that the sensation was of the man in question. Thus, we shall not even have in the case of knowledge by acquaintance all that is implied by the term "knowledge" if this involves certainty. But all this is beside the point, for the sense of "knowledge" I wish to consider is not what goes by the name of "knowledge by acquaintance," but rather that sometimes called "knowledge about" or "knowledge that." And to this I now turn.

The conception in question may well be called "the classical conception of knowledge." For it is roughly what I take to be Plato's conception as formulated by him in *Theatetus* that is here under discussion. According to this well-known conception, knowledge is true opinion or belief combined with reason, i.e., for which the claimant to knowledge can give adequate grounds, or a rational account or justification. Among contemporary authors this conception plays a central role. Thus Hintikka in his recently published work *Knowledge and Belief*[1] seems to be working with a special form of this general conception; and Ayer in his *The Problem of Knowledge*[2] tells us that "the necessary and sufficient conditions for knowing that something is the case are first, that what one is said to know be true, secondly, that one be sure of it, and thirdly, that one should have the right to be sure." He puts the main stress on the third condition and devotes much of his discussion to elucidating "the legitimacy of the title to be sure" (p. 35).

My own version reads as follows: A knows that P if and only if (1) P, (2) A believes that P, and (3) A can[3] give adequate evidence that P, where the variable "P" stands for a proposition or statement; this being understood as a cognitively meaningful declarative sentence, i.e., one which when uttered is governed by truth rules, rules specifying its necessary and/or sufficient truth conditions, as the user understands it.

The first requirement is the familiar and generally accepted one according to which one cannot know what isn't so; the second, a rather weak requirement, is useful nevertheless among other things for eliminating the so-called "logical oddity" involved in *A*'s saying, "I know that *P*, but I don't believe it"; and the third, the crucial element, is introduced to enable us to distinguish between chance true belief and genuine knowledge. So-called "knowledge by acquaintance" may be understood as simply that special case in which the whole content of the proposition is assumed to be exhausted by the sensa, the sensing of or acquaintance with which is supposed to give the knowledge by acquaintance, and where seeing is, so to speak, believing, that is, the limiting case in which giving adequate evidence that *P* is identical with pointing to the data constituting a sufficient condition that *P*. As it may be doubted that such cases are very common even if possible (I shall not go into this now), what follows will be concerned solely with *knowledge about* or *knowledge that*.

I take it for granted that such knowledge does exist and in abundance. If I did not think so I could see no reason for trying to clarify the concept itself, for it seems to me that it would be an obvious waste of time to try to formulate a concept of knowledge that applied to nothing. While not going so far as to infer the existence of an entity or process from that of a term purporting to name it, I yet think that we are, in general, justified in assuming that, subject to correction, a designative term constantly in use is not without denotation in at least some of its senses.

Thus it is a source of amazement to me that intelligent men should be found who demonstrate, for instance, that there are and can be no synonyms in a language. What is astonishing is not their often impressive cleverness but why they think it worthwhile to define a familiar term in such a manner that it could have no possibility of application. Similarly, when someone formulates the sense of "knowledge" in such a way that it is extremely unlikely, if not impossible, that there be any knowledge, I am perplexed, and want to know why they think it worth their while to formulate such a sense. As I said, I would certainly not prevent them from doing so, even if I had the power, but I think it only fair that in return they should not try to prevent others from formulating a sense ac-

cording to which the term might find application. That there
are senses of "knowledge" in which the term has denotation
I consider to be beyond question. Thus I take it for granted
that some men know more than others, that modern technology
rests on a vast amount of knowledge, that the last two centuries
have witnessed an unprecedented increase in knowledge and
the rate of its growth, etc. And I should think that theory of
knowledge or epistemology would have among its tasks elucidating the sense or senses according to which the above assertions are true, not demonstrating that they can't be.

And speaking of theory of knowledge, allow me to register
a mild complaint against the prevailing use of the term "theory"
in philosophical discussions. Where I come from the term
"theory" is more or less a synonym for "hypothesis," usually
general in character. Theories, at least in the sciences, contain
theorems, ideally testable, and in any case such as to allow *truth*
or *falsity* or at least *probability* or *confirmability* to be predicated
of them. But in philosophy it seems quite in order to call any
kind of talk, especially systematic talk about or in support of
a terminology, "a theory." Thus theory of value generally appears to consist in telling us what, for example, value is, in
the sense of what the speaker means by the term "value";
ethical theory, the elucidation of a vocabulary of ethical terms;
and theory of knowledge, the laying out of a terminology involving the word "knowledge" or "to know"; but explaining
and enstating a vocabulary seem to me to be at most prelimi-
naries to the formulation of a theory, which, using these terms,
tells us something about the relations among their denotata,
if any.

Now a systematic way of talking about a subject matter
is certainly a fine thing, and one may deplore the extent to
which much philosophic discussion is vitiated by failure to prepare an adequate vocabulary; but the best such vocabulary
seems to me not yet a theory in what I would like to call
"the proper sense" of the term, namely a system of testable
general hypotheses concerning a certain subject matter. But
enough of this. For, while I should be much happier if there

were less pretentious talk about philosophical theories amongst us, I must admit that no one has given me any kind of valid certificate authorizing me to be happy, so back to the theory of knowledge once more.

An adequate theory of knowledge (in the sense of "theory" here deplored) would, in my opinion, be one that explained what it means to know something, in that sense of "knowledge" in which the earlier-mentioned views turn out to be correct. A sense of "knowledge" that failed to do justice to these claims would appear to me to be of little interest, except perhaps for generating philosophic squabbles or that masochistic pleasure that many perverse souls find in denigrating the human race and its achievements—the pleasure in self-belittlement and abasement that characterizes so much dogmatic skepticism. In short, if we do not in contemporary science have knowledge then we ought to find another term that enables us to distinguish between what we have there in abundance and lack in certain pseudo sciences: Few if any men know when they will die, while most of us know when, or at least that, we were born; we do not know whether intelligent beings inhabit other heavenly bodies, but we do know that there is hydrogen in the sun; and some but not all men know the nature of electricity in the sense that they are familiar with the equations describing electrical phenomena and are able with their help and other knowledge to harness such energy and use it in the variety of ways known to all of us.

I want now to show how the classical sense of "knowledge" mentioned above does justice to these claims and distinctions, and how that sense establishes that knowledge is not sensation, although it often does involve sensation; and that certainty, being sure, in the sense of incorrigibility or impossibility of being wrong or mistaken, is not a necessary condition of such knowledge and is in fact incompatible with it; and that, finally, we can know that there are other minds and much about them even if we cannot share other people's feelings, and must admit that with respect to any knowledge claim, however justified, we must answer "yes" to such questions as: "But couldn't you be mistaken?" or "Isn't it possible that what you claim to know isn't so?"

My version of the classical definition runs, you will recall, as follows: *A* knows that *P* if and only if (1) *P*, (2) *A* believes that *P*, and (3) *A* can give adequate evidence that *P*. It should be noted that in the above formulation the sentence (propositional) variable "*P*" appears in all of its occurrences unquoted. That is, the sentence represented by "*P*" in the formula is to be understood as not about expressions but about states of affairs in the world so to speak. Of course, in view of the well-known equivalence of " '*P*' is true" and "*P*" (I am aware of the precautions necessary here), I could have said equally well that *A* knows that *P* if (1) "*P*" is true, (2) *A* believes that "*P*" is true, and (3) *A* can give adequate evidence that "*P*" is true—"*P*" here being replaceable by some sentence in a language understood by *A*, and expressing a certain definite proposition. But I prefer the form given above if only to avoid certain sources of possible confusion. I have in mind, for example, Ayer's requirement, laid down in his *The Problem of Knowledge,* that "what one is said to know be true." This seems to me to suggest strongly that Ayer holds that what we know when we have knowledge are propositions, for it is of these that I suppose truth and falsity are predicated. But in my view what we know are not propositions but, if I may use the term, facts. That is, when I seek knowledge it is of the nature of things or of certain states of affairs. But although propositions are in my view made true by their correspondence with matters of fact, i.e., states of affairs, the object of knowledge, what we know when we know, is not primarily something linguistic or logical, but something that is the case. It may of course be the case that a certain proposition is true, but even then it is not in my opinion (or vocabulary) the proposition that is known, whatever it means to know a proposition, but its truth, or being true. But there may be no real issue here, for Ayer may be simply careless in stating his view, or interpret it in a sense that might leave it not different from my own.

Now when we assert *"P,"* or "that *P,"* or even *" 'P'* is true" we do so by uttering in some form or other certain sentences. And if our assertion be cognitively meaningful, as it must if we are to understand it, or be understood by others when asserting what we assert, there must be in the language of which the sentence is an element some well-understood rule which assigns to this sentence, assuming it to be a proposition, some specifiable—and I would add ascertainable—state of affairs such that, if it exists, the proposition in question, i.e., that expressed by the sentence uttered, is true; or such that, if it does not exist, the proposition is false. At least this holds if we are talking about propositions that enter into knowledge claims. And if our knowledge claim be affirmative, *"P"* must be governed by a truth rule specifying a sufficient condition for its truth; and if negative, then by a truth rule specifying a necessary condition for its truth; and if the claim is to be possibly true as well as possibly false, then both kinds of truth conditions must be specifiable.

Thus if we assert that in a specific instance knowledge is (or isn't) had, this presupposes that we understand what it is to have knowledge, and the same for denials. Hence if radical skepticism, the denial (perhaps even of the possibility) of knowledge, is to make sense, it must at least be possible, unless the matter be foreclosed by some definition, that radical skepticism be mistaken, and that we know how to ascertain whether it is or not. I apologize for repeating these old truths, but constant neglect of them seems to me to justify occasional timely repetition. Among these truths that need repeating when talking about knowledge, its nature and possibility, is the following: both the affirmation and denial of knowledge claims presuppose a subject matter concerning which the claims are made. That is, if I claim to know that tomatoes are edible this presupposes, in addition to knowledge being possible, that there are tomatoes and that some things are edible, or at least that there might be such things as tomatoes and such properties as edibility. And these presuppositions in turn themselves presuppose that the speaker understands what he is talking about when using the terms that enter into the propositions expressing these presuppositions.

Thus if, for example, I claim that *A* knows that tomatoes are edible, this claim of mine presupposes that there are knowers, since it is assumed that *A* is one; that there are propositions, since "tomatoes are edible" is taken to be or expresses one; that some propositions are true and some false, since my claim implies that "tomatoes are edible" or some synonymous statement is true; that there are facts describable, such as tomatoes being edible, whose existence makes propositions asserting them true; that there are therefore tomatoes; that likewise some people have beliefs, since my claim involves the assertion that *A* believes that tomatoes are edible; that some people can give adequate evidence in support of propositions, that therefore there is a category of facts that are evidential; that there exists a criterion or scale for rating evidence with respect to adequacy, etc., etc.

It is evident, even if further analysis leads us to the view that the presuppositions of "*A* knows that tomatoes are edible" be finite, that they constitute a very large number and that in any instance of making and supporting a knowledge claim it is impossible to go into all of them, attempting to establish them all prior to taking up the knowledge claim itself. Only when it is assumed, taken for granted, that all the presuppositions are satisfied does the question of the truth of the knowledge claim legitimately appear on the scene, and it is only the requirements that *A* believes that *P*, that *P*, and that *A* can give adequate evidence that *P* that we are under obligation to establish if we are to establish our knowledge claim. This does not imply of course that these assumptions are true.

Only if our question be not whether, say, *A* knows that tomatoes are edible, but rather the question whether there be any tomatoes, need we take up the question as to whether this object before me is a tomato—the currently favorite object of "epistemological" investigations. The questions thus as to whether what I see before me is a tomato and if so what is

affirmed or denied when it is affirmed or denied that I can or
do *see* the tomato or any part of it, however important they
be, seem to me not to be *central* ones in the theory of knowledge properly understood. The questions: "Is this a tomato?"
"What do I see when I see a tomato?" "Are tomatoes classes
of sense data or physical objects?" seem to me, that is, to
have very little to do with what it means to say that someone
knows that something is a tomato or that tomatoes have certain
properties. Some of these last questions are, I believe, the
proper concern of pomology, assuming the tomato is a fruit;
some have to do with linguistics, those that concern the senses
of the verb "to see"; and some possibly with what ought to
go by the name of "philosophical theory of perception," whatever that is. But none of them in my opinion has much to do
with theory of knowledge.

Percepts, sense data, sensation, ideas, impressions, the given
in experience, do not in my opinion in the least play the role
in theory of knowledge which the epistemological tradition
usually assigns to them, namely, the role of being themselves
the ultimate objects of knowledge or constituents of its objects.
Percepts, sensations, the given in experience, ideas, etc., are in
general, to begin with, simply natural signs of the presence of
objects or facts that knowers seek to know, in that sense of "to
know" that the theory of knowledge, if one wishes to call it a
theory, seeks to explain.

To raise the question whether a certain person or anyone
has knowledge about tomatoes presupposes in general, as I
said, that there are tomatoes and that they can be recognized
by reliable signs. To ask whether it is possible for someone
to know something about another mind presupposes that there
are, or at least may be, other minds and that one can locate
the individuals the knowledge of whose mentality is in question;
and it presupposes as well that there be signs of mentality,
evidence available from which it is possible to infer the presence of that quality of mind the possible knowledge of which
is presupposed in the question as to whether someone knows
that there is such a quality in such a mind. Unless we under-

stand what it means, i.e., what the truth conditions are, for someone to have knowledge of someone's mentality, the question cannot legitimately arise as to whether someone or anyone can know anything about it; but if we have this understanding then it is by that very fact *possible* to get evidence for or against the claim itself.

I wish now to argue that just as it is not the case that to have knowledge about a tomato requires that we be given in sense awareness the qualities whose correct attribution to the tomato would make true a statement about it (whose truth is entailed by a correct claim to have such knowledge), so it is not the case that in order to have knowledge of another's mind, even in fact of his feelings or pains, one must have given in sense awareness the quality correctly attributed to that mind in a true knowledge claim about it.

But it is required in order to have knowledge about a tomato that there be such and it is the primary role of sensation to locate for us the object to be known. It is by means of, among other things, the perceived-round-redness that we become aware of the presence before us of a tomato concerning which we may wish to come to know something. That round redness is not of course itself the tomato, but it normally is a reliable sign of the presence of one, a sign whose reliability we may put to the test in a wide variety of ways and which we normally find confirmed. And even if, contrary to the most obvious fact, the tomato could be conceived as identical with our percept of it, the having of the percept would not constitute *knowledge* of the tomato but merely *perception* of the tomato, which is obviously something other than the knowledge of it. At most in this case awareness of the tomato percept would constitute evidence that a tomato is there, which is not knowledge of the tomato but of something else, namely, that a tomato is there. To have knowledge of *it* presupposes that it is there, and its being there first makes possible learning something *about* what is there other than that it is indeed there. If it is there I may claim to know that it is soft and mealy or firm and tart, and by suitable tests establish the truth of what

I assert. And this brings to light the second main role of sensation or awareness in knowledge, namely, that of giving us evidence tending to verify or confirm the proposition whose truth constitutes one of the three necessary conditions for establishing the knowledge claim, according to the conception of knowledge based on the classical definition as given above.

Sensation, that is, enters into knowledge in two main ways: (1) it locates for us the thing to be known, and (2) under suitable conditions presents us with data entering into the confirmation or testing of the correctness of our knowledge claim, by presenting us with evidence that bears directly or indirectly on the truth value or probability of the proposition whose truth constitutes one of the necessary conditions for the correctness of our knowledge claim. The perceived data that follow on certain operations on the object to be known constitute direct evidence for the truth of the statement in question just to the extent that the proposition in question is given content identical with or entailed by the data in question making their appearance upon the relevant test operations being performed. It is evident that this is not always the case. Generally the data observed consequent on the relevant operations are indirect evidence for, or perhaps against, the truth of the proposition in question, lend to it at best some probability, confirm it only to some degree or other, or the contrary.

But this point can be made too strong. Assuming I have a tomato before me, I can ascertain with little effort that it is soft and mealy or firm and tart; I can with practically no difficulty establish that diamond scratches glass, and glass copper and the like; or, if too much is assumed in affirming that this is diamond, glass, or copper, I can at least determine with as much confidence as I wish that this piece of stuff scratches that and that that in turn scratches the other. I can determine that this stuff which, perhaps with the best of reasons I take to be sugar disappears when dropped into that liquid I take to be water; that this animal jumps when I jab it with a pin, growls menacingly when I attempt to take away its food, wags its tail when I pet it, and so on. And these determinations which I can make allow me to make certain inferences via certain rules that greatly increase the scope of the knowledge I can base on these observations. Thus if A scratches B I can infer that A is harder than B; if this disappears when dropped into that liquid, then it is soluble; if this jumps when I jab it with a pin I infer that it is alive and sentient; if it growls when I attempt to remove its food I infer that it is angry; if it wags its tail when petted I infer that it is pleased. And if one asks with what right I make these inferences the answer is that I understand "being harder than" in such a way that A scratching B is a sufficient condition that A is harder than B; and I understand "being soluble" in such a way that if A disappears when dropped into a clear liquid B then A is soluble in B; and "being sentient" in such a way that if something animal-like jumps when jabbed with a pin it is sentient; that an animal is angry if it growls menacingly when I attempt to take away its food, and pleased if it wags its tail upon being petted.

Note that I do not *identify* scratching and being harder than, disappearing and being soluble, growling and being angry, etc., but relate the first to the second as at best a sufficient condition for it only. This is not an unimportant point since the identification of objects or properties with sense data, or sequences of them arranged according to some natural law or formula, appears to many including myself most implausible. Such identification lies at the root of phenomenalism in the form made familiar by Berkeley, Kant, and many modern authors. But the crude identification of the thing with the class of sense data said to be of it cannot account for the predictive element in our knowledge of things, for from the mere class we can form no idea of the order and connectedness of the elements. Hence some authors have replaced the idea of a class by the law itself connecting the members, seeing in the idea of substance or thinghood the notion of the permanent amidst change, which at once underlies and explains its appearances.

But I find as objectionable the view that a thing or sub-

stance is a law connecting sense data as I do that it is a class
of sense data, although it must be admitted that if one had to
choose, the idea of law or function certainly seems more
adequate. It seems to me, however, that it is unnecessary to
define "substance" or "thing" or "physical object" or "property" in order to make use of such terms in describing and
explaining the world. What is necessary is only that we understand our concepts and statements into which they enter
sufficiently to enable us to establish the truth or falsity (or
some would say probability) of statements we make about
things and substances and properties. Thus it is only necessary
to lay down partial truth rules for this to be possible, that is,
to specify rules according to which it will follow from the
presence of certain data or facts that certain statements are
true or probable or confirmed to a certain degree; or that
they are false, or improbable or disconfirmed to a certain degree given the absence of certain data or facts.

Thus above, when I affirm that a substance is soluble if
it disappears in a liquid this does not rest on a *definition* of
"soluble" but only on the specification of a sufficient condition
for solubility; and when I affirm that A is harder than B I
require only the specification of a sufficient condition for this
to be the case, not in addition a necessary condition, although
if I want negative knowledge such specification will be
required.

Phenomenalism thus, I should think, requires only that the
truth of some statements follows from the presence of certain
data, not that objects be reducible to sense data, impressions,
or ideas. But it is not my purpose to defend phenomenalism.
I want only to argue that there are at least some concepts such
that we can determine the truth of some propositions into which
they enter in terms of what we find given in experience. And
this I think is often or at least sometimes the case. But while
it may be granted that if A scratches B (in the sense dealt
with above where A and B are hard substances, e.g., glass,
copper, diamond) A is harder than B, it is less likely to
be granted that if it is an animal and jumps when I jab it

with a pin, it is sentient or feels pain; that if when I threaten
to remove its food it growls, it is angry; or pleased if it wags
its tail when I pet it. In these cases it will be held by many that
there is no strict logical connection of entailment (not to speak
of identity) between its jumping when I jab it with a pin
and its being sentient, or angry if it growls when I threaten
to remove its dinner. Hence I cannot affirm with certainty that
it is angry if it growls when threatened, etc., etc. This may
well be the case, although it would occur to no one with any
knowledge of animals and feelings to question the judgment
in ordinary contexts, and this, if not decisive with respect to
correct usage, ought still not be assumed as wholly beside the
point concerning how data are connected logically with certain
statements. Stranger definitions or truth rules are to be found
in the most exact sciences than that according to which jumping when jabbed is a sufficient condition for being sentient,
which, if not identical with being in pain, presumably is equivalent to having some or other feelings akin to pain, one of
which might in a given case be identical with it. If parallel
lines can enclose an area, or meet at infinity, if holding a
five-hundred-pound weight on one's shoulders is not work, as
it need not be, I fail to see why jumping when jabbed should
not entail sentience, or growling under certain conditions, anger.
But I shall concede the opponents' point in order to make my
case stronger by resting it on a weaker one.

Knowledge does not require that the given data when we
report evidence in support of a statement be related to that
statement by a relation of entailment. It is enough if the conditional connecting the data with the inferred fact be simply
true, not necessarily true. Thus if it be true that if it jumps
when jabbed it is sentient, I may correctly infer sentience
from such jumping without having to directly observe the
sentience inferred. If it be true that if it growls then it is
angry, I may infer the state called "anger" without directly
observing it, given the growl, and so on.

The question then is whether any such conditionals are
true. Now it is obvious that the conditionals in question are

not material conditionals in the sense that any such will be true merely if its antecedent is false or its consequent true. The conditionals required for such inferences in cases in which we wish to infer from what may be called "indirect evidence" are, it seems (as I have maintained elsewhere in a paper called "Evidence"[4]) nomological conditionals, that is conditionals entailed by laws. If there exists what we suppose is a law in a given domain, there will be formulable an infinite number of conditionals entailed by that putative law, and true if it not be false, and having exactly that degree of probability or confirmation possessed by the supposed law from which they are derived.

We have, that is, precisely as strong grounds for inferring anger from menacing growls under appropriate conditions as we have for supposing that the conditionals such as "if A growls menacingly when its food is threatened then it is angry" are true, and for the truth of these conditionals we have whatever grounds there are for maintaining the nontrivial generalization to the effect that (x) (Growls $x \rightarrow$ Angry x). So the question becomes: how much if any support do we have for this universal statement which might be a law?

It is clear, I think, that such a universal statement that is possibly to qualify as a law cannot be verified in the strict sense. That is, as a law it is understood to be not a *restricted* universal such that it might be replaced without loss of content by a finite conjunction. It is and must remain open-ended. Thus even if we could directly observe states of anger in other animals and could for as large a number of cases as one wishes observe such anger whenever menacing growls are forthcoming, this would not enable us to establish the law beyond possibility of refutation by the next relevant case. Of a strict law, that is, the most we can reasonably and sensibly demand is that it have been put to the test many times and never found wanting. Under these conditions we speak of it as well confirmed and use conditionals derived from it with complete confidence in making predictions.

Hence to give adequate evidence in support of a proposition it is enough to make use of a conditional derived from a well-confirmed generalization. If the prediction based on the use of this conditional premise is verified, as in some cases is possible, we establish the correctness of our original knowledge claim by satisfying the three necessary truth conditions making up the content of the classical definition of "knowledge," assuming, that is, as follows from our example, (a) that what is predicted occurs, (b) that we believed it would, and (c) that we gave adequate evidence in support of our claim, by adducing a well-established generalization in support of the conditional premise which, together with that describing our initial conditions, led to the correct prediction. As a concrete illustration, observing what I establish by the usual tests to be a piece of sugar, I assert that it is soluble in water. I make this claim on the basis of the well-confirmed generalization that pieces of sugar of the kind in question dissolve in water. Putting it in water, I observe that it dissolves. Hence the proposition expressing my knowledge claim is true, assuming I believed it was, of which the knowledge claim itself constitutes adequate witness, and that I based the prediction on the conditional "if this is sugar then it will dissolve in water," which qualified as a nomological conditional by virtue of being entailed by the well-confirmed generalization "(x) (sugar x $\rightarrow$ dissolves in water x)." For it follows that I have given adequate evidence in support of my claim, and hence the knowledge claim is established in the sense of the classical definition.

But how about the case of the dog alleged to be angry? Well, assuming that I believe it is and that it is (we must assume that we know what fact is asserted in this claim, and that it is capable of existing, otherwise we cannot raise the question whether I do or do not know that it is angry), then all that remains is to adduce a well-confirmed generalization to the effect that all dogs whose food is threatened in the manner described earlier are angry. But suppose that we cannot directly observe his anger and that we do not treat growling under the conditions described as logically a sufficient condition for being angry, what then? I answer that here we confront a more complicated sense of "well-confirmed generalization." Instead of being directly confirmed by the regular satisfaction of necessary truth conditions, as I assume to make the opponents' case as strong as possible, we have a somewhat different situation. We infer the not-directly-testable hypothesis of the dog's being angry when he growls under the specified conditions, and then test the correctness of this hypothesis by means of observing consequences we have reason to expect if the hypothesis be correct. That is, we know from much experience of ourselves and reports of other human beings that the hypothesis of anger being aroused by threats to the food supply of an animal can itself be confirmed in turn by overt action, typically taking the form of attacks on the source of the danger. Thus anyone who is made angry by another is likely, all other things being equal, to turn upon and attack the person assumed to be the source of danger or offence. When then we observe not merely that the dog in question growls when I pretend to take its food, but actually turns upon and attempts to bite and possibly succeeds in biting me, the evidence in support of the anger hypothesis becomes very strong. Such confirmation of the inferred hypothesis strengthens our grounds for accepting it as correct and constitutes the kind of ground one can give in support of the view that the anger hypothesis is indeed a well-confirmed one, in the only sense in which this concept has application to the situation in question, namely when we have no access to what might be thought of as direct confirmation of the hypothesis. On the basis of such well-confirmed hypotheses we assume the truth of conditionals derived from them and in this way proceed to give adequate evidence in support of our knowledge claim, the adequate evidence obviously altering its character with the type of case involved.

In general, what constitutes adequate evidence in support of a hypothesis or law is a function of the subject matter, and what counts as such, say, in physics possesses a higher degree of reliability than what we have in even ideal cases in, say, historical knowledge, where the hypothesis regarding the past also finds confirmation in even more roundabout ways. In fact such indirect types of confirmation of generalizations being well confirmed are typical of highly involved and complex theoretical structures such as we find in the more advanced sciences. I should like to stress here the *relativity* of the concept of well-confirmed generalization, and the absence, in general, of simple direct confirmations, although they do exist. Obviously the concept of giving adequate evidence in support of a knowledge claim possesses exactly the same relativity to particular types of cases, and our formulation of the concept of *knowledge* must take this into account.

That the fact that we may have no direct confirmation of an alleged law when making inferences via conditionals derived from it to other pains or feelings carries with it no special significance can be shown by making clear that we are in a similar position when, say, claiming to know the chemical constitution of stars. Here there exists the spectroscope which we know to be a reliable instrument for ascertaining the constituents of incandescent bodies or gases. The existence of certain lines in the spectrum of light coming from some distant body is taken with complete confidence as implying the presence in it of certain elements, which we shall probably never test directly by more familiar test tube chemical methods. But the well-confirmed hypothesis that the star contains certain elements can in its turn be tested by deducing from that hypothesis other testable consequences such as emission of typical radio waves that can be detected by suitable equipment.

If one argues here that there is, at least in theory, a method of directly testing the hypothesis of there being hydrogen in the sun one must ask: precisely which of the many possible tests for hydrogen qualify as ascertainment of direct evidence for hydrogen as contrasted with indirect? It is, it would seem, highly arbitrary as to which tests give us direct evidence, and which indirect. In fact the same holds for knowledge of terrestrial bodies of average size and accessibility. When I "see my friend" is it actually my friend that I see? At what distance and from what angle do I really see him and not some appearance of him or some sense datum? What is it such that if and only if I see it or other things of the same class do I actually see *him* as opposed to inferring his existence indirectly?

It is, I think, quite incorrect, except by way of arbitrary convention, to speak as if things or objects had *essential* characteristics. By far the larger part of what constitutes a thing (a very poor concept, really) exists in it only potentially, as it were. Thus of all the true propositions about an object most are surely hypothetical in character telling us, to the extent of our knowledge, about what *would* become accessible to observation *if* certain operations were performed. Most of these operations are never performed and we must suppose that their totality is infinite. There is no end to the ways in which we might come to possess adequate evidence for the existence of something.

Suppose then I cannot sense directly another's sensations, whatever this might be supposed to mean, if anything, what has this to do with knowledge of them or even of their existence, which is quite something else. The hypothesis that someone is in a certain mental state can be tested in many ways, and it is mere dogmatism to suppose that the only adequate test is sharing that state itself, even assuming the sense of this can be unraveled. It is not even true to suppose that a man always knows his own feelings, even in the sense of being aware of all of them, which is as minimal a sense of "know" as one could hope to find. And if we distinguish *knowing* one's feelings (i.e., their character, or that we have them) from *having* them, that is, if we distinguish, as was done earlier, between confronting the object to be known with the knowing of it, it is fairly obvious that probably the person who *knows* least about the feelings of a man is that man himself who has them. If this were not so psychology instead of being the latest comer on the scientific scene would have been the earliest of sciences. Instead of self-knowledge being the hardest kind of knowledge it would be the easiest, and Socrates' injunction would have had no point at all.

Much discussion about knowing other minds has in fact been predicated on a wholly false assumption, namely, that *the mind* is a thing that can be sensed, not to speak of being reducible to a momentary feeling, say, a pain. In the proper sense of the term, we know another man's mind when we know its products: his habits of action and speech, his writings, his behavior tendencies and responses, his values, his goals. His intelligence shows itself only in his acts, likewise his nobility or baseness; his brilliance or dullness, his wit or stupidity, his courage or cowardice—all these qualities that make up his mind, in the only sense that does justice to the concept, are knowable and known as well by outsiders as by himself, and for that matter generally much better by outsiders than by himself. It is a very wise man indeed who knows himself. And if a man who is his own physician has a fool for a patient, then the man who thinks he knows himself probably has a conceited ass for the object of his knowledge.

I return now to knowledge in general and its classical formulation as I have given it. It will be evident that knowledge is not sensation, but rather the object of knowledge is first given or located through sensation; and that sensation again enters the process of coming to know in those confrontations of data which give us whatever evidence we have or can get that that process has been successful. These data do not in and of themselves constitute evidence, but only in the context of laws and nomological conditional statements that connect these data with the propositions whose truth constitutes a necessary condition for knowledge. In every case of knowledge the fact that we *could* be mistaken is no evidence at all that we are. That what we infer on the basis of our nomological conditionals and observations *might* not be the case is no evidence at all that it is not; the fact that what we take to be a nomological conditional may be inferred from a well-confirmed generalization that further experience might show to be mistaken likewise has no bearing on the question whether what we claim to know we do indeed know. To know does not require that we either be sure or have the right to be sure, Ayer to the contrary notwithstanding.

All that is required for knowledge is that what we claim to know be the case, that we believe that it is, and that we can give adequate evidence that it is. And all these conditions are capable of being satisfied in quite objective terms, and *even in the absence* of our knowledge that they are satisfied. The evidence that I offer that P may be adequate in the sense here involved even if I have serious doubts that it is; it may be the case that P even if I do not know that it is; I may believe that P although not P, and may doubt that P although P. What may *not* be the case is that I should know that P although not P, or if I did not believe that P, or could not give adequate evidence that P. But if these necessary conditions are satisfied then in the sense called "classical" I know.

The fact that one can know even though one is neither sure nor has the right to be sure that one knows, whatever be the nature of the right, will seem odd only to those who suppose that to know that P entails that one knows that one knows that P. This conclusion does not follow from my formulation, although it is demonstrable, at least for certain cases, according to Hintikka's formulation given in his work mentioned earlier. I shall not try to explain his view or the grounds for it, but simply report that I have been informed by him that his view is not in fact incompatible with mine, despite appearances of incompatibility.

If one assumes that if one knows that P then one must know that one knows that P, or be sure that P, and if it be granted that one could be mistaken unless one knows that one knows, it would seem to me that there could be no knowledge, for in my view one could always be mistaken, i.e., one could never be sure in the intended sense. Similarly, if it is demonstrable that if one knows then it follows that one knows that one knows it would seem to me very difficult if not impossible ever to know, for it seems clear to me that this infinite process soon takes us beyond comprehension. Now I use "belief" in such a manner that one cannot believe what one does not understand. Hence at some step in this infinite iteration A will come upon a proposition, perhaps "A knows that he knows that he knows that he knows that P" that he does not understand, hence does not believe—hence the knowledge chain will snap for him as I use the term "to know."

But there is another reason why for me it does not follow from the fact, say, that I know that P, that I know that I know that P. For if I know that P then it follows in my sense that I can adduce a well-established generalization that shows every sign of being a law, from which I can derive a nomological conditional that justifies me in making the inference to the truth of the proposition expressing what I claim to know; but it does not follow that I can do anything of the sort with respect to the claim that I know that I know. For (a) this would have to be true, (b) I would have to believe it, and (c) there would have to be a nomological conditional, i.e., one derived from a well-established generalization, such that from it together with the statement constituting its antecedent I could validly infer the truth of the statement that I know that I know. But even this soon I am quite lost and hardly any longer understand what I am talking about, not to speak of knowing a confirmed generalization from which I might derive the nomological conditional required to make possible the inference that I know that I know.

I conclude that knowledge is achievable, even of other minds and other pains, without involving that dizzying and dangerous prospect of infinite knowledge, appropriate not to men but to gods. And I am thankful for this, since I am much impressed by what happened on a well-publicized historic occasion; and if Berkeley is not precisely Paradise, still, I do not yet know of a better place.

Finally, if sad experience had not taught me otherwise I would not now consider it necessary to inform my readers that I have not been trying to tell them what knowledge *really is*, as if God had once and for all settled the matter, and I by virtue of Promethean cleverness had managed to steal the secret. There are extant a good many other senses of the term, some less interesting than others, which I have not found it relevant to my purpose to discuss. I leave it to the vagaries of philosophic fashion, or perhaps the historians of our age, to render judgment on some of these occupying the center of attention in certain circles. My goal has been simply to try to formulate a conception more or less adequate to what I take to be the paradigm cases of knowledge-that, shown to be such not by my "say so" or by reference to "what we would say," but by the rather more cogent evidence which is nothing other than the very existence and character of our scientific civilization. That the formulation is far from novel in its general outlines I am ready to admit, and have done so; my excuse for putting it forth is that the views it is directed against are perhaps even less so, which does not prevent them from being widespread and even, I regret to say, influential—at least among some philosophers.

NOTES

1. Jaakko Hintikka, *Knowledge and Belief: An Introduction to the Logic of the Two Notions*, Ithaca, 1962.
2. A. J. Ayer, *The Problem of Knowledge*, New York, 1956.
3. I do not define this difficult term, but rest content with the fact that if *A* does give adequate evidence, then he can.
4. *Synthese*, XII, no. 1, March, 1960.

ON KNOWING THAT WE KNOW

ARTHUR C. DANTO

I

Austin advanced a view to the effect that the descriptive content of the sentences *s* and *I know that s* is exactly the same, the latter giving no information not already given by *s*, but only, as it were, underscoring the fact that the information is being given by the speaker. Thus the operative fragment "I know that —" is descriptively vacuous; it constitutes an act of speech by him who voices it; and it has the force of asserting whatever sentence may follow it without contributing to what is asserted. Perhaps, then, the iterated fragment "I know that I know that —" merely adds emphasis. Obviously, if I must assert that I assert, infinite regressions yawn. But perhaps I can, as occasion demands, assert emphatically, so that "I know that I know that —" is, as it were, an italicized "I know that —" with an implicit exclamation point. So not only do I add nothing to the descriptive content of whatever sentence may be emphatically asserted; I add nothing to the performance of assertion save, perhaps, energy. Indeed, we may argue to such a conclusion if we take "I know that —" as the form of words with which to advance a knowledge claim, whether we also suppose (as Austin plainly and—I believe—wrongly did not[1]) that it is descriptive in its own right.

Were a man *m* to utter the sentence "I know that *s*" we all would recognize something weirdly wrong were he to add "But I don't know that I know that *s*." The entire "I know that *s*

I am grateful to the Columbia Council for Research in the Humanities for support of the project from which the present essay is extracted.

32

but I do not know that I know that *s*" is *somehow* inconsistent, though not formally so. Well, if it is inconsistent, "I know that *s* and I know that I know that *s*" is tautologous in whatever way the other is inconsistent. The question is only how the inconsistency is to be explained. There is, of course, an immense temptation to explain it with reference to certain features of knowledge as such. Thus there are philosophical views that knowledge is a cognitive condition—a state which the knower is *in*—and that when he is in this state, his being so is transparent to himself. So, when he knows, he knows that he knows in virtue of the reflexive transparency of the cognitive condition. We could not know without knowing that we knew. This could be so; but the original conjunction would sound weird to anyone with an ear tuned to correct English, and, since few native speakers are aware of the transparency theory and since fewer still believe it to be true, the weirdness cannot be explained with reference to that theory. So the theory is not needed and, more important, the weirdness need lend no support to the theory invoked to explain it. Let us explain it on the level of language as such.

Consider the schema (1) "*p*, but I don't know that *p*." Let *p* = "I know that *s*." Upon substitution, we derive (2) "I know that *s*, but I don't know that I know that *s*." Now (2) happens to make reference to its speaker twice over, and the double reference back to the speaker might appear to lend some support to the transparency theory. But we get something quite as weird as (2) no matter what sentence we may put in place of *p* in (1). Thus, let *p* = "The Prussians are coming." This yields (3) "The Prussians are coming, but I don't know that the Prussians are coming." And it is simple enough to see what is wrong with (3), and indeed with any sentence we might get upon uniformly substituting in (1). The pronoun "I" which is embedded in the schema works retroactively upon the first occurrence of the substituent to render it as an *assertion*, that is, not merely as a sentence but as an asserted sentence. But then the fragment "I don't know that —" constitutes a disclaimer, a refusal to assert whichever sentence fills the blank. To utter (3) or any sentence sharing parity of form with it is to assert and to withdraw the assertion of the identical sentence, the two pieces of behavior neutralizing each other. It is like promising with crossed fingers. And since this leaves things exactly as they were—as though one were simultaneously to administer a poison and its antidote—it is in effect a self-stultifying performance. The performance is *incoherent,* and the transparency theory of the cognitive condition is merely irrelevant, since we need never leave the surface of language to clarify the matter. We have no instances of tautology in the domain of action quite so clear as the instances of inconsistency. But doing twice what need be done but once—like crossing one's heart while one promises (or swearing on the Bible)—is perhaps as clear an instance as we need. To assert that one asserts that *s* is just to assert that *s*. In Fregean idiom, the second ⊢ in ⊢⊢ is but a shadow of the first. It brings no substance of its own.

And here the matter would end, but for the sobering thought that we have shown only that "I know that *s*, but I don't know that I know that *s*" is not something we can *say*. But it does not follow that, with suitable changes in grammatical person, where the performative resonances die away, it could not be said of *us*. Or, if it could not be said of us, some reason better than those which derive their force from the illocutionary circumstances of first-person utterance would have to be given. *Is* it possible to know without knowing that we do? I think it is. But some philosophers whom I admire have thought otherwise. The purpose of this paper is to show that they are wrong and I am right.

II

Prichard writes, in a celebrated paper, as follows:

We must recognize that whenever we know something, we either do, or at least can, by reflecting, directly know that we are knowing it, and that, whenever we believe something, we similarly either do or can directly know that we are believing it and not knowing it.[2]

In support, or perhaps in intended explanation of this claim, Prichard says that knowing and believing are so transparently distinct that confusion of one with the other is all but impossible.

Let *s* be a sentence not about *m*, or such that at least one truth condition for *s* is independent of *m*. And let us suppose as beyond controversy (since it is common ground for all the philosophers I shall discuss) that "*m* knows that *s*" entails *s*. If *s* is true, then whatever the truth conditions for *s* may be, they must be satisfied. The question is how, by reflection alone, *m* should know that the truth conditions for *s* are satisfied when one of these truth conditions is independent of *m* and, hence, presumably opaque to *m*'s reflection? Thus let *s* be the sentence "The magnetic moment of the nucleus lies between -6 and $+2$ nuclear Bohr magnetons." We ask *m*—a physicist, say—whether he knows or believes that *s*. Perhaps he replies that he knows. Asked how he knows, we should be surprised (at the least) were he to say that, having reflected, he has discovered that his condition is one of knowing and *not* of believing. So what could Prichard have meant? He was no less a master of language and of reflection than we who are puzzled by his view. A clue to his intention, perhaps, lies here:

> We should only say that we know something when we are certain of it, and conversely, and . . . in the end the meaning of the terms is identical; whereas when we believe something, we are certain of it.[3]

Well, the difference between knowledge and belief *could* be the difference between certitude and incertitude. But are we to allow that the question whether or not we are certain can be dissolved by reflection? Reflection will tell a man whether he *feels* certain (in case he has to reflect to know this). But then "*m* knows that *s*" cannot be synonymous with "*m* feels certain that *s*" if the former entails *s*, while the latter is notoriously compatible with its falsehood. Or, if the entailment is to be preserved, then we are unlikely to suppose "*m* feels certain that *s* means what we thought it did when we conceded it could be determined through reflection. So it is just a distraction to shift from knowledge and belief to certainty and incertitude. But Prichard was clever enough to have seen this. So there must be an important point sunk beneath the obvious vulnerabilities of the argument: if Prichard was misled, it must have been for reasons powerful enough to blind him to plain fact.

Prichard very likely thought that, when I believe that *s,* I in the nature of the case know that I believe that *s.* For he thought the contents of our minds are always directly accessible. This is perhaps creditable with belief, at least for those in the Cartesian tradition, for whom "I believe that —" is a Cartesian report that any *res cogitans* can effortlessly make to itself. Then, thinking that knowing was here on a footing with belief from the point of view of philosophical psychology, Prichard regarded it as similarly open to the unimpeded perception of inner vision. We then know that we believe—or that we know—in just the same way. True, the evidence and inference demanded for such a sentence as "The magnetic moment of the nucleus..." is complex. But no one was saying he knew *that* sentence by reflection. The claim was that given that this sentence is known, then the further sentence that it *is* known by *m* would require no such evidence or inference. It would be a basic sentence for *m*. He could know it directly. How otherwise could he know it, Prichard would ask. And he would say that we had confused knowledge as such with knowledge *of* knowledge. It was exactly the thesis that knowing is a condition of the knower that Austin was hoping to wash away with his performative account of "I know." But Prichard thought it *was* such a condition. And then, if it were so, it surely would be open to reflection. And so what we have here is the transparency theory, alluded to before. This theory, if correct, would not *entail,* of course, that I must know that I know that *s* if I know that *s*. For I might not have reflected. So Prichard's theory is weaker than it might seem at first to be. Besides, it presupposes that knowing *is* a condition of the knower, and hence a thesis in psychology. I shall

therefore consider a somewhat stronger thesis, and one which
alleges to make no psychological assumptions. Then I will come
back to Prichard.

III

Jaakko Hintikka has argued that "*m* knows that *s*" and "*m*
knows that *m* knows that *s*"—or, in his notation, K*ms* and
K*m*K*ms*, respectively—are virtually equivalent.[4] As I understand him, we would say that *p* and *q* are virtually equivalent
when we cannot, either with *p* and not-*q* or with not-*p* and *q*,
consistently describe any state of affairs. This means that *p*
cannot be true with not-*q*, nor *q* with not-*p*. So *p* and *q* would
have to be true together if either of them is true at all. To say,
then, that K*ms* and K*m*K*ms* are virtually equivalent is to say
that we cannot consistently describe any state of affairs with
either the pair K*ms* and NK*m*K*ms*, or the pair NK*ms* and
K*m*K*ms*. That no state of affairs may be described with the
latter pair admits of a trivial proof. Let us suppose ourselves
entitled to make uniform substitutions. Then replace K*ms* with
r. This yields the pair N*r* and K*mr*. But, by comment consent,
K*mr* entails *r*. So this gives us the conjunction of *r* and N*r*. So
the original pair would not be cotenable. Such a semiformal
proof of this half of Hintikka's thesis differs, of course, from
his. Hintikka sets up very nice rules which prevent the two
sentences from forming part of the same formal system. But
proof here scarcely is needed, it being more or less the common
sense of the matter that, if a man does not know that *s*, he
hardly can know that he knows that *s*! It is the other half of the
thesis that is more vexing and less open to common sense. And
my style of proof yields no noncotenability of K*ms* and
NK*m*K*ms*. All we get from it is *r* and NK*mr*. And these seem
plainly enough compatible. There must be many things that
m does not know. True, I can't *say* "*s*, but I don't know that *s*."
This is an inconsistent performance. But surely someone could
say "*s*, but *he* does not know that *s*." Well, perhaps the general

case won't serve to show that NKmKms and Kms might after all be incapable of describing any possible state of affairs. So perhaps semiformal proofs and common sense are unreliable here. For Hintikka has what he claims to be a proof that they are not cotenable.

The notion of a model set is that of a system of sentences that describe or partially describe a possible state of affairs. If two sentences cannot together enter the same model set, there is no possible state of affairs that they may jointly describe. Hintikka deduces a contradiction from the assumption that Kms and NKmKms are entered in the same model set, and concludes that no possible state of affairs could sustain a description consisting of their conjunction. His discussion here is sophisticated and complex, but, since it is a relatively simple matter to provide an actual state of affairs that the two sentences jointly describe—I shall do this in the concluding sections of my paper—either something is wrong with Hintikka's rules or he is simply using a defective translation of the words "— knows that —," and no genuine connection holds between them and his K—.[5] But in fact he has indicated his intention to capture usage by means of his epistemic operators.[6] So I shall later argue that he has failed. He would certainly have failed if, for example, KmKms had a truth condition distinct from the set of truth conditions for Kms and if satisfaction of the truth conditions for the latter did not exhaust the truth conditions for the former or *entail* their satisfaction. In Prichard's analysis, Kms could be true while KmKms was false, notably in cases where m had not reflected upon his condition to determine whether it were knowledge or belief or what.

Hintikka wants his proof to go through without appeal to psychological operations of any sort. And indeed, in a gloss on his proof, he endorses a thesis of Schopenhauer to the effect that "m knows that s" and "m knows that m knows that s" mean just the same thing. If they do, then of course they cannot have distinct truth conditions. But do they mean the same thing? Prichard would not have said so. And who is right? I don't think we would depend so much upon the apparatus of model sets to discover this as we would upon the canvassing of native speakers. Hintikka supposes we are dealing with different forms of words. But nobody, I think, would suppose that "*m* believes that *s*" and "*m* knows that *m* believes that *s*" are merely different forms of words for the same thing; for it is open to dispute whether, Descartes notwithstanding, we might not hold beliefs we do not know we hold. True, *I* cannot say "I believe that *s* but I don't know that I believe that *s*." But someone can tell me, perhaps demonstrate to me, that I have beliefs I would not have said I had because I did not in fact know them to be mine. First-person utterance, once again, is merely misleading. But why can one not have knowledge that one does not know one has? To say this is impossible because "*m* knows that *s*" means nothing different from "*m* knows that *m* knows that *s*" raises the question whether they do mean the same thing. Prichard thought they did not. So in what way has Hintikka solved "Prichard's problem"? He has demonstrated only a virtual equivalence between K*ms* and K*m*K*ms*, thinking wrongly that *K* represents what philosophers mean by "knows —." So he will have achieved here only an interesting irrelevancy. Let us therefore return to Prichard.

IV

Prichard not only believed that we each can know in a direct way whether we know or whether we believe that *s;* he also held a thesis which he either did not distinguish from this one or else would have offered in support of it, namely, that knowing and believing were simple and unanalyzable conditions of an individual. Knowing that I know is *direct*, and it is so because nothing tells me that I am in a knowing way except the fact that I *am* so, and the reason for this is that knowing is a simple, unanalyzable condition of myself. That our knowledge of our knowledge is direct, is stated here:

> The knowledge is . . . in both cases direct; we do not know, for example, that our state is one of knowing that the noise

we hear is loud indirectly, i.e., by knowing that it [NB: the knowledge, not the noise!] has some character, other than that of knowing—such as that of being a clear and distinct perceiving; we know directly that it is of the sort which knowing is; and so, too, with our knowledge that our state is one of believing.[7]

And that these are simple and unanalyzable conditions is suggested here:

In knowing that some state in which we are is one of knowing or of believing . . . we are necessarily knowing the sort of thing which knowing is, and the sort of thing which believing is, even if it is impossible for us or anyone else to define either, i.e., state its nature in terms of something else.[8]

These two points are connected in Prichard's polemic against Descartes. He wants first to say that nothing tells me that I know that *s* except the fact that I *do* know that *s* and, accordingly, that no criterion (as we would say these days) is needed for knowledge, or no criterion is possible. So there is nothing such that I first must ascertain that it holds in order to know that mine is a case of knowing. But, secondly, I cannot know anything at all without in the nature of the case knowing what knowledge is, and accordingly a generalized doubt is impossible. Thus, suppose I say I know nothing, but only have beliefs which may perhaps be mistaken ones. Well, I must then know what beliefs are, Prichard argues, and so it is false that I know nothing. Indeed, even if it were true that I knew nothing, if I only knew *that*, then I would know something, namely, that I knew nothing. So I never could know nothing. Descartes, of course, was a master of such argumentation. Consider only his besting of the *malin génie*. Descartes proved he could not always be mistaken. He could not because, in order to make a mistake, a man has to *assert* something. If you do not assert, you are never wrong (though of course never right). So, on the hypothesis that I am always mistaken, it follows that I am always asserting something, and then I cannot doubt that I make assertions (= think). So there is at least one thing about which I am not mistaken on the hypothesis that I always am mistaken, and that hypothesis is accordingly self-defeating. *Tant pis* for the *malin génie*. But of course it does not follow that I ever make correct assertions, or have correct thought, except in the one case where my thought is about thinking, or where I assert that I must assert if ever I am mistaken. So there is cold comfort in such argument. Prichard's point is that, in knowing what knowledge is, I automatically have an *instance* of knowledge. But one ought to draw a distinction between what after all amounts to understanding what "knowledge" means and having an instance of knowledge. Prichard's thesis is that merely to understand the word is to have an instance of what it applies to, which is vaguely reminiscent of the Ontological Argument. But at best this works only in one case. If *comprendre, c'est savoir* works at all, it does so only in the one case where it is *savoir* itself that is the object of *comprendre*. There is, then, one clear win against the skeptic. But he, like the *malin génie*, can cut his losses. That one win guarantees the intelligibility of his own position, but does not make that position further untenable. It is quite compatible with my knowing what knowledge is that, other than this, I should know nothing whatever.

It is a curiosity of Prichard's position that it works even when I don't understand what knowledge is—or "knowledge" means. For even if I misuse the word, I must at least know how I am using it, and so there is something I do know. Prichard himself could not have understood very well what "knows that —" means. Otherwise, he never would have thought either that knowledge was a simple unanalyzable condition of persons, or that we know directly whether we are in a knowing way or only in a believing way. Some such view *might* be worked out for believing. It could be argued that, for instance, if I could determine whether or not I believed something only by first consulting evidence of some sort, then (a) this evidence could be grounds for belief only if it consisted of lawlike connections which themselves presupposed an antecedent ability on the part of whoever built them up independently to identify beliefs, e.g., just as the laws that connect Angstrom measurement on spectra with colors presuppose the antecedent ability to identify colors directly; and (b) he who could not identify his beliefs save through taking note of evidence and inferring that he had such and such beliefs would be an Other Mind to himself. And the question would then arise in what sense the beliefs were *his*. But no such argument will work for knowledge. Moreover, if "*m* knows that *s*" entails *s*, then the truth conditions for *s* must be among the truth conditions for "*m* knows that *s*." So either we know *s* only when the truth conditions for *s* happen to be part of ourselves and open to autoinspection—which entails a form of solipsism—or else knowing cannot be *simply* a condition of ourselves. And then neither can knowing that we know that *s* be a simple condition of ourselves, since the truth conditions for *s* would be among the truth conditions for "*m* knows that *m* knows that *s*." So how could I know directly that I know that *s*, in case what knowing that *s* involves is a *relation between* us and whatever it is, independent of us, that makes for the truth of *s*? So Prichard is a bad master of usage, and it little matters that *his* usage is not captured by Hintikka. I turn, therefore, to one for whom usage is a matter upon which he maintains a certain connoisseur's authority. This is Professor Malcolm.

V

According to Malcolm, there is a strong and a weak sense of the word "know," and, if we take the strong sense, we have something reasonably close to Prichard's claim, so close that the latter may be reconstructed by registering the criteria for this strong sense. The *weak* sense appears to be this. The man *m* asserts that *s*, and, upon investigation, *s* turns out to have been true. We then allow that *m* knew that *s*, though, had *s* turned out false, we would say instead that *m* only believed that *s*. Nothing then need be different with respect to *m* himself for there to be a difference between his knowing or his believing that *s*. The only difference is external, and concerns the truth value of *s*. "As philosophers," Malcolm writes, "we may be surprised to observe that it *can* be that the knowledge that *p* is true should differ from the belief that *p* is true only in the respect that in the one case *p* is true and in the other false. But that is the fact."[9] Malcolm leaves no room here for the possibility of true belief, which so vexed the agonists of the *Theaetetus*, but this is of less concern to me than the claim that there is no subjective difference between knowledge and belief. So it follows that, by mere reflection, I could scarcely determine whether or not I knew or only believed that *s*. For the weak sense of "knows," then, Prichard was wrong. And perhaps, in my own criticism of him, it was the weak sense that I had in mind. But if *he* had in mind the *strong* sense, then we were arguing at cross-purposes.

A person employs the strong sense when, in claiming to know that *s*, he will not allow that there can be against *s* any compelling counterevidence. He would not, according to Malcolm, "call anything evidence against it. The person who makes the statement would look upon nothing whatsoever as evidence against it."[10] He might not be able himself to *show* that a certain bit of alleged counterevidence was not so in fact. But he would rule out, nevertheless, that it could really *be* counterevidence. Now there are in fact certain things we all could claim to know, and such that we would simply never suppose, and could not tolerate, that so-called counterevidence could actually turn out to be such. We know that certain classic problems having to do with rulers-and-compass solutions will never be solved in those terms, that no one ever is going to square the circle, or duplicate the cube, or trisect the angle by those means. Proofs, so-called, rain down upon mathematics departments, but it would merely be charity that would ever motivate mathematicians to examine them for their flaws. They know in advance that there must be a flaw, and the question only is how, and whether it is worth the while, to identify it. In much the same way we know there will be no perpetual-motion machines, however ingenious candidates might appear. I once found a "proof" that if any pair of propositions p and q are compatible, then, if r is compatible with p, r is incompatible with q. This is the sort of startling discovery out of which metaphysical systems take their rise, but I regarded it as only a parlor addition to the paradoxes of material implication. One day a colleague recognized that if I were right, every non-Euclidian geometry had to be inconsistent if Euclidian geometry were consistent. But there is a famous proof by Klein that every non-Euclidian geometry has a model in Euclidian geometry, so all are consistent if it is. So my colleague now knew that there had to be a flaw in my argument, and by dint of application it was found (it was not, by the way, a surface find!). All these might be counted as instances of Malcolm's case, I suppose, but for the fact that the reason we will not allow the counterevidence is that we know the sentence in question, and, hence, know that whatever is truly incompatible with it has (logically) to be false in case "m knows that s" entails s. But it is not merely a matter of our not *allowing* counterevidence. It is, in each case, a justified disallowance, and perhaps it is not obvious that we are dealing with a different sense of "know" or a "stronger sense." So I shall consider just Malcolm's examples.

Malcolm claims strongly to know that $2 + 2 = 4$. He knows this, he says, not because he has a proof, nor because of anything. He simply knows it, as everyone does. Proofs for it can be found, but these do not bring, as it were, a sigh of relief that an old, familiar, but possibly dubitable proposition has been vindicated. Rather, they merely illuminate the foundations of mathematics, and should any proof go *against* the proposition, that would be sufficient for rejecting the proof. We will not allow that there can be a valid proof that terminates in the denial of $2 + 2 = 4$. But this is not because it happens that this sentence is, perhaps, a tautology or a priori or analytical in some way. For there are other sentences, which are none of these, and which I would insist that I know as well, and there are bona fide sentences in mathematics that

I would hesitate to say I knew in the strong sense at all. This part of Malcolm's thesis is interesting and important, for it cuts across a distinction which, at the time his paper was written, was considered unfilterable. Let me try to reconstruct what I take his point to have been.

In both arithmetical calculations and in empirical hypotheses, there are what we might term "checking procedures," simple operations by means of which we determine whether or not an empirical claim is false, or a computation is in error. In checking a calculation, I break it down into such simple steps as $2 + 2 = 4$. But this is about as simple as I can get: $2 + 2 = 4$ is not in the typical run of things itself computed. And, in the sense in which a man might commit an error of calculation, there is no way in which he can have miscalculated here, since there is no calculation to begin with. There is a *kind* of error that is excluded. But, comparably, suppose I claim (using Malcolm's example) that there is an inkpot in the dresser. I can be wrong, and do not know whether I know until I have checked up. I open the dresser and have a look. I see an inkpot, and have validated my claim. Now nothing stands to this checking-up procedure as *it* stands to the initial claim—a fact which might be lost sight of through the fact that the very same sentence might be used to express the claim and to announce the results of the checkup. All empirical checkings up are perhaps resoluble into such simple operations of looking and seeing. And with these there is nothing further to be done. These are the operations with which we make checks, and any way in which we might check up on these would involve operations of just the same sort. So how could one coherently trust *those* if one mistrusts *this*? Such doubts are incoherent.

There are disanalogies between empirical claims that are shown false and calculations that are in error, but the analogies here are striking and important. Yet it is absolutely necessary, Malcolm's interesting thesis notwithstanding, that we emphasize that these simple cases do not guarantee us against being wrong. They guarantee us against being wrong only in a *certain*

sort of way. It is only that our errors, if there be any, cannot
be discovered through repeated operations of checking up in
which the appeal to these simple cases consists. It would have
to be a different sort of error altogether. Malcolm would not
have shown that error is impossible, but only that it would not
be discoverable in the same way in which we discover errors
through these simple "checking procedures." Now it may very
well be true that, as the notion of evidence is used, there would
be no sense in saying that evidence could count against such
claims as "Here is the inkpot" or "$1 + 1 = 2$." It is because
just these are the sorts of sentences with which our evidence is
ultimately expressed. But then consider, by contrast, such sentences as these: "Every non-Euclidian geometry has a model
in Euclidian geometry"; "It is mechanically impossible to derive energy from bodies by cooling them below the tempera-
ture of the surrounding object"; "A straight line cannot be
constructed equal to any given arc of a circle." These sentences
are appealed to in connection with our claims to know that the
circle cannot be squared, that perpetual-motion machines are
impossible, that "Danto's theorem" is false. And it was the
latter which, on the basis of such considerations as the former,
we might strongly claim to know. Yet it makes sense, because
these are not *ultimate* expressions of evidence, to speak of evidence going against these. They express evidence. But not
ultimate evidence. Accordingly, the sense in which I might
claim to know that the circle cannot be squared, or that perpetual-motion machines are impossible, is different from the
sense in which I claim to know that $2 + 2 = 4$ or that I see an
inkpot. In both cases, I know that there cannot be compelling
evidence against these claims. In the first case it is a matter of
knowing that there can be no such evidence; in the second
case it is a matter of how evidence is defined. For in the
second case what I claim to know just *is* evidence, though for
higher-order sentences. In the first case what I claim to know *is*
a higher-order sentence, for which evidence is required and
may, in the end, consist of the sorts of simple sentences Malcolm
discusses. But what has any of this to do with resolutions? What

has any of this to do with any resolution on my part? It has to
do, at best, with the definition of evidence. Perhaps it is true
that I can know when I am *resolved to act* in a certain way and,
hence, that I am resolved to tolerate nothing as counterevidence.
But this way of restating Prichard's point is utterly discon-
nected from what Malcolm was talking about *really*—or from
what Prichard was talking about.

Let us now consider the disanalogies between the two sorts
of ultimate checks. If a man were told he was wrong in asserting $2 + 2 = 4$, it is unlikely that the charge against him would
be that he had miscalculated. But if *not* miscalculation, then
what his error might consist of is not easy to see. Were someone
to urge against him that $2 + 2 = 5$, the latter could not urge
on his own behalf that he had correctly computed. At best he
would be working with a different base, or using one of the
terms differently from the rest of us. No fact, other than a fact
of usage, is in order here. Consider, by contrast, the beholding
of an inkpot, an ultimate check in the domain of experience.
There could be an analogous quarrel, e.g., were someone to say
it was an apple, not an inkpot. It would turn out he meant, by
"apple," what we mean by "inkpot." But there is another sort
of case which does not arise in the example of $2 + 2 = 4$
(which is precisely why Descartes placed them on different
levels). I can reach for the inkpot and find my hand *closes on
nothingness!* Malcolm in fact considers this possibility. He does
not say it could not happen. He only says that he would consider *that* an hallucination, and would persist in claiming that
what he saw was an inkpot. He will not allow his grasping
emptiness to count as contravening evidence. But surely, in
point of ultimate evidence, grasping is of a piece with seeing.
They both are in the order of ultimate checkings. So you
can't, as it were by definitions, decide that the one is not evidence if the other is. So you decide arbitrarily. You make
a resolution. But that is all it now is. It is no longer knowledge.
To be sure, you cannot use evidence to decide issues when our
evidence itself is inconsistent. But that is exactly what the
skeptic was saying all along. You have not met the skeptic by

retreating into decisions, when it was precisely his claim that
what you call knowledge is ultimately only a decision.

It is perhaps not interestingly controversial that I can
know what I have decided, or what I am resolved to do. So
the defense of Prichard here is rather barren. For knowledge
in "the strong sense" cannot be coupled with that logical feature which we took all along to be common ground, viz., that
"m knows that s" entails s. If we took it in conjunction with
that principle, we would get untoward results. We need, as
Richard Taylor pointed out,[11] simply to find the true believer
who has resolved never to count in evidence anything against
the proposition that God exists in order to "prove" that God
exists. But there are, let me add, as many adamant atheists, so
that one need only find one of them in order to prove that
there is no God. So we get inconsistent results. The "strong"
sense of "knows" renders "m knows that s" compatible with
the falsity of s, and so fails to preserve the logical feature of
the concept of knowledge I take as common ground in our
discussion. The "weak" sense *does* preserve that feature, since
the criterion for differentiating "m knows that s" from "m believes that s" is that s must be true in the former case. So, in
the *weak* sense "m knows that s" is compatible only with,
and so entails, the truth of s. But since there is no *subjective*
difference between knowing (in the weak sense) and believing,
we cannot, in the typical case, know by mere reflection on
our own condition that we are knowing or that we merely are
believing that s. The *strong* sense, let us grant (since nothing
in the controversy turns upon granting it) applies in cases
where a man "strongly knows" means only that he has resolved
never to allow contravening evidence. A man might know
when he has reached that point, but this is compatible with
total ignorance everywhere else. And it has not the slightest
interest for epistemology unless there are some interesting or
important doubts about this sort of self-knowledge. But it
would not at the best be a matter of knowing that we *know*,
but only of knowing where we stand. Where Malcolm touches
upon knowledge, he fails to rescue Prichard, and, where he

rescues Prichard, he loses touch with knowledge. And so far as anything positive in his analysis is concerned, it is quite possible to know without knowing that we know. The only thing that remains (perhaps) impossible is that we take a stand without knowing we have done so. And these are different things indeed, unless one could show that some condition of myself—that condition which Austin (correctly) was loath to designate "knowing"—were a sufficient condition for the sentence for which knowledge was claimed, when that sentence should have, among its truth conditions, factors independent of us. So let us find our own way.

VI

I shall not endeavor in this paper to offer an adequate analysis of "m knows that s." I shall content myself, rather, with the mere specification of an element, the absence of which would render any purported analysis *in*adequate. I submit that "m knows that s" entails, and hence presupposes, "m understands s." And I believe this would be required whatever our analysis, and invariantly as to whether we subscribed to a performative or a descriptive account of "I know that s." For even if it were merely a matter of giving my word regarding s when I use the form of words "I know that s," it scarcely could be maintained that I would be in a position to do so if I did not understand what I was saying. So I shall suppose it would be common ground that m must, if he knows that s, understand s, just as I supposed it common ground that s itself is entailed by "m knows that s." And I shall suppose that this is not controversial, however controversial might finally be the question of how "understanding" is itself to be analyzed. My discussion will presuppose no special analysis of that concept.

Let s now be the sentence "m knows that t," and let us replace the dummy variable s with this, transforming "m knows that s" into "m knows that m knows that t." But now it is quite

obvious that "*m* knows that *m* knows that *t*" must satisfy a
truth condition in excess of the truth conditions for "*m* knows
that *t*." For the latter to be true, it is required only that *m*
understand *t*. But for the former to be true, it is required, in
addition, that *m* understand the sentence "*m* knows that *t*." The
latter requires no such thing. And surely it is possible that
men might know a great deal, might understand a great deal,
and yet not know that they know these things because they
do not understand what knowledge is—or what "knows that —"
means. We have discussed three philosophers in this paper, for
example, whose knowledge in many matters I utterly respect,
but who plainly do not understand what "knows that —" means.
For otherwise they could not have argued as they have. Or,
if *they* are right, then I am wrong. So at least I don't know
what "knows that —" means. Unless I am to be held ignorant
of all things (including what they said), *I* at least would have
some knowledge I do not know that I have. So the fact that
polemic of the sort I have been engaged in is possible indicates that I am right (which is a near relative to a Cartesio-
Prichardian argument). But I think it generally true that we
often have a great deal of knowledge which we would not
acknowledge ourselves as possessing—because we hold to an
incorrect *theory* of knowledge. "We need only draw the curtain
of words, to behold the fairest tree of knowledge, whose fruit is
excellent, and within reach of our hand."[12] And what word
has stood more opaquely between us and the knowledge we are
entitled to claim than the word "knowledge" itself? It is for
this reason, then, that I should reject Hintikka's proof of a
virtual equivalence between K*ms* and K*m*K*ms*. For I have
described a state of affairs within philosophy itself where, although it is true that *m* knows that *s*, it is false that he knows
that he knows it. But, at the same time, it should be plain that
nobody could *say* that he knew but did not know that he knew
that *s*. But that is due merely to the logical vagariousness of
first-person usage.

We do not need, after all, any special psychological assumptions regarding the instantaneous transparency of the

knowing condition, the pellucid reflexivity of the knowing mind. Knowing that one knows could only have arisen as a concept when men came to be self-conscious about knowledge, when, as it were, the sorts of speculation in which we ourselves are interested actively took their rise with the first epistemologists, whomever they may have been. There is, then, a reflexiveness here. It is a reflection upon our own condition. This is Prichard's word, but not his meaning. For it is not psychological in any interesting sense. It is but a further instance of that sort of circumspection and self-consciousness which is the mark of philosophical investigation, whatever may be its subject. Men had knowledge all along. By reflecting upon knowledge, we did not *add* to it. We only, at best, analyzed what it was to be in possession of it. But until these facts were reflected upon by philosophical wits, men did not know that they knew; they only knew.

There would of course be no room for the word "know" in the language if we had not, as it were, already placed a distance between us and our primary occupations with the world, and begun to analyze the nature of that occupation and its justification. Someone could be so occupied, as indeed men have been from the beginning, without reflecting upon it. But they would already have achieved that distance when the word "know" entered the language, and *for that reason* they have already some notion of the criteria of the application, and so think they know what knowing is. Yet they may have incorrectly rendered that occupation, and so there is no warranty that they know what knowledge is, although they know. So a man can misapply the word to himself—or to his fellows —or he can (as we saw before) not yet be in a position to apply it at all. There are two reasons, then, why there is no virtual equivalence between K*ms* and K*m*K*ms*.

But, in mitigation of Hintikka (and of Schopenhauer), let me hasten to add that there is a virtual equivalence between K*m*K*ms* and K*m*K*m*K*ms*. The reason is this. Once we have mastered the concept of knowledge—the logic of "knows" —there is nothing further about knowledge—or "knows"—

to understand. So these two expressions would indeed be only different forms of words, and there would never be an extra truth condition for K*m*K*m*K*ms* over and above what is required for K*m*K*ms*. The former would, I dare say, be extremely rare. And its analysis would be a matter of sociolinguistical, rather than logical interest. I imagine it *would* be only a matter of emphasis, as repetition so often is, e.g., "I told you and I told you." It certainly suggests nothing of that infinite series of concentric interreflexive selves which the literal mind of the metaphysician is prone to postulate.

With this, I hope, the problem of whether we must know that we know, in case we *do* know, has been solved. And it has been solved with appeal to little more of psychology than is required for the understanding of a sentence. In fact, little more in the nature of self-consciousness is required for "*m* knows that *m* knows that *s*" than for "*m* knows that *m* digests onions poorly." For the latter to be true, *m* must (however it is done) understand the sentence "*m* digests onions poorly.' And for the former he must understand the sentence "*m* knows that *s*." But think what a gratifying solution this is! It entails that, unless we have a correct theory of knowledge, we may have as much knowledge as you wish and yet not know that we have it. In order to know that we have knowledge, epistemology is logically required. Epistemologists, then, contribute nothing to the world's stock of knowledge. They merely are internally related to the possibility of our knowing that we have it. And if to be properly human is to know what we are about, there is an internal connection between being human and being an epistemologist: man is the animal that tries to know what knowledge is, i.e., a philosophical animal.

NOTES

1. I discuss this issue in my "Seven Objections Against Austin's Analysis of 'I know,'" *Philosophical Studies*, XIII, no. 6.

2. H. A. Prichard, "Descartes," in *Knowledge and Perception*, Oxford, 1950, p. 86.

3. *Ibid.,* p. 86.

4. Jaakko Hintikka, *Knowledge and Belief: An Introduction to the Logic of the Two Notions,* Ithaca, 1962, chap. 5. For consistency, I employ the letters m and s in place of Hintikka's a and p in the context K–. And I use the Polish N for similar reasons.

5. See, for example, Roderick Chisholm, "The Logic of Knowing," *Journal of Philosophy,* LX, no. 25, 784. We should remind ourselves, of course, that the sentence that is thus demonstrated may not be the one with which philosophers have been concerned when they have asked "Can we know without knowing that we know?"

6. See note 1, p. 105, of his book.

7. Prichard, *op. cit.,* p. 88.

8. *Ibid.*

9. Norman Malcolm, "Knowledge and Belief," *Mind,* LXI, no. 242, 60.

10. *Ibid.,* p. 62.

11. Richard Taylor, "A Note on Knowledge and Belief," *Analysis,* XIII, March, 1954; and his "Rejoinder to Mr. Malcolm," *Analysis,* XIV, March, 1954.

12. George Berkeley, *The Principles of Human Knowledge,* "Introduction," par. 24.

IF I KNOW, DO I KNOW THAT I KNOW?

E. J. LEMMON

Is it analytic that, if *a* knows that *p*, then *a* knows that *a* knows that *p*? Or does *a*'s knowing that *p* entail that *a* knows that *a* knows that *p*? The answer to this question, both recently and less recently, has tended to be affirmative. I would like in what follows to suggest some doubts and reservations.

In an earlier article, I suggested an analysis of "know" in terms of "learn" and "forget," in the light of which, I claimed, there could be seen to be counterexamples to the principle that, if I know, then I know that I know.[1] However, what I then said was briefly said, and has in any case been subsequently attacked by others;[2] so it may be as well to begin with an expansion of what I still think is correct in those opinions. I shall then attempt to meet the objections raised against them, and go on to argue that, even on other analyses of knowing than mine (such as Ayer's and Hintikka's), counterexamples appear to be forthcoming. Finally, I shall discuss Hintikka's "proof" that, if I know, then I know that I know, and make some remarks concerning the enterprise of epistemic logic.

I

The verb "know" belongs to a fairly small class of verbs in English which have somewhat remarkable characteristics. Besides "know," the class contains "remember,' "recall," "forget," "learn," "find out," "discover," "teach," "see," and "hear" (there are doubtless others). One characteristic shared by the class is the roughly similar range of constructions by which its members can be followed. I can know that . . . , know whether . . . (or not), know whether to . . . (or not), know how (a car is driven), know how to (drive a car), know where (the key is hidden), know where to (find the key), know when (my lecture is), know when to (give my lecture), know what (an emergency is), know what to (do in an emergency), know which (dictionary contains the answer), know which (dictionary) to (turn to for the answer), know why (bandages are applied to a wound), know why to (apply bandages to a wound), know who (will solve the problem), know whom to (go to for a solution). The reader will, with more difficulty in some cases than in others, be able to construct similar examples for each of the verbs in the above list.[3]

A second characteristic fairly widespread in the group is that, in the "that" construction, I . . . that p entails that p. This is well known in the case of "know": if I know I can't be wrong. But if I remember I can't be wrong either, in just the sense that if not-p then I may think I remember that p but cannot actually remember that p. For special reasons, "I forget that Brutus killed Caesar" is "self-defeating,"[4] but "I never forget that . . . ," "I forgot that . . . ," "he forgets that . . ." all entail that . . .[5] "Find out" ("discover") fairly obviously has this characteristic, presumably because "find" in contrast with "seek" is a "success" verb. "Learn" is not so straightforward: when it means "find out" then it has the property; but when it means "is taught" it does not. At school I learned that Cicero killed Caesar, but then the Roman history teacher was no good. Similar cases show that "teach" lacks the property too: "he teaches that the end of the world is coming." "See" is an odd case. "On looking out the window I saw that it was raining" does entail that it was raining (otherwise I only thought I saw); but "I saw in the paper that the Vietnamese war was over" does not entail that it was over, for, even if it isn't, I did (in a way) see the *proposition* that it was. And "hear" has the same ambiguity.

However, one must not exaggerate the similarities. All these verbs take objects, but in rather different ways. Knowing people ("John"), places ("Paris"), tunes ("The National An-

them") is paralleled by remembering and forgetting people,
places, and tunes; one can learn tunes and languages (though
not find them out) but hardly people and places (though one
can come to know them). Teaching John is very different from
teaching French—compare teaching John French.[6] Bear in
mind also "I discovered (saw, heard) him in the shrubbery,"
"I found him out in a lie."

Another oddity is that many of these verbs take a "neat"
infinitive: "I forgot (remembered) to put the kettle on." "He
knows to put the kettle on" may be a little odd, but is idiomatic
English, and does *not* mean the same as "He knows how to put
the kettle on."[7] "He is learning to swim" seems close in meaning to "He is learning how to swim," but "The dog is learning
(being taught) to bark for his food" is not like "The dog is
learning how to bark for his food."

A sharply contrasting class of verbs is "believe," "think,"
"suppose," "imagine" (and others). The members of this class
take the "that" construction, but none of the others. And none
of them, in the "that" construction, have the second characteristic
mentioned above. Indeed, in the past tense, "I believed (thought,
supposed, imagined) that it was raining" would tend to suggest that I was wrong rather than right in so believing (thinking, supposing, imagining).

"Be certain (sure)" is a little tricky. We *can* say "I am
not certain how to solve the problem," "I am not sure where
the key is," "I am not certain whether Brutus killed Caesar."
Thus it appears to share the first characteristic, though not
the second, with the first class of verbs. In this usage, "I am
not certain" seems to mean "I do not know for certain" or
perhaps "I am not certain that I know." On the other hand,
"I am certain where the key is" *is* odd, except as a possible
ellipsis for "I know for certain where the key is." This suggests
that there is a sense of "be certain that" in which it means
"know for certain that" and in which, presumably, "I am
certain that . . ." does entail that . . . . This may be the sense
in which I say "I was quite certain the horse would win"
after it has won. But of course there *is* a sense in which I can

say "I was (felt?) quite certain it would win" after it has *failed* to win; and clearly this sense must be different since it has different entailments. I hope to throw a little more light on "certain" later on. It may be that "be certain" should be classified with "doubt" rather than with either of the two previously distinguished classes.[8]

II

What, if anything, can be learned from these purely linguistic facts that may have a bearing on our initial problem? It seems to me that, in the case of the first class of verbs, the constructional similarities are an indication of semantic interconnections. Very roughly, all these verbs have to do with a man's store of information—the facts at his disposal, the answers he has to questions, and so on—together with his grounds and evidence, his rational backing, for that information. Thus, to take perhaps the least problematic cases, "I see (hear) that it is raining" means "I have the information that it is raining, and I have come by that information on the strength of the evidence of my eyes (ears)." (Here I use "I have the information that . . ." in such a way that it entails that . . . .) "I remembered that it was his birthday" similarly means "I had the information that it was his birthday, and I had it on the strength of evidence from my memory." From this standpoint "I know that . . ." means something like "I have the information that . . . , together with evidence to support it"—though we shall need to qualify and clarify this later.

What are the kinds of ground or evidence that can be used to support a knowledge claim? They include at least the following: evidence of the senses; good authority; evidence of memory; suitable experiments; a piece of scientific theory; a deductive argument from premises already known. If the claim to know involves the claim to have supporting evidence, then the question "How do you know?" is the question *"What kind* of supporting evidence?" Thus "how?" here has the mean-

ing "in what manner?", as it would in the question "How did
you swim the channel?" meaning "In what way—on your back,
doing the crawl, or what?—did you swim the channel?" not
"How (on earth) did you (manage to) swim the channel?"
It is the request to be specific concerning the manner of evidence. We may contrast "How (on earth) did you (manage
to) forget (something as obvious as) that?" and "How (on
earth) did you (manage to) remember (something you learned
as long ago as) that?" "How do you remember?" cannot be
asked in the same sense of "how?" as in "How do you know?"
precisely because the claim to remember *answers* the "How do
you know?" question.

By contrast, "believe," "suppose," and so on, as their far
narrower constructional pattern suggests, have little to do with
information and evidence for it, but have rather to do with
our attitude (rational or irrational) towards propositions: to
believe that p is to be inclined to assent to p. Thus "I couldn't
help knowing that he was still alive" suggests that evidence for
his being still alive was pushed under my nose, whilst "I
couldn't help believing that he was still alive" suggests that I
was unable psychologically to face his death, that I was unable
to resist the inclination to assent to the proposition that he
was alive. Hence it seems to me unlikely that knowing entails
believing. From the fact that I have certain information and
certain evidence to support it nothing follows *logically* concerning my attitude to that information; though I shall in general
be inclined to assent to it because of the evidence, I still may
find myself unable to face the truth of the proposition. This is
why I think we should take seriously the common idiom "I
know perfectly well (that he is dead) but still cannot (really)
believe it."

Attention to the linguistic facts concerning "know," and
in particular its range of constructions, enables us to evaluate
more adequately Ryle's familiar contrast between knowing
how and knowing that. Roughly, knowing how, when, where,
etc., as opposed to knowing how to, when to, where to, etc.,

is simply knowing the answer to the questions "how?" "when?" "where?" etc. Hence it is in a way reducible to knowing that: knowing *where* the key is hidden is knowing *that* the key is hidden in . . . place, knowing *how* a car is driven is knowing *that* a car is driven in . . . manner. Of course, in saying "I know that the key is hidden in the desk" I *give away* where the key is hidden in a way that I do not when I say merely "I know where the key is hidden." This is the difference between the claim that one has the answer to a question and the claim that the answer one has to a question is . . . . But there is a far bigger difference between knowing how to and knowing how than there is between knowing how and knowing that. If I know how a car is driven, it follows that I know that a car is driven in . . . manner, for some suitable filling of ". . ."; and vice versa. But I may know how a car is driven without knowing how to drive one (I may have watched my parents drive, and be able to describe precisely what they do in the correct order, and yet have never sat at the wheel). In other words, it is knowing how (when, where) *to* that contrasts with both knowing that and knowing how (when, where); and the contrast appears to involve in some way the contrast (such as it is) between *practical* and *theoretical* information. I may know (in theory) when I ought to speak and when I ought not to, but I do not know when to keep my mouth shut unless I am able (in practice) to keep silent on the right occasions.[9]

The semantic connections between these verbs seem to be such that various interdefinitions are possible. The one that for present purposes is the most interesting is the following:[10]

(1) I know that p if and only if I have learned (found out) that p and have not forgotten that p.

Analyses similar to (1) are also forthcoming for the other constructions that can follow "know"; thus I know how to swim if and only if I have learned how to swim and not forgotten how to swim. However, since our original problem is posed in terms of knowing that, and does not seem even to be meaningful in other constructions (what would knowing how to know how to be?), we shall in the sequel restrict attention to the "that" construction.

(1) may seem self-evident; nevertheless let us test it step by step. First,

(2) If I know that *p* then I have learned (found out) that *p*

appears to be analytic. To know, one must have come to know. This is partly to say that "know" is a static verb in Kenny's sense;[11] "I have known for 7 years that . . ." entails "I know that . . . ," as "I have loved her for 7 years" entails "I love her." "I know that . . ." reports a state I am in; but I further claim that it is a state I am in as a result of having done something, namely, having acquired, in whatever way, suitable evidence for . . . . This is the performance that is brought to an end by the state of knowing, and this performance may be called, with slightly different implications, "learning that . . . ," "finding out that . . . ," "discovering that . . . ," or "coming to know that . . . ." It seems that the only potential counterexample to (2) would be innate knowledge; on a crudely Platonic view, it may be true that I know that $2 + 2 = 4$ without it ever having been true that I was coming to know that $2 + 2 = 4$. Even this is not enough, however; for, even if one accepts certain forms of innate knowledge, if there is a time at which I came into existence, then at that time I came to know that *p*, where *p* is a piece of innate knowledge. Hence a counterexample to (2) would require some such doctrine as the reverse immortality of the soul. With these somewhat tenuous reservations, I accept (2) as analytic.

Second,

(3) If I know that *p* then I have not forgotten that *p*

is surely analytic. There might in many cases be uncertainty as to whether I have or have not forgotten that *p*; but in such cases there will also be uncertainty as to whether I (still) know that *p* or not. And if I really have forgotten that *p*, then I cannot (any longer) be truly said to know that p, even if I did indeed once find out (come to know) that p.

Hence the two right-hand side conditions in (1) appear to be necessary. Are they also sufficient? The situation here is not entirely clear, and the obscurity will be relevant in what follows, so let us be cautious. Let p be the proposition that the square on the hypotenuse of a right-angled triangle is equal to the sum of the squares on the other two sides, and suppose that John, age 12, found out that p, in the sense that he followed, and accepted, one of the standard geometrical proofs that p. Now suppose that, ten years later, John recalls that p is a proposition that he once accepted, but does not recall the proof of p. Then it could be said that John once learned that p, and has not now forgotten that p, but it could be doubted that John any longer knows that p.

Now in fact this case is far from simple, and can be distinguished into several subcases, which depend on what is meant by "John recalls that p is a proposition that he once accepted." First, and at one extreme, there is the subcase where John can formulate the proposition that p (might even recall that it is called Pythagoras' theorem), recalls also that he once accepted it, but has no recollection of whether he had good evidence, bad evidence, or none at all, at the time when he accepted it. In this case it is dubious whether we would really agree that John had not forgotten that p; for can it be said that John remembers that p when he has no idea what kind of evidence there might be for p, when in fact all that John remembers is that at one time, for whatever reason, he accepted p? A second subcase is that in which John recollects not only p, and that he accepted p, but also that he had at the time good evidence for (in the form, let us say, of a deductive proof of) p, though he does not recall what the evidence (proof) actually was. A related subcase is that in which John recalls that he was told that p by a geometer whose competence he still accepts; for here again he recalls that he had good evidence for p, though of a different kind, and even recalls the nature of the evidence (good authority). I am inclined to say of these cases that John indeed has not forgotten that p, but also to that extent *still knows* that p. Indeed, to insist that John does not really know that p unless he can actually produce a proof of p would seem to set a quite unrealistically high standard for knowing. For example, I think I would be justified in claiming to know that the predicate calculus is undecidable, since I recall having been through Church's proof of this with some care, though I gravely doubt my ability to reproduce the proof spontaneously. And I think I am justified in claiming to know that the axiom of choice is independent of the other set-theoretic axioms, since I have it on Cohen's authority that this is so, though I have not been through his proof at all. There are other subcases where the line between remembering and not remembering is even harder to draw: for example, suppose John, as in the first subcase, can formulate p and also knows it is Pythagoras' theorem; he is not certain what the word "theorem" means, but is inclined to think it means "proposition for which there exists a valid proof"—does he remember that p? But then does he now know that p?

For the moment, despite these uncertainties, I shall accept (1). In any case, we shall see later that similar difficulties surround the notion of "having sufficient evidence for"; so we shall have to tackle the same problem in a related form.

III

If (1) gives sufficient and necessary conditions for knowing that p, what will "I know that I know" mean? At this point it will be convenient to introduce certain abbreviations. Let Kap mean "a knows that p," Lap mean "a has learned (found out, come to know) that p," Fap mean "a has forgotten that p."[12] Then (1) can be expressed in the form

(1)′ $Kap \longleftrightarrow Lap \,\&\, \text{-}Fap.$

Hence "a knows that a knows that p" will have the property

(4) $KaKap \longleftrightarrow LaKap$ & $-FaKap$.

Our basic question—does $KaKap$ follow from Kap?—becomes now the question whether the right-hand side of (4) follows from Kap. *Since* by (1)′ Kap is analytically equivalent to Lap & $-Fap$, the question transforms into whether

(5) Lap & $-Fap \rightarrow La(Lap$ & $-Fap)$ & $-Fa(Lap$ & $-Fap)$

is analytic.

At this point, I need to remark that one may indeed have learned that p and yet have forgotten that one has learned that p: this despite the fact that one has not forgotten that p. Suppose, for example, that someone asks me at 10:30 what the decimal expansion of π is to 10 places; I in fact learned this at school, but, when asked, do not recall having learned it and indeed decline to answer the question; at 10:35, however, I say suddenly 3.1415926536, realizing that this is the decimal expansion of π to 10 places. Now it is clear that at 10:35 I *do* know the decimal expansion of π. It seems to me also clear that my ability to produce the answer at 10:35 shows that I had not forgotten even at 10:30 this expansion. Hence at 10:30 both Lap and $-Fap$ are true, where p is the proposition that the decimal expansion of π to 10 places is 3.1415926536. However, it is not true at 10:30 that I have any evidence that I have not forgotten p; indeed, I may be so surprised at my own remark at 10:35 as to suggest that at 10:30 I was actually inclined to think that I *had* forgotten the answer. Hence I am tempted to say that at 10:30 I had forgotten that I had learned that p: in symbols, $FaLap$.

A natural logical principle concerning forgetting would seem to be the following:

(6) $-Fa(p$ & $q) \rightarrow -Fap$ & $-Faq$.

If a man has not forgotten the conjunction p & q then he has not forgotten p and has not forgotten q. As a special case, taking p as Lap and q as $-Fap$, we have

(7) $-Fa(Lap$ & $-Faq) \rightarrow -FaLap$ & $-Fa-Faq$.

Since, in the example above, the consequent of (7) is false, so is its antecedent. But its antecedent is one of the conjuncts of the consequent of (5), whence this consequent is also false. But its antecedent is true. Thus (5), and with it $Kap \rightarrow KaKap$, is false in the imagined example.

A possible objection would be this. It may be true that at 10:35 I have not forgotten p, since then I actually state that p; but at 10:30 my refusal to answer the question shows that I have *temporarily* forgotten that p. In other words, it is true that at 10:30 I do not know that I know that p, but then I do not really know that p either. I can only be said really to know that p as from my answer at 10:35; but at this time, as my awareness of my own answer shows, I also know that I know that p. Hence the case cited is no true counterexample to (5).

This reply is, I think, specious. In the first place, when we ask others questions, we normally allow others a little time to reply. The fact that it *takes* them a little time we do not normally construe as showing that they did not really know the answer or had temporarily forgotten. Of course, if they go on *too* long, we are inclined to say they have forgotten or perhaps never knew, certainly no longer know, the answer. And we should be hard put to say *how* long the absence of an answer has to be to reveal their having forgotten. (If it takes a year, could we ever be safe in saying they "knew all along"?) In the second place, we may in fact revise the case so that the answer is immediate but nonetheless takes the answerer by surprise—"I'd no idea I knew that" is a common enough idiom. In this case, it is unrealistic to say that I did not really know that p at the time the question was asked; for I could not have *shown* my knowledge any more quickly than I did. However, before the answer "popped out" in such a way as to amaze me, I did not know that I knew, had perhaps forgotten that I had ever learned the answer.

Let me put the case a little more dramatically. Imagine that I am confronted with a test which takes the form of a series of questions; what I am asked to do, however, is to mark in the space provided, not the answer, but whether *I think I know* the answer or not. Question 6 is "What is the decimal expansion of π to 10 places?" I have dreaded mathematics since school and am at once inclined to say no, I don't think I know the answer. At the same moment the answer comes to my mind, remembered distinctly from the distant and hated past. At that moment, of course, I both know and know that I know the answer; but I also discover that *up to* that moment I knew but did *not* know that I knew.

IV

Cohen[13] objects to my example in these words: ". . . this argument rests on an equivocation between the occurrent and dispositional senses of 'know.' If a man knows dispositionally that so-and-so he may well not know occurrently that he knows dispositionally that so-and-so. But if he knows anything dispositionally he surely knows dispositionally that he knows it." I have carefully refrained in my earlier discussion of "know" from talking about dispositions and episodes, partly because I am suspicious of Ryle's suggestion that "know" is a dispositional word. It is true that a distinction in sense can be made between the simple present tense of many verbs ("I walk") and the continuous present ("I am walking"), and similarly in the past and future, such that one might call the first tense dispositional and the second episodic; it is also true that "know" lacks a continuous present tense. But this fact, of course, by no means forces us to say that "I know" is dispositional. I would rather say that "know" is a success or achievement verb, like "win" or "cure," except that in these cases to mark the achievement we use the perfect tense ("I have won," "I have cured him") whilst for "I have come to know (and not forgotten)" we use the simple present "I know."[14]

In any case, there is no suggestion in Ryle that "know" has both a dispositional and an occurrent sense, so that I am unclear how Cohen is using these terms. Aristotle[15] contrasts two senses of "know," in the first of which a sleeping man

may be said to know, whilst in the second only a man who is
"using" his knowledge may be said to know; this may be
what Cohen has in mind. For the second sense, I doubt
whether the English word "know" can be used; perhaps the
correct English would be something like "I am currently
aware of the fact that," which I shall abbreviate to "I am
aware that." If this is what Cohen means, then of course he is
right that one may know that *p*, e.g., in sleep, but not be
(currently) aware that one knows that *p*. However, this was
not the kind of case I had in mind; nor was my case like
this. My case is rather one in which a man is disposed (to
use this terminology) to answer a question correctly, and so
knows the answer (dispositionally, if you like), but is not
disposed to answer correctly the question whether he knows
the answer correctly, and so does not know (dispositionally)
that he knows (dispositionally) the answer. Hence I cannot see
that Cohen's objection is very cogent.

Hintikka also objects to my thesis.[16] The context is
Hintikka's own defense of the thesis that $Kap \rightarrow KaKap$ is
a logical truth, and I shall return to this defense later. However,
he says of my reasons for rejecting (5): "They are in terms
of what 'the rational man' might (rationally?) forget. They
are therefore ruled out by the initial condition that only
statements made on one and the same occasion are considered
here." Hintikka is referring to page 7 of his book where, in
explaining the boundaries of an "occasion" in his sense, he
stipulates: "the notion of forgetting is not applicable within
the limits of an occasion." Here he clearly has in mind that,
if an occasion is allowed to cover a length of time during
which a man may forget that *p*, then at the beginning of the
occasion *Kap* is perhaps true and towards the end false,
which makes the study of the logic of knowledge very difficult.
Whilst I am sure he is correct in making such a stipulation,
it fails to rule out my case; for in my case it is *at one and
the same time* true that *Kap*, yet false that *KaKap*. Certainly,
a moment (or five minutes) later, I realize that I have not
forgotten that *p*, so that *KaKap* becomes true the moment

I give the correct answer realizing what I am doing. But if we restrict the occasion so as not to include this later moment, then Hintikka's stipulation is met and yet $Kap \rightarrow KaKap$ is falsified on that occasion, as my later answer, together with my surprise at myself in giving it, shows. Hence I conclude that Hintikka, here at least, has not shown my thesis to be false.

V

My case against the analyticity of $Kap \rightarrow KaKap$ has so far rested on my analysis of "know" in terms of (1). Hence it is open to an objector simply to reject this analysis. I am inclined to think that (1) is correct, but, rather than attempt to justify it further, I prefer to argue that, even if alternative analyses of "know" are favored, similar difficulties concerning the analyticity of $Kap \rightarrow KaKap$ arise.

Suppose a philosopher (Plato?) were to suggest that knowledge was true belief together with reason. We might take this to mean that sufficient and necessary conditions for Kap were (i) that p be true, (ii) that a believes that p, and (iii) that a has sufficient evidence for p (can give a *logos* for p). An immediate question would be: what counts as sufficient evidence? Should it be conclusive (compare Woozley[17]) or merely adequate (compare Chisholm[18])? This question, however, turns out to be mainly irrelevant to our present question; let us merely say, for (iii), that a had ϕ-evidence for p— what makes evidence ϕ-evidence can be left to philosophical taste, provided it be assumed that having ϕ-evidence for p precludes logically having ϕ-evidence for not-p. Abbreviating "a believes that p" to Bap and "a has ϕ-evidence for p" to Eap, we may write our current suggestion in the form

(8) $Kap \longleftrightarrow p$ & Bap & Eap.

As before, this gives

(9) $KaKap \longleftrightarrow Kap$ & $BaKap$ & $EaKap$,

which in turn, by substitution in accordance with (8), gives

(10) $KaKap \longleftrightarrow (p \ \& \ Bap \ \& \ Eap) \ \& \ Ba(p \ \& \ Bap \ \& \ Eap) \ \&$
$\quad Ea(p \ \& \ Bap \ \& \ Eap).$

Our question now becomes that as to whether the right-hand side of (8) entails the right-hand side of (10). The first conjunct of the right-hand side of (10) is just the right-hand side of (8), so that presents no problems. To simplify matters, let us also assume that "*Ba*" and "*Ea*" distribute through conjunctions, i.e., that

(11) $Ba(p \ \& \ q) \longleftrightarrow Bap \ \& \ Baq$

(12) $Ea(p \ \& \ q) \longleftrightarrow Eap \ \& \ Eaq$[19]

are both analytic. These will be seen to be at least plausible, if the reader considers the intuitive meaning of "*Ba*" and "*Ea*." Our question now becomes whether

(13) $p \ \& \ Bap \ \& \ Eap \to Bap \ \& \ BaBap \ \& \ BaEap \ \& \ Eap \ \&$
$\quad EaBap \ \& \ EaEap$

is analytic. And this in turn is the question whether

(14) $p \ \& \ Bap \ \& \ Eap \to BaBap \ \& \ BaEap \ \& \ EaBap \ \& \ EaEap$

is analytic.

I think it can hardly be conceded that (14) is *obviously* analytic *or* synthetic. For one thing, the meaning of the conjuncts on the right-hand side is far from clear. For example, what does it really mean to *have* ϕ-evidence that *p?* Suppose someone, without my knowing it, slips into my pocket a correct formal proof of *p;* do I then have ϕ-evidence that *p?* If this is what is meant, then it is easy to falsify (14): *p* may be true, I may (irrationally) believe that *p,* and I may (unknown to myself) have ϕ-evidence that *p,* but I certainly need not believe that I have ϕ-evidence for *p* (*BaEap*). If, at the other extreme, *Eap* means that not only is there ϕ-evidence for *p* in my possession but also that I am currently aware of having it, then of course the *left*-hand side of (14) ceases to be a plausible analysis of *Kap* in anything other than its dubious "occurrent" sense.

In fact in most normal cases to say *Eap* is to say that φ-evidence for *p* *has come* into *a*'s possession *in such a way as to be taken by* a *as grounds for* p and that *a* has not "lost" φ-evidence for *p*—where "lose" might mean anything from failure of memory to literal loss of one's experimental notes. (In a similar way, owning a horse means that the horse has come into one's possession in such a way as to make it *legally* one's own and that one has not "lost" possession of it—where "lose" might mean anything from giving it away to its dying.) For example, let *p* be "there are Russian missiles on Cuba." By October 22, 1962, President Kennedy knew that *p;* what this means, on our present analysis, is that *p* was true, Kennedy believed it, and Kennedy had come into possession of φ-evidence (in the form of photographs) for *p* in such a way that he took this as evidence for *p* and, further, had not "lost" the evidence. On the same date, however, Khrushchev did *not* know that Kennedy knew that *p* (according to Theodore Sorensen); and part of what this means is that, even though Kennedy did know that *p*, and even if Khrushchev (irrationally perhaps) believed that Kennedy knew, nonetheless Khrushchev did not have φ-evidence that Kennedy knew. Now Khrushchev had φ-evidence that *p*, though different φ-evidence from Kennedy's, and he might have had φ-evidence for Kennedy's believing that *p* (Kennedy might have told him on the hot line that he couldn't help believing that *p*). What Khrushchev lacked was φ-evidence that Kennedy had φ-evidence for *p*.

It is clear from this example that, on our present analysis, *Kap* → *KbKap* is not analytic (not that anyone might suppose it was), and this because *Eap* → *EbEap* is not analytic —*a*'s φ-evidence that *p* may well be different from suitable φ-evidence for *b* that *Eap*. Can a similar counterexample to *Eap* → *EaEap* be devised? Let us turn to our previous case, where I am asked the decimal expansion of π. Here *Eap* is true; I did indeed come into possession of φ-evidence for *p*

at school in the right way and have not "lost" it, as my correct
answer shows. However, what about my evidence for *Eap?*
I certainly came into possession of ϕ-evidence that *Eap* at
the same time that I came into possession of ϕ-evidence that
p, for presumably I realized what I was learning. But it cannot, I think, so readily be said that I have not "lost" this
evidence; at the later date, I in fact have *two* pieces of evidence
relevant to *Eap*—my correct answer and my own surprise at
this answer—so that the correct answer can no longer be taken
as ϕ-evidence for *Eap* in view of the surprise (compare the
proviso made earlier on the nature of ϕ-evidence). Reverting to
(14), I am again inclined to say that, whilst the left-hand side
is true, the right-hand side is false because *EaEap* is false, so
that (14) is not analytic.[20]

VI

Let us consider one other recent attempt to give sufficient
and necessary conditions for *Kap*, that of Ayer.[21] Ayer begins
by maintaining that necessary conditions for *Kap* are (i) that
p be true and (ii) that *a* be (completely) sure that *p*—let
us abbreviate to *Sap*. He argues, however, that (i) and (ii)
are not together sufficient for *Kap*. A man walking under a
ladder might be convinced that he will have an accident, and
he might indeed have one, but we should not agree that he
knew he would. When we say he knows, we "concede to him
the right to be sure." The three conditions (i), (ii), and (iii)
that *a* has the right to be sure that *p* are collectively both
sufficient and necessary, according to Ayer.

We may begin by questioning whether (ii) *Sap* is indeed
a necessary condition for *Kap*. If Ayer is using "*a* is sure that
p" in the sense "*a* fully and confidently believes that *p*," then
doubts concerning *Kap* → *Sap* can be raised on the same lines
as doubts concerning *Kap* → *Bap* raised earlier. For *a* may know
rationally that *p*, in the sense that he has the best possible
grounds at his disposal for *p*, and yet be unable to feel sure
(confident, certain) that *p*, to have the right attitude of assent

to *p*. It is interesting that Ayer passes, in the ladder example, from "be sure" to "be convinced"; for it is quite natural to say "I gave him all the evidence for *p*, and he accepted it, but he wasn't really convinced." Thus Ayer seems to take "be sure" to mean what I would prefer to call "feel sure." On the other hand, quite apart from the sense of "be sure" discussed earlier, in which it means "know for sure," there may be a sense of "be sure that *p*" in which it *does* mean "have *ϕ*-evidence for *p*." Thus "I wouldn't say I *was* sure, but I certainly *feel* sure that *p*" might mean "I have a confident attitude to *p*, but not the proper rational grounds for *p*." In this sense, being sure is no doubt a necessary condition for knowing. But, as we shall see, it is probably redundant in the presence of condition (iii).

What does Ayer mean by "having the right to be sure"? Ayer makes[22] three suggestions: (a) it may imply that a man has "followed one of the accredited routes to knowledge"; (b) it may imply that a man has an "adequate basis" for his conclusion; (c) it may imply (the case of the man who makes regularly successful predictions without our being able to find an adequate explanation for how he does it) merely that a man is "successful in a given domain." Ayer himself regards the third suggestion as questionable, so let us drop it: it is surely dubious whether we should be willing to say more, of the case Ayer mentions, than that the man *appears* to know the outcome, so long as we are entirely ignorant of his procedure (if any). As to the first suggestion, though it is doubtless true that if I follow one of the in fact accredited routes to knowledge I know, it is not clear that this can be what is *meant* by "having the right to be sure." For crystal gazing may be a route to knowledge accredited in a certain society, yet it is dubious whether if I crystal gaze that *p*, then I have the right to be sure that *p* (either in that society or in any other). The second suggestion seems closer to what Ayer must mean. But then having an adequate basis for *p* is presumably just what we were trying to capture earlier by the notion of having *ϕ*-evidence that *p*. I conclude, then, that, of Ayer's conditions (ii) and (iii), either they come to the same thing,

Eap, in which case one is redundant, or (ii) (in the sense "feel sure") is not even a necessary condition for *Kap* and may be dropped from the analysis.

It will be seen that, thus revised, Ayer's analysis is very like the earlier "Platonic" analysis in (8), except that now *Bap* is dropped. We have in fact

(15) $Kap \longleftrightarrow p \& Eap$,

which gives us in the usual way, for $Kap \rightarrow KaKap$,

(16) $p \& Eap \rightarrow p \& Eap \& Ea(p \& Eap)$.

There is now no difficulty in using our earlier counterexample as a counterexample to $Kap \rightarrow KaKap$ on Ayer's analysis. For in that example it was true that *p* and also that *Eap* but false that *EaEap,* and so presumably false that *Ea(p & Eap)* [compare (12)]. Hence (16) as a whole is false in this case.

For reasons already given, I am more inclined to support (15) than I am to support (8)—indeed I chiefly followed out the argument in connection with (8) to show that my case against $Kap \rightarrow KaKap$ in no way depends on my case against $Kap \rightarrow Bap$ or $Kap \rightarrow Sap$. Hence it might be useful to compare (15) with the initial analysis (1)'. Suppose then that *Lap & -Fap* [compare (1)']. Clearly *Lap* in the sense we are giving to it entails *p.* Further it is reasonable to suppose that finding out that *p* involves the appropriate acquisition of ϕ-evidence that *p.* Also *-Fap* presumably entails that *a* has not "lost" ϕ-evidence for *p.* Hence *p & Eap.* Conversely, suppose *p & Eap.* Then *a* at some time acquired ϕ-evidence for *p* which he used as a ground for *p;* hence at this time he clearly found out that *p, Lap.* Further, ϕ-evidence is still at his disposal, so that he cannot have forgotten that *p, -Fap.* Thus the analyses (1)' and (15) are "intuitively equivalent."

VII

There are two further difficulties that need to be discussed. The first concerns Hintikka's defense of $Kap \rightarrow KaKap$:

Hintikka purports to prove this principle, so that if his proof is correct there must be something wrong with my proposed counterexample to it. This matter I take up in the present section. The second concerns the justification for a logical maneuver used in our earlier discussion, namely the substitution of analytic equivalents inside "know"-contexts, and this I shall take up in the following section.

Let us begin by asking just what "ϕ" means in "ϕ-evidence." After citing Ayer's discussion of the right to be sure, as well as Urmson's and Chisholm's similar position, Hintikka writes:

> I think that the three suggestions . . . are also right in stressing that one can be justified in saying "I know" only if one's grounds are "conclusive" or "adequate" in some sense. I am not in a position to say "I know" unless my grounds for saying so are such that they give me the right to disregard any further evidence or information. . . . Whoever says "I know that p" proposes to disregard the possibility that further information would lead him to deny that p. . . . He commits himself to the view that he would still persist in saying that he knows that p is true—or at the very least in saying that p is in fact true—even if he knew more than he now knows.[23]

On this very plausible view, having ϕ-evidence that p is having evidence for p such that one is justified in disregarding the possibility that one may come by evidence for not-p. I hope it is by now clear that, in this sense, Eap may be true and yet $EaEap$ false; I did (before my correct answer) have ϕ-evidence that π is approximately equal to 3.1415926536, but I was not at that point justified in disregarding the possibility that I might come by evidence for not-Eap, since the fact that I had not done mathematics for years was just such evidence—witness my surprise.

Nonetheless, this passage from Hintikka is part of his defense of a rule for the logic of knowledge which later leads him to accept $Kap \rightarrow KaKap$. Let us therefore retrace his argument. He introduces the notation *Pap* to mean "it is possible for all *a* knows that *p*." In terms of this, the rule in question[24] may be stated thus: if $Kap_1, \ldots, Kap_n, Paq$ form a consistent set of sentences, then so do $Kap_1, \ldots, Kap_n, q$. Other rules then determine an equivalence between *Pap* and *-Ka-p* analogous to that between $\diamondsuit p$ and $-\square -p$ in modal logic. Thus an obvious consequence of the rule is that, if $Kap_1, \ldots, Kap_n, -Kaq$ are consistent, then so are $Kap_1, \ldots, Kap_n, -q$. Now we can argue that, if *Kap, -KaKap* were consistent, so would be *Kap, -Kap*, which is absurd. Thus $Kap \rightarrow KaKap$ is demonstrated.[25]

The proof is of course formally correct. Everything therefore hinges on the acceptance of the original rule A.PKK* (I do not question here the equivalence of *Pap* and *-Ka-p*). Hintikka argues for the rule in the following passage:

> That *q* is the case can be compatible with everything . . .
> *a* . . . knows only if it cannot be used as an argument to
> overthrow any true statement of the form "*a* knows that *p*."
> Now this statement can be criticized in two ways. One may
> either try to show that *p* is not in fact true or else try to
> how that the person referred to by *a* is not in a position
> r condition to know that it is true [in effect this is (15)].
> n order to be compatible with everything he knows, *q* there-
> fore has to be compatible not only with every *p* which is
> known to him but also with all true statements of the form
> "*a* knows that *p*." [26]

Hence, Hintikka concludes, if the set $Kap_1, \ldots, Kap_n, Paq$ is consistent, then so is the set $Kap_1, \ldots, Kap_n, q$, and not just the set $p_1, \ldots, p_n, q$. Since this argument depends on an analysis of "know" on the lines of (15), this leads Hintikka to endorse Ayer and others who have favored this sort of analysis in the passage quoted earlier.

However, the first sentence of the above passage begs the whole question. If *q* is compatible with all *a* knows, then presumably for any proposition *p* such that *Kap*, *q* is compatible with *p*. But it by no means follows that *q* is compatible with *a*'s *knowing p* (*Kap*). Hence there is no *logical* reason why q, though compatible with all p such that Kap, should not be used to overthrow Kap for some p, and this precisely *because*, as Hintikka implies in the next sentence, Kap makes a larger claim than p. Indeed, in my view, this is exactly what happens in the test case. Kap, that is p & Eap, is true, but then so is *-KaKap;* in Hintikka's language, *-Kap* is compatible with all a knows. This is possible because, though Kap is true, a does not have ϕ-evidence for Kap (though he does for p). Thus suppose *all a* knows *is p;* then clearly *-Kap* is compatible with p, as Hintikka's own analysis of Kap shows. Hence there is no reason for maintaining that Kap and *-KaKap* are inconsistent.

This same switch, between saying that q is compatible with all p known by a and saying that q is compatible with all true propositions of the form Kap, appears in a variant form in the last sentence of the first passage quoted. Hintikka's real view is that to say Kap is to commit oneself to p and to the claim that no further evidence could lead one to deny p. But in that sentence he suggests the different claim that a man who says Kap commits himself to maintaining Kap, and not just p, in the face of other evidence. This switch is obviously very easily made; it *is* a switch, however, and it is only by making it that Hintikka achieves his "proof" that $Kap \rightarrow KaKap$ is analytic. I conclude then that this proof is faulty—or at least on inspection can be seen to assume what it sets out to prove.

VIII

At various points in this paper, I have tested the thesis $Kap \rightarrow KaKap$ by translating it in accordance with a supposed analytic equivalence; thus by means of $(1)'$ it turned into (5), by means of (8) into (14), and by means of (15) into (16). I then hoped, by revealing the nonanalyticity of the translation, to show the nonanalyticity of the thesis itself. Tacitly employed in this translation was a substitution principle, namely that, if $A \longleftrightarrow B$ is analytic, then A may be substituted for

B in *all* contexts, whether they be *"Ea," "Ba,"* or *"Ka."* Since
these contexts are all, in Quine's terminology, referentially
opaque, it may be questioned whether this principle is correct.
This in turn raises the whole question of the correct formulation
of epistemic logic, the logic of knowledge. In what follows,
I shall largely concern myself with analytic substitution in
"know" contexts; but what I say seems to apply with equal
or more force to the other cases.

Epistemic logics have been put forward by several authors,
including von Wright, myself, and, most recently, Hintikka.[27]
For axioms, the most favored foundations have included

(17) $Kap \rightarrow p$

(18) $Ka(p \rightarrow q) \rightarrow (Kap \rightarrow Kaq)$

together with the rule

(19) if $\vdash A \rightarrow B$ then $\vdash KaA \rightarrow KaB$.

This basis (together of course with the propositional calculus) gives von Wright's system, which I called E2. I later[28]
recommended a system equivalent to the modal system T of
Feys, and Hintikka's is equivalent rather to the modal system
S4, in that he accepts, as we have seen, the thesis $Kap \rightarrow KaKap$.

It is quite clear, however, that (18) and (19) are implausible in several respects. (18) affirms that what *a* knows
is closed with respect to detachment, whilst *a* may well be such
that, though he knows that $p \rightarrow q$ and knows that *p*, has not
yet come to realize that *q*. Similarly (19) implies that *a* knows
all the *logical* consequences of what he knows, which is even
less plausible. I suggested that we must view epistemic logic
as giving the logical truths concerning a logical fiction, a sort
of "ideal knower" the rational man. Hintikka suggests instead
that we regard the theorems of epistemic logic not as recording logical truths but as giving *self-sustaining* propositions.[29]
Thus a defense of (19) might be that, if $A \rightarrow B$ is a logical
law, then if *a* does know A but denies he knows B once the
logical truth of $A \rightarrow B$ is pointed out to him, he is open to

the charge of unreasonableness. Whatever justification of epistemic logic along these lines may be given, it still seems interesting—and relevant to our present issue—to ask what a more realistic logic of knowledge would be like.

If we abandon (18) and (19) but hold on to (17), is there anything else we should add? The principle mentioned at the beginning of this section would take the form

(20) if $\vdash A \longleftrightarrow B$ then $\vdash KaA \longleftrightarrow KaB$.

(20) is certainly weaker than (19), and seems more plausible: if A is logically equivalent to B then surely knowing A is just knowing B. Another apparently satisfactory principle is

(21) $Ka(p \ \& \ q) \rightarrow Kap \ \& \ Kaq$,

if a knows the conjunction $p \ \& \ q$ then he already knows the conjuncts p and q separately. However, (20) and (21) together yield the undesirable (19) again. For suppose $\vdash A \rightarrow B$. Then by propositional logic $\vdash A \longleftrightarrow A \ \& \ B$, so that by (20) $\vdash$ $KaA \longleftrightarrow Ka(A \ \& \ B)$. Hence on the supposition KaA we have $Ka(A \ \& \ B)$, whence KaB by (21). Thus $\vdash KaA \longleftrightarrow KaB$, which gives (19). In other words, a system which possesses the rule (20) but lacks (19) must lack (21) as well.

On reflection, (21), though no doubt in general *true*, begins to look less like a *logical* truth. For may not a particularly stupid person know that $p \ \& \ q$ and yet not realize that p is a consequence of what he knows? Of course, if a knows A, and B is a *very* simple logical consequence of A, we (and a) are tempted to say that a *must* have known B all along.[30] But it does remain possible that we (and a) are wrong, that he simply had not realized that B.

But very similar intuitive objections can be raised against (20) itself. If A is logically equivalent to B but a has not realized this, it may be true that KaA and yet false that KaB. For example, suppose that $2 + 2 = 4$ is logically equivalent to $4 = 4$ (their biconditional is a theorem of arithmetic at least); if a knows the law of identity but no arithmetic, he may

well know that $4 = 4$ but not that $2 + 2 = 4$. To say this is
simply to repeat the observation that propositional attitude contexts, including the "know that" context, are more referentially
opaque than "it is analytic that." It begins to look as though a
realistic logic of knowing contains no distinctive theorems apart
from (17) and its logical consequences.

How open is our previous argument to criticism on the
score that (20) and similar rules for other contexts fail? I
presented a case in which p, Eap, and $-EaEap$ were all supposed to be true, and we assumed earlier the analyticity
of $Kap \longleftrightarrow p \& Eap$. Then it is clear that Kap is true, and
that to show the falsity of $KaKap$ we need to show the falsity
of $Kap \& EaKap$, which is equivalent to showing the falsity of
$EaKap$. What we *cannot* do is assume the equivalence of showing this to showing the falsity of $Ea(p \& Eap)$. This is
because "Ea" is as referentially opaque as "Ka": having ϕ-
evidence that p has to be interpreted, as we saw earlier, as
meaning that a has come into possession of the evidence in
such a way as to *take* it *as* grounds for p, and it is the notion
of *taking* evidence *as* grounds for p that here generates
opacity.[31]

We are thus faced with the curious possibility that $EaKap$
might be true though $Ea(p \& Eap)$ is false: a may have good
evidence for Kap, taking it to be such, but not have good
evidence for $p \& Eap$, taking it to be such, because he does not
realize (or accept?) the equivalence of Kap and $p \& Eap$.
And there is a further snag. The falsity of $EaEap$ only entails
the falsity of $Ea(p \& Eap)$ in the presence of a principle such
as (12), $Ea(p \& q) \rightarrow Eap \& Eaq$; this principle may also be
doubted on the lines of the doubts just raised concerning (21)
—a may have ϕ-evidence for $p \& q$ but not for p or for q
separately precisely because he has not realized that each is
a logical consequence of $p \& q$. Thus showing the falsity of
$EaEap$ is not enough to show the falsity of $Ea(p \& Eap)$,
and, even if it were, this would still not show the falsity of
$EaKap$.

It is true that our earlier arguments depended upon principles like (20), and that anyone rejecting these principles can reject those arguments. But the fact remains that the supposed counterexample to $Kap \rightarrow KaKap$ is intuitively as successful in showing the falsity of $EaKap$ as it is in showing that of $EaEap$. I *did* know that p, but had only mixed evidence (my answer together with my surprise, and so on) for my knowing that p, not enough to be called ϕ-evidence for Kap. I conclude, then, that these somewhat formalistic objections, though correct as objections to my procedure, go no way towards saving the analyticity of $Kap \rightarrow KaKap$.

IX

In conclusion, it may be worth mentioning certain cases that either might be or have been supposed to be counterexamples to $Kap \rightarrow KaKap$ but which do not seem to me to be such; I mention them mainly to indicate that my present position in no way depends on such cases. The most obvious one has already been mentioned: the sleeping man who knows that $2 + 2 = 4$ but, while asleep, does not know that he knows. Unless more is added to the description of the case, it just will not do; to the extent that he knows even though asleep, he also in *that* sense of "know" knows that he knows.

Hintikka mentions another kind of case,[32] in which a man (implicitly) knows that p but has not yet realized that the evidence he has points that way: for example, Oedipus knows that he is the murderer of Laius (has the evidence) but (at a certain point in the play) does not know that he knows. A somewhat similar case would appear to be Plato's slave in the *Meno:* he knows that p all along (as is shown by his following and accepting the proof) but at the outset does not know that he knows; this is no doubt one sense of "I suppose I must have known all along, and never realized I knew." But again it seems that two senses of "know" are involved; perhaps there is an "implicit" sense in which the slave knows the theorem all along; but I can see no reason why he did not also "implicitly" know that he "implicitly" knew. On the other hand, in the sense of "know" with which we have been mainly concerned in this paper, he did not know that he knew until he had followed the proof; but then until that moment he did not know *simpliciter* either—did not have the evidence in the way of taking it as grounds. Indeed, following the proof is precisely *coming* to know. Hintikka's Oedipus case, if I understand it correctly, is similar; of it I am inclined to deny that Oedipus *did* know that he was Laius' murderer; he has in a way evidence for this proposition, but does not take the evidence as grounds for its truth. Oedipus resembles the man mentioned earlier who has the proof in his pocket but does not realize that it is there.

A third case, mentioned by Hintikka[33] is that in which a man may say "I know but don't *know* that I know" in the sense "I have the grounds, but don't feel certain I have the grounds." This is no doubt idiomatically correct, but again the second occurrence of "know," in the sense "feel certain," is different from the sense of the other two occurrences, so that no counterexample to $Kap \rightarrow KaKap$ is here given.

Indeed, it is fairly clear from the present analysis that, if there is to be a counterexample to $Kap \rightarrow KaKap$ of other than a punning kind, it will have to be one in which a's ϕ-evidence for p is distinct from the ϕ-evidence for Kap, and further where though the former evidence is at a's disposal the latter evidence is not. Reflection on these conditions will lead the reader, I suspect, to the conclusion that the only counter-examples to $Kap \rightarrow KaKap$ are on the lines of the one stressed in this paper. Indeed, if I can be persuaded that this counter-example is after all not one, then I shall be strongly inclined to believe that it *is* analytic that if I know then I know that I know.

NOTES

1. E. J. Lemmon, "Is There Only One Correct System of Modal Logic?" *P.A.S.*, Supp., vol. 23 (1959), pp. 38–39.

2. See L. J. Cohen, *The Diversity of Meaning*, pp. 223–224, and J.

Hintikka, *Knowledge and Belief: An Introduction to the Logic of the Two Notions,* Ithaca, 1965, pp. 105–106.

3. Perhaps "hear" is the hardest verb, and "why to" the hardest construction. But why not "I heard on the radio this morning why to wash lettuce before eating it"?

4. In what way? To say it is in most circumstances (not all: compare "I always forget that . . .") to falsify it. In this it is a bit like "I am not thinking": see my "On Sentences Verifiable by Their Use," *Analysis,* vol. 22 (1962), pp. 86–89.

5. Admittedly in a rather odd way. If not-*p*, it does not follow that he *thinks* he forgets that *p* but doesn't really; rather, when *I* say "he forgets that *p*," I imply that I know that *p* but he doesn't. Perhaps "he forgets that *p*" entails *p* in the way that "he doesn't know that *p*" sometimes does. Compare Hintikka, *op. cit.,* pp. 12–13.

6. Compare also the *Shorter Oxford Dictionary,* s.v. "learn": "learn him a lesson," 1889. It is not clear that the classical direct and indirect object distinction does full justice to such cases.

7. I suppose we don't say "he knows to swim" in the sense *il sait nager.*

8. "Doubt" takes "that" and "whether" but not "where," "when," etc. Contrast "wonder," which takes any of the constructions except "that."

9. Yet knowing how to is *not* the same as being able to; I may know how to play the piano—have learned how to, practised, have indeed been a concert pianist—but have lost both hands.

10. This was suggested in my article mentioned in footnote 1.

11. See A. Kenny, *Action, Emotion, and Will,* chap. 8.

12. Other logical symbolism employed from here onwards, it is hoped, is perspicuous. I might add that throughout I have been more careless than I should have been concerning quotation conventions and the like.

13. Cohen, *op. cit.*

14. J. L. Austin once suggested to me that "I know" was a "disguised perfect" tense.

15. Aristotle, *Nichomachean Ethics,* bk. VII, chap. 3.

16. *Op. cit.*

17. A. D. Woozley, *Theory of Knowledge,* p. 192.

18. R. Chisholm, *Perceiving, a Philosophical Study,* p. 16.

19. It is arguable that the implication from left to right in (12) is a good deal more plausible than that from right to left: this depends partly on what "ϕ" is in "ϕ-evidence." However, in fact only the former implication is relevant to what follows. For doubts concerning even that, see pp. 75 ff.

20. Of the four conjuncts of (14)'s right-hand side, I have avoided discussing the three involving belief, since this would take us too far afield. However, I think a good case could be made out for the falsity of at least *BaBap* and *BaEap* in the case imagined.

21. A. J. Ayer, *The Problem of Knowledge,* New York 1956, chap 1.

22. *Ibid.,* p. 33.

23. *Op. cit.,* pp. 20–21.

24. A.PKK*, p. 17.
25. Cf. *ibid.*, p. 105.
26. *Op. cit.*, p. 18.
27. See G. H. von Wright, *An Essay in Modal Logic*; E. J. Lemmon, "New Foundations for Lewis Modal Systems," *J.S.L.*, vol. 22 (1957), pp. 176–186; Hintikka, *op. cit.*
28. In the article mentioned in footnote 1.
29. Cf. *op. cit.* pp. 31–32.
30. *Ibid.*, pp. 34–35.
31. Chisholm, *op. cit.*, chap. 11.
32. *Op. cit.*, pp. 112 ff.
33. *Ibid.*, p. 115.

2

THE OTHER MINDS PROBLEM

P-PREDICATES

TERRY FORREST

I

To say of another that he is in pain, depressed, angry, hopeful, expectant, resentful, disappointed, thinking about his promotion, doubtful that it will rain, convinced that the Tories are intellectually bankrupt, or wondering whether to take a bath, are some from among the wide range of terms that have come to be called "*P*-predicates," the ascription of which

The philosophical world suffered the loss of a great young talent when Terry Forrest died of a heart seizure at the age of 34. Mr. Forrest, who was a lecturer in philosophy at the University of British Columbia, was working on a manuscript on the Other Minds Problem at the time of his death. He had planned to submit this work to the Department of Philosophy at the University of California, Berkeley, as his thesis for the Ph.D. degree. Mr. Forrest and I had had a number of lengthy conversations about his approach to the Other Minds Problem, and on the basis of these discussions, I requested that he rework some of the material from his thesis into an article on "*P*-predicates" which I would include in this book. Unfortunately, he died before he was able to bring either the thesis or the article to completion. The executors of his estate, Professors R. J. Rowan and D. G. Brown, were kind enough to send me all the manuscript material found in his study after his death. From this material, I have extracted two self-contained sections which deal with *P*-predicates. Since this material was in "first draft" condition, I have rewritten large portions of it with the aim of improving its readability while retaining the essential structure of its arguments. No doubt Mr. Forrest would have had reservations about publishing it in this state; nonetheless, it seems to me a very interesting piece of work and well worth inclusion in this volume. (A.S.)

to a creature, in at least some of their uses, are descriptions of, or statements about, its mind. Likewise, the question whether a particular creature has a mind is not different from the question whether at least some from among this range of *P*-predicates can in fact, or could with sense, be ascribed to it. This is to say no more, but no less, than that the conceptual connection between "mind" and "pain, depression, conviction, belief" and the rest of the members of the class of *P*-predicates is such that the ascription of the former logically entails the ascription of some of the latter, and vice versa, without engendering any commitment as to the logical equivalence or conceptual identity of the former with some from among the latter, or even an indefinite disjunction of members of the latter.

It seems incontestable that behavior, including what a man says, is the primary basis upon which others make their ascriptions to him of various *P*-predicates. "Behavior" is, however, a term of such breadth that more needs to be said about how we are to understand it.

It is obvious that some among the items which form our basis in particular cases for ascribing a *P*-predicate to a man would be called actions of his. "Action" is itself a difficult term to get clear about, as has been demonstrated by the volume of philosophical writing recently dedicated to its explication.[1] One of the primary difficulties about "action" is that any attempts at explication immediately involve concepts such as that of intention, purpose, voluntary, and free, which are themselves of equally problematic status. For our purposes we need not enter this area. I wish only to say that I mean to include under the generic term "behavior" what can properly be called action, whatever the proper account of this latter may in detail turn out to be. It should also be mentioned that in typical cases action involves the making of more or less gross physical movements, although it is by no means to be identified with such movements, for the reason among others that one and the same set of bodily movements may properly be involved in different actions, and the same action may involve different sets of bodily movements; care must also be taken to remember that action may involve the suppression or restraint of such movements as well as the making of them.

Activity is again distinct from action, but it is necessary for our purposes to include it under the notion of behavior. That a creature is engaged in some activity of a specific sort, or engages in it on occasions over a span of time, may well be for us one—or even the leading—item on the basis of which we should be willing to ascribe a *P*-predicate to it. There are other items falling under the rubric of behavior, besides those of action and activity, such as response or the lack of response; attitude, in the sense of bodily position, both of the whole body and of particular parts such as the limbs.

Besides the items which would properly fall under behavior in the broad sense described above are things such as states or conditions of the body or of its parts. Flushing, perspiring, twitching, smiling, pallor, muscular tension, trembling, groaning, wincing, and frowning would be examples. Some of these lead a kind of double life: flushing may be simply a visible redness or reddening of parts of the face or ears, and may also be blushing. Groaning and frowning may refer in a natural way to a particular kind of sound emanating from a creature's mouth or to the characteristic disposition of the skin on a creature's forehead, and may also carry an additional implication lacking in the former uses which brings them onto a level equivalent to a kind of behavior or even action.

There may be already a strong disposition to say that the Other Minds issue has already been begged. The problem posed is whether we can know that another creature has a mind, and with right or justification ascribe to it particular *P*-predicates from among the class of those the ascription of which is a part of what it is to say that it has a mind. But the very list of items on the basis of which I have claimed that we do make such ascriptions includes things which are themselves at issue, or if they are not themselves at issue then they involve items that are. To mention actions, activities (and, therewith, intention and purpose), wincing and frowning, is to cite as the basis for the ascription of *P*-predicates other *P*-predicates, or predicates involving them. But this is just what is at issue, and the original problem can be simply shifted to asking of them with what right or justification, if at all, we can identify a set of bodily movements as, for example, "holding one's cheek" rather than as "his hand moving to and remaining in contact with his cheek"—or "his lashing out with his fist" rather than "his balled hand moving suddenly outward from his body." The justification for the ascription of a class of predicates cannot be carried on in terms of that class itself.

My rejoinder to this objection would be as follows: It is certainly true that in many cases where we are prepared to say of a man that he is angry or depressed or in pain, the things we would mention as the basis for saying that he is include such things as "He is holding his cheek," "He winces when his tooth is touched," "He is clenching his fist," and "He seems to have little interest in diversion or amusement." And it is no doubt true that these latter items cited as grounds for the former fall themselves within the class of *P*-predicates in question. But we must distinguish two different questions, which the objection overlooks. They might be called "internal" and "external" questions. The internal question is of the following nature. We have within language a range of terms which we can characterize as *P*-predicates, and which we ascribe to creatures other than ourselves as well as to ourselves. In the case of other-ascription, the basis upon which we do so in particular cases with particular predicates consists in a range of phenomena of the sort outlined above. The question that has been raised is whether the grounds upon which we ascribe the particular predicate, say, being angry, are items of behavior which are not themselves in whole or in part identical with what is ascribed on their basis; and, further, since this latter is not itself open to direct observation or inspection in order to determine its existence, or presence, whether it follows that we are always making an inference or drawing a conclusion which we can never in any case confirm.

The very posing of the question in this way requires, *ex*

hypothesi, that the status of the basis as so identified be not itself questioned, but only questioned as to its status as a basis for the supposed inference to something else. This is not to say that one could not raise the external question, but only that one cannot do it at the same time as one raises the internal question if the latter is to have sense. The external question concerns the general nature and validity of inferences of the kind in question, while the internal question does not.

Perhaps the following analogy will illuminate these remarks. One may well raise a question as to whether, and in what way, a conclusion drawn from certain premises is supported by them. But sensibly to raise this question requires the presupposition or admission of canons of valid inference in terms of which this inference is to be assessed. An independent and different question may be raised about the soundness or legitimacy of these same canons of inference which in the former question must be assumed. In skeleton form, the distinction amounts to this: To ask whether items such as A, B, C provide sufficient evidence to draw the conclusion X can only make sense if one does not at the same time raise a question as to whether what is referred to as A, B, C is legitimately so referred to. But this does not preclude raising the question about A, B, and C as an independent question. Translating this into a case of the kind at hand, we may say that the two questions take the following form. We may ask whether, and in what way, a man's holding his cheek, wincing when his tooth is touched, and being careful not to chew food on that side of his mouth, is evidence, or sufficient evidence, for his having a toothache. But the question only makes sense provided we accept the identification of the movement he makes as correctly identified in the posing of the question. A different question one might raise is whether, and how, we identify the movement consisting in his hand's rising from his side until the palm comes into, and remains, in contact with his face, as a case of "holding his cheek."

The question with which we are faced, then, is that of describing in sufficient detail a range of cases concerning the

application of some particular *P*-predicate with a view to determining the nature and legitimacy of such ascription. We
observe a man who has just been struck on the forehead
with a stone. A swelling begins to appear at the point of
impact. The skin is broken and he is bleeding slightly. He is
gingerly touching the swelling and looking at it in a mirror.
He contorts his face and makes short sudden intakes of breath
each time his finger touches the swelling. Anyone would say
in such circumstances not only that the man has hurt his
forehead, but that his forehead hurts him. And to say that his
forehead hurts him is to ascribe the predicate "hurts" in the
way of a *P*-predicate (unlike: his forehead is hurt, or he
often hurts his forehead). The force of saying that the predicate is being applied as a *P*-predicate is to indicate that the
man is suffering, that not only is he doing what we can all
see that he is doing but that he is doing it *because* he is in
pain, *because* his forehead hurts him.

    There are a number of ways in which the skeptic may
question the ascription to him of "pain." His first argument
might run as follows: "I acknowledge all the things that you
have said about this man. He certainly was hit in the way you
describe, and he is certainly doing all the things you say he
is doing. But surely it is obvious that a man might do all these
things in these circumstances and still not be feeling any pain,
not be suffering, not be doing them *because* he is in pain.
Everything that you have noticed is entirely consistent with
saying that he is not in fact suffering. What you have adduced
doesn't prove it, although I grant that it makes it improbable,
even immensely improbable, that he is not suffering, is not in
pain." We may call this a moderate skeptical argument.

    The question we must ask the skeptic is this: When you
admit that he did undergo what we said he did, and further
admit that he is doing all the things we said he is doing, what
do you mean to suggest when you say that still he may not be
feeling pain, may not be doing what he does because he's in
pain? What, in such a case, is the cash value of "may not be
feeling pain"?

There are a number of possible responses. It might be claimed that it is possible the man is only faking, that often when one is hit sharply the shock of the blow temporarily numbs one so that there is no pain for a while. Or it may be that he is faking because he has been anesthetized in the forehead, or perhaps he hasn't the typical nerve pattern a person normally has in his forehead.

Having cited some of the responses that the skeptic might produce to our query, "What is the cash value of 'may not be feeling pain'?", I think it is worth meeting forthwith a further objection. The objection is that there is no reason why the skeptic needs to produce any of the specific ways above mentioned which constitute explanations of what he means to suggest when he says that the man may have undergone what was described, and has done what he was said to have done. Isn't it perfectly intelligible and sufficient that he simply reply "What I mean is plain enough. I mean no more and no less than that the man is behaving as you say, gingerly touching his swelling, sucking in his breath, and the rest, but that in fact he just isn't feeling any pain, isn't suffering. Surely this is not hard to imagine, for feeling pain and acting as a man who is feeling pain acts, are two different things. You are claiming, on the ground that he is acting as a man in pain might well act, that he is in fact acting this way *because* he is in pain, and all I am saying is that he may not be. Hume made it quite clear that what is distinguishable is separable, and these are certainly distinguishable and certainly separable, and the presence of the one is no proof of the presence of the other. So the burden falls on you and not on me. It is up to you to show that he is in pain; it is not incumbent on me to say in just what way he may not be."

There isn't any satisfying short answer to this objection. It has to do with issues that have been raised and discussed at considerable length in recent years, in particular by J. L. Austin.[2]

In discussing a possible question raised about an item which takes the form, "But is it a real one?", Austin seems to me to be making the same point in that connection as what is at issue here. He says that "The doubt or question, 'But is it a *real* one?' has always (must have) a special basis, there must be some 'reason for suggesting' that it isn't real, in the sense of some specific way or limited number of specific ways in which it is suggested that this experience or item may be phony. Sometimes (usually) the context makes it clear what the suggestion is: the goldfinch might be stuffed but there's no suggestion that it's a mirage, the oasis might be a mirage but there's no suggestion it might be stuffed. If the context doesn't make it clear, then I am entitled to ask, 'How do you mean?' 'Do you mean it may be stuffed or what?' *'What are you suggesting?'* "

I take it that what Austin says of "But is it a real one?" is true also of "But isn't it possible he may not be in pain?" or the variant "Mightn't he not be in pain?" But what Austin says on this matter, although in my opinion right, needs filling out. Whether the way in which I expand on this would be entirely consonant with Austin's own views is immaterial. It is at any rate a view which I am prepared to defend. I might also say that there is a tempting but wrong way to answer this objection. An example of the wrong way occurs in Norman Malcolm's "The Verification Argument,"[3] in which Malcolm argues essentially that in certain circumstances it is not possible; that given the behavior, the man *must* be in pain. As I shall want to argue, Malcolm's thesis seems to be typical of the responses to skepticism which, in seeking to deny its claims, are forced to assert claims which are equally untenable, equally indefensible.

The kinds of ways in which I provided content to the skeptic's suggestion that the man might not be in pain, although he was acting just as a man in pain acts, are I think ones that anyone would acknowledge as making it understandable how it might be that this is so. It is important that we can all understand these, and that any of us might ourselves have suggested these, or others like them. The question as to whether the man might in these circumstances do what he does and still not be in pain is not an open suggestion. The "possibility" envisaged by the question is conceptually restricted to a range of specifiable circumstances which would be the respective situations in which such possibility consists. Leaving aside for the moment the further question of when, or under what circumstances, it makes sense to raise or bring into question some one from among this range of possibilities, what we are now considering is whether some one of them must be forthcoming if the question of "possibility" is raised. If the skeptic responds to "what do you mean?" by saying, "It's possible he isn't in pain," and if all he means by saying this is that although the man is behaving in the way he does he is nevertheless not feeling any pain, then I think that this explains nothing, for that much was already clear. The point is that the possibility which the skeptic is suggesting, if it should turn out to be realized, will be such that we shall be prepared now to say that the man is not, after all, in pain, although he appeared in every way to be so. But in whatever way this "turns out to be so," in whatever way the possibility is "realized," it must be in *some* particular way, and furthermore that way must be in principle (if not in *this* case), something for which there are, in Austin's words, "recognized procedures (more or less roughly recognized, of course) appropriate to the particular type of case." A "possibility" which, when specified, could in no way ever be discovered, is not a possibility, but merely an empty form of words.

All of the specifications which I provided as examples of how one might fill out the assertion that "It's possible . . ." are ones which are such that at least in principle (in favorable cases) could be discovered. Whether a man is feigning pain, or lacks normal nerve patterns, or is merely examining the swelling out of interest, are things that could be checked. We can, if we really do entertain these suggestions, try to observe him when he thinks no one is looking, or subject him to a series of physiological tests. Of course, he may be too spry for us to catch him off guard, or our tests may be carelessly run: but he might have been less spry, and we might have had a careful

technician helping us. If in no cases such techniques would be
of avail, then the very suggestion that perhaps he's feigning
would lack sense. It is not just that one could never tell, but
that in such circumstances there would be nothing of which
to tell.

There is another faint parry that the skeptic could make.
He might reply that all the talk of specific possibilities has
its place, but he meant nothing more by saying that it's possible than that one is not contradicting oneself by stating that
the man is acting in every way as a man in pain acts, and
that he is not in pain. "It's possible that . . ." means "It's not
impossible," and "It's not impossible" means "It's not a contradiction." And surely your own examples show that it's not
a contradiction, for what do they amount to but the admission
of behavior, and the denial of pain.

My response is that they mean more than this, and that
"It's possible" as used in the circumstances cited doesn't mean
"It's not a contradiction." If we granted that all that one meant
to be saying by saying "It's possible" is that it is no contradiction, then this would be of no interest, would have no point.
Although I have reservations about the distinction between
"relations of ideas" and "matters of fact" (analytic-synthetic),
these reservations have more to do with its employment in
too indiscriminate and ubiquitous a way, rather than with
whether it does indeed mark out a broad and useful division
which needs to be delineated. With this caveat, there is no
doubt that our original statement that the man is in pain
would fall within the category of statements intended to record
matters of fact. But it is one of the distinguishing, if not defining, criteria of this class that its members are not logically
entailed by any one, or a number of, its other members. Hence,
to tell me that "It's possible he doesn't feel any pain, despite
all of his behavior," where "It's possible" means "It's not a
contradiction to assert all of the statements which describe his
behavior and to assert the negation of 'He's in pain,' " is tantamount to telling me that the statement which I uttered concerning his being in pain, and uttered as a statement of fact, is

indeed a statement of fact. But if that isn't what one meant, which of course was not what the skeptic meant, since he wishes to insinuate a doubt about whether the man is in fact feeling pain, then the wheel has come full circle, and he *must* be prepared to specify in what way the man might be behaving as he is, and still not be feeling pain.

I claim, in short, that the response "I mean by 'It's possible' that he's faking in order to get off from work" means more than, amounts to more than the admission that he may be behaving thus, but not be feeling pain. It certainly involves this, but it adds, importantly, that this may be a case of feigning. What *does* this add? It tells us in what way the behavior can be as it is, and still allows for the man not to be feeling pain. It provides a mode of explanation of the discrepancy, the disparity, which will account for the absence of the phenomena ascribed by means of the *P*-predicate, despite the presence of all the normal phenomena on the basis of which the *P*-predicate is properly applied. To feign pain is intentionally to act in the ways that a man in pain would act, to do this in order to deceive others, and to induce them to believe that one is in pain. Thus to say that a man is feigning is to say not only that although he is acting as a man in pain would, nevertheless he is not in pain, but it also serves to explain the manner in which this is so by providing a concept which designates an intelligible and known pattern of human behavior. It casts the elements of the situation into a new framework.

Furthermore, the concept of feigning in general entails, although in the particular case does not guarantee, that relatively specific sorts of lapses from the normal course of the pattern of subsequent behavior of a man who is in pain will occur. In addition, I think it presupposes that certain situations of a broadly describable sort obtained antecedent to the occurrence of the pain behavior. What I have in mind is that if a man is feigning, which involves his acting in order to deceive, then in general there will be reasons for his engaging in deception which will have to do with his situation before he engaged in the deception. Things, for example, such as his relation to

those whom he intends to deceive, or perhaps the existence of
an insurance policy which would pay him some amount if
he were to be suffering from a bad back. Feigning is a kind
of action which, like all action, in general flows out of antecedent circumstances and yields a train of subsequent traceable
behavior.

II

As I pointed out earlier, to discuss whether a particular
item has a mind is the same thing as asking whether we can
with sense (not necessarily truth) say certain kinds of things
about it. This can also be put by saying that it is the same
question whether a range of predicates can with sense be
ascribed to it. People are the paradigms of the kind of creatures to which we apply such predicates, although we do so
to animals as well. It is obvious that we are willing to apply
certain predicates to people, say certain things of them, which
we are unwilling to say of anything else, or are only willing
to say of these other things with reservation. It is primarily to
persons that we ascribe pain, anger, hope, expectation, intention, belief, puzzlement, depression, melancholy, vanity, jeal-
ousy, and astonishment. The list is obviously indefinitely ex-
tendable. Let us call such ascriptions "*P*-predicates." As well
as these, we also say of people that they are upstairs, getting
heavier, six feet tall, cut, lying on the ground, or underwater.
Let us call such ascriptions "*M*-predicates." These latter sorts
of things we say equally of a wide range of physical objects
as well as of people. It is in the applicability of the former
group that we are inclined to say that the distinctiveness of
persons resides, and in the applicability of the latter that their
community with the rest of the natural world belongs. If it is
in the possession of rationality that man's distinction within
the animal kingdom lies, then it is in the ascribability of *P*-
predicates that his distinction within the natural world lies.
We could say that the distinctiveness of a type of entity can be

identified by specifying a unique range of predicates which apply to it. Persons are such a type of entity in virtue of the applicability to them of both *P*-predicates and *M*-predicates.

Although we have given a sample list of the kinds of predicates which fall into each class, we have not even begun to say what the features of the classes are. We have not begun to describe that, in virtue of which, a predicate is to be classified either as a *P*-predicate or an *M*-predicate. On what grounds should we assign or refuse to assign a suggested candidate to one class or the other?

Not on the ground that *P*-predicates are those which we apply only to persons, since we are trying to explain what it is to be a person in terms of the applicability of a restricted range of predicates. It is crucial then to be clear what the character is of the classes whose members are respectively *P*-predicates and *M*-predicates.

P. F. Strawson, who introduced the terminology of *P*-predicates and *M*-predicates, although of course not the conception of the two classes so referred to, has surprisingly little to say about them beyond listing a few of each. About all he says is that "although not all *P*-predicates are what we should call 'predicates ascribing states of consciousness' (e.g., 'going for a walk' is not), they may be said to have this in common, that they imply the possession of consciousness on the part of that to which they are ascribed."[4]

But this is no help at all, for consciousness is itself a central one among the class of *P*-predicates, and cannot therefore be of any use in delineating the nature of the class.

In the literature two features are suggested as distinctive of the class of *P*-predicates. It is these features which presumably separate this class from the class of *M*-predicates.

The first is that they suffer from a peculiar sort of systematic ambiguity or equivocation. Take anger as an example. When I say "I am angry," and likewise when you, or any other person says of himself, "I am angry," the criterion or basis upon which he says this is a feeling of anger which he, and only he, feels. But when I say of you, or of anyone other than myself, or when anyone else says of me, or any other person than himself, that he is angry, the criterion or basis upon which I, or you or they say it, is the behavior of the other, and not the feeling which only he can feel. Thus, since the criteria of ascription are systematically different, not as between persons and nonpersons, but as between the speaker and other persons, this constitutes a distinctive feature of their use which is not true of M-predicates.

It should be remarked that this feature is sometimes held, but need not be, also to entail that there is a systematic ambiguity of meaning coincident with and dependent upon this systematic asymmetry of grammatical person. Why it need not follow I shall explain later. Granting (what is highly contentious) that there does exist such an asymmetry, is it the case that this is not true of M-predicates?

"Is six feet tall" is an M-predicate. It does seem true that my basis for saying "I am six feet tall" is fundamentally the same as my basis for saying that anyone is six feet tall, and is the same as your basis for saying this of me. Any measuring device used by you on me, or by me on you, is the same as I would use on myself, or you on yourself. And there is none that is in principle or in practice unavailable to either of us in either instance. (Consider whether placing myself against a measuring rod is "egocentric.")

But there are other M-predicates which seem without doubt to be M-predicates, of which this doesn't seem true. Consider the predicate "mouth is open." Normally I can say whether my mouth is open without looking to see whether it is, or touching it with my hand to find out. But I cannot determine whether your or anyone else's mouth is open without doing one or the other of these things. And the same is true of you and of everyone else vis-à-vis me and any others. (Although I may in some circumstances need to look at or touch my own face, normally I need not. But I must, or someone must, look at or touch your face to tell.)

However, the situation is even worse than this. Not only can we find cases such as the above, where what is held to be a unique feature of *P*-predicates happens to be true of an *M*-predicate, we can also find cases of *P*-predicates of which it is not true.

A weak case is found for any of the wide range of predicates which we could call "capacity" or "character trait" predicates. Vanity, courage, loyalty, wit, and intelligence are among these. There is little question that there is not the suggested asymmetry between first-, and second- and third-person uses of these predicates. I come to know in the identical ways of myself whether they are applicable or not to me, as I do whether they apply to you, and equally for you vis-à-vis me. The reason I call these "weak" cases is because I think they do lie closer to the periphery of *P*-predicates than do many others. The reason, in short, is that they all presuppose the applicability of more basic *P*-predicates such as "thinks," "conceives that," or "views as." In order to be a prospective candidate for vanity or loyalty, the subject must already be viewed as a creature having a conception of himself, and of others as self-conceiving creatures; because vanity involves holding a view of oneself which is a possible object of the view that another has of one; and loyalty involves seeing oneself as related to others who are of a like type, and who might relate themselves in a like manner to you.

A strong case can be found with "angry." Although it is no doubt normally true that I know that I am angry without reference to how I am behaving, it is still not rare (even common) to find to one's surprise that one is angry by noticing that one is stuttering, perspiring, and saying rude things. And if these are, as often they surely are, the same ways in which I can tell that you're angry, and you of me that I am, then we have a case of the lack of asymmetry claimed to be unique to *P*-predicates.

Some objections might be raised to my examples. It might be claimed that the case of "mouth is open" is spurious. I asserted that in normal cases I can say whether my mouth is open without looking or touching. The counterclaim might be that even though this is true, the fundamental criterion is still sight, or even better, touch. This for the reason that, should there be a discrepancy in a particular case between what I say without looking or touching, and what I should then see or feel, the nod would go to the latter. If this is true, then the final test is nonasymmetric in the case of the first-, and second-or-third-person uses, and preserves the feature mentioned. I am skeptical, however, that this is so. It is easy enough to imagine cases where I might yield to sight or touch; for example, if I had just had a tooth filled under anesthetic. But I can equally imagine situations in which sight or touch would yield to non-observational knowledge; situations in which there were other visual or tactual aberrations which would put these senses in question. And they might also lead me to wonder, if you say of me that my mouth is not open, whether your sight or touch was abnormal.

A different objection would take the following form. Rather than relying upon an argument as to which criterion would in particular cases be decisive, since this will depend upon the circumstances of that case, it might be maintained that sight and touch are the fundamental criteria in the sense that I never could have come to have such nonobservational knowledge of the state of my mouth unless I had repeated prior experience of seeing it in mirrors and feeling it with my hands, including opening and closing it and inserting spoons and items of food into it. So that nonobservational cases are derivative from the cases of observation. I am inclined to think the genetic account plausible, but irrelevant, since once acquired, it yields no order or primacy for the respective criteria.

A different sort of objection may be raised in connection with the case of anger, of being angry. I was claiming the availability of cases where the asymmetry is lacking, where my basis for saying "I am angry" is identical with your basis for saying of me "He is angry." The objection would run as follows: Of course there *are* cases such as you describe. But they are not only statistically in the minority, they are conceptually derivative and parasitic. The normal case is that one feels angry, and also behaves in the way described, as well as in more violent ways such as striking out or pounding the table. It is important in your description that the man is *surprised* to find that he *is angry*. He is surprised just because he doesn't *feel* angry, or at any rate hadn't noticed that he did until he noticed that his behavior was the typical behavior of an angry man. It is his *feeling* angry which is his primary criterion. Normally, in fact, when a person is angry, he doesn't even notice that he is stuttering or perspiring. And if he did, then attending to this would normally reduce his anger.

It is not odd to say "I am most angry, although I am not behaving in any of the ways that angry people behave," but it is odd to say "I am angry, but I don't feel the least bit angry." This serves to reinforce the point that it is the feeling that the man has which is his primary criterion for saying he is angry, while his behavior is a secondary criterion, something that he notices only incidentally as having accompanied the feeling of anger in past cases.

My reaction to this objection is this: I don't think that I really need this case to make my point. As long as the case of the *M*-predicate above described holds, it serves well enough. I am proving more than I need. But in fact, I think this case is not open to the objection imagined. The "feeling" mentioned as being fundamental, the feeling of anger, is suspect. In any relevant sense of "feeling," I can see no difference in my feelings when I am angry, or indignant, or extremely irritated. The difference is in the context, the situation, and the so-called behavior. In other words, the feeling of anger so-called, is only identifiable as such given a good deal besides what the objector means to refer to by "the feeling of anger." At least a part of what is needed in addition is constituted by the behavior and the situation, which I come to know about by observation in ways no different from those in which you come to know about them.

I conclude then that this suggested feature of *P*-predicates, which is supposed to distinguish them from *M*-predicates, is without merit. What is the second suggested feature? It is that

the particular to which a given ascription of a *P*-predicate refers is in some sense nontransferable. What is meant by "nontransferable" and what is the intended sense?

We may follow Strawson's account in this connection. In
considering what he calls the "no-ownership" or "no subject"
doctrine of the self, he says that it gives an incoherent answer
to the question "Why do we ascribe our states of consciousness to anything at all?" where he understands by "states of
consciousness" the ascription of any of the *P*-predicates we
previously cited. The no-ownership theorist is viewed as holding that the unique causal relation which one's body has to
one's experience provides sufficient reason for the idea that
"one's experiences can be ascribed to some particular individual
thing, can be said to be possessed by, or owned by, that thing."
The theorist is viewed as holding that so long as the possessor
is thought of as the body, the idea of possession makes sense,
since this is a contingent fact, due to the possibility of the
experience having been dependent on the state of some other
body. But once one begins to assign experiences to something
else, a self, or an ego, then the relationship is no longer contingent, but necessary.

Strawson holds this view is incoherent because the theorist,
in denying the legitimacy of a necessary sense of "possession,"
is forced to make use of the selfsame sense of "possession." In
trying to state the contingent fact that a class of experiences
are causally dependent on some body, he must state it in some
such form as "All my experiences are uniquely dependent on
body *A*." But the "my" is ineradicable, for the class of experiences he wishes to refer to is defined by their being mine, and
this is just the sense of "ownership" he means to be denying.
Strawson claims that this incoherence is a serious matter because
it denies what is prima facie so, namely, that we do in fact
ascribe our experiences to something, ourselves, in precisely
the logically nontransferable sense denied. We do not coun-
tenance the possibility that the identical pain which was in
fact one's own might have been someone else's. Strawson thinks
the explanation of this fact is found in the requirements of

identifying reference: such particulars cannot be identified except as the experiences *of* some particular identified person, and in order for this to be possible they must be possessed or ascribable in just the way denied by the theorist.

This argument is difficult to assess, since the idea that "the identical pain which was in fact one's own might have been someone else's" is not itself very clear. I gather that if *this* seems to Strawson not to make sense, that he would think that its negation makes perfectly clear sense: namely: "This identical pain which was mine mightn't have been anyone else's." But that seems to me as hard to understand as does the affirmative version. We shall have to return to the examination of the sense which can be made out of such assertions, but granting for the moment that we understand what is meant, then it seems to me that in the same way, and to the same extent, we should not be prepared to admit the sense of a parallel ascription of an *M*-predicate being logically transferable. Consider the case of "cut" or "bruised." These would both seem to be *M*-predicates, in the untutored and unexplained sense in which we have introduced that notion. It seems to me that to whatever extent we are prepared to withhold sense from "The identical pain which was mine might have been someone else's" we should be prepared to deny it to "the identical bruise (cut) which was mine might have been someone else's." This alone seems sufficient to allow us to say that logical nontransferability, if it is a characteristic of *P*-predicates, is equally a characteristic of *M*-predicates, and so an unsuitable feature upon which to base any supposed distinction between them.

What Strawson refers to as the "requirements of identifying reference in speech to *particular* states of consciousness," namely, that they must be identified as (via) the states of some identified person, is, I think mistakenly, thought of by him as unique to particulars of this sort. But it is in fact a general requirement of identifying reference to a wide range of particulars that they can only be identified as the states, processes, or conditions *of* identifiable particulars of some kind. Cuts, bruises, germinations, flows, weights, textures, densities, misfires, and shapes are all only identifiable as being *of* some particular of another type than themselves, which is in turn identifiable. Having said that certain particulars are identifiable only via the identification of particulars of another sort, it is another question to what extent, if at all, the rules of identity for them, as so identified, preclude our reidentifying them via another particular of the sort which they were originally identified by means of; or reidentifying them at another time with the same particular. Some examples may help.

Suppose I have a spasm in my gut. Five minutes later I have another. I say "It was the same each time." Is this to be understood as "I had two different spasms which were qualitatively indistinguishable from one another," or that "I had one spasm which affected me on two different occasions"? Probably the former, since the time of occurrence is one of the criteria for identifying spasms. It is also important to note in such a case that we do not have criteria for the continued existence of such a spasm during the time when it is not observable or felt.

A different case is that of a pain. In the case of a rheumatic knee, we are inclined to say that the twinges of pain I felt today were qualitatively the same as, but not identical with those I felt yesterday. But with an aching tooth that hurts, is anesthetized, and hurts again when the anesthetic wears off, or a headache which one suffers, relieves with aspirin, and later suffers again, or is, as we say, unnoticed for a while due to a pleasant distraction, or being startled, we should incline perhaps to say that it is one and the same pain, the identical pain, felt before, not felt for awhile, and now felt again. And it need not even be qualitatively the same: we may say that "My headache is not as bad as it was before I took aspirin," or "This headache is worse than it was before."

Perhaps it could be objected that these are cases where the material body via which the identification is made, is in each case the same. Instead, what is required is a case of a *P*-predicate, and of an *M*-predicate, identified as a particular, and the same particular, first via one and then via another particular of the sort by means of which it is identified. Consider "heat" as an *M*-predicate. Suppose we place cold water in a very hot metal container. We notice after a few minutes that the container is much cooler, and the water much warmer. "The heat is passing from the container to the water." We were originally prepared in such a case to identify the heat as a particular via the container, and are prepared to reidentify it later via both container and water, or even perhaps via the water alone. There is little temptation, if any, to want to claim that the heat which the container had was one particularized bit of heat, and that which the water now has is another, numerically distinct bit of heat. In such a case the overriding picture is of an absorption, or transfer of the heat from the one to the other, analogous to the way osmotic processes permit the passage of a bit of liquid from one body of liquid to another through a membrane. Electric current transfer would be a similar type of case, as might a discoloration bleeding from one fabric to another. We have then, cases of *M*-predicates which, when particularized, require identifying reference via particulars of another kind, but which do not have logically nontransferable association with them. They require the identifying mediation of some specific particular, but are not conceptually bound to them. Are there similar cases for *P*-predicates?

Primitives apparently believe that many bodily maladies can be "cured" by placing compresses and pads of various sorts on the affected parts, which serve to "draw out" the disease, or the spirits as the case may be. They provide a more attractive refuge than the afflicted body. Children will sometimes say that they wish you could have their cold, or hurting forehead, although when I catch your cold, you don't lose yours; I now have my own cold, and you still have yours. Colds are progenitive rather than nomadic. Fear or excitement may be contagious, but the contracted fear constitutes new instantiations of fear and not dispersions of the original. What we would seem to need in the case of, say, pain, would be something on the order of my feeling pain in my finger tip, and upon touching the tip of your finger with mine, you would

feel pain in the tip touched, and I would no longer feel pain
in my finger tip. We might say in such circumstances that you
now had the pain which I had previously had. Or if I still felt
pain, we might say that the pain was now dispersed, that I felt
a part of it, and you felt another part of it. But our experience
is not like this, although the possibility of imagining such
cases shows that it might be, that it is contingent. It is these
contingent facts which lead us to have the logic of the concepts
we do have, to employ the criteria of identity which we do.
To say "I can't have his toothache" is to make a logical (grammatical) remark about our concept of toothache; the logic of
which is determined by our experience. But, as Wittgenstein
remarks, "Of course, if we exclude the phrase 'I have his toothache' from our language, we thereby also exclude 'I have (or
feel) my toothache.' "[5] And Austin remarks "The man doesn't
'know his pain': he feels (not knows) what he recognizes as,
or what he knows to be, anger (*not his anger*), and he knows
that he is feeling angry."[6]

We say of people that, for example, "He has his father's
nose" as well as "She has her mother's grace and charm" or
"her mother's wit." Having the nose, grace, wit, or charm of
another is not the same as having his gloves, pocketbook, or
comb. In the former cases, there is not an independently identifiable particular which is now associated with one person, and
now with another; it is rather that each has an item of the
same generic kind which is in striking or important ways
similar in appearance. He may break his nose, without his
father's nose being broken, but she cannot soil her gloves,
without her mother's gloves being soiled.

I think that the cases described of cuts, bruises, and germinations are sufficient to show that at least some *M*-predicates
are such that they share with *P*-predicates the feature that
identifiable particulars of their kind are, in the sense explained,
logically nontransferable. I believe that the cases mentioned
of heat, electrical current, and discoloration show that others
do not share this feature. But the fact that some do is in itself
sufficient to warrant scrapping logical nontransferability as a
unique and distinguishing feature of *P*-predicates.

I am also inclined to think, although cases might be produced, that there are not any cases of *P*-predicates which are in this sense logically transferable. But the possibility of describing conditions under which we should say things that are tantamount to providing them with this feature, although in fact such conditions are not realized, poses an interesting question. (The possibilities I have in mind are those of the fingertip transfer of pain as described, and also cases such as Wittgenstein mentions, of pain patches.[7])

The interesting problem posed is this: We are inclined to say that "I can't have this toothache" and "Only I feel my pains" are statements which express part of the "logic" of the concept of toothache, or of pain. Or, in the idiom of Wittgenstein, they are "grammatical" statements. But it is easy to shift from saying something like this, to saying that they are logical truths, or tautologies. I have no wish, nor competence, to investigate what a logical truth is, but my understanding of what is meant by this is that it involves at least that the negation of a truth of logic is a contradiction. And people are inclined to say that it is a contradiction to speak of "his suffering from my toothache."[8]

But we have imagined cases where this might well be just what we should say. We have imagined certain things happening which don't. So if these are logical truths whose negations are contradictions, we have the curious phenomenon that if contingent matters which don't in fact happen did happen, they would be true, and their negations not contradictions, but simply false. But this is *not* the status of logical truths as ordinarily conceived. Nothing different in our experience would render "This vixen is not a female fox" true, or "Someone can count to the end of the series of natural numbers." So we must beware of understanding that when statements are described as "expressing part of the logic of a concept" or as being "grammatical statements" that this is equivalent to saying that they express logical truths, or that they are tautologies.

Rather, what seems to be meant, is that they are, *given* the character of our experience, expressive of the internal logic of the concepts we have and use and which are derived from and applied to that experience. What strikes one when it is put in this way is that a statement, which fails to accord with *that* logic, implies or entails that our experience would have to be different from what it is. This suggests that perhaps some of the seemingly paradoxical statements of skeptics and metaphysicians are not in the strict sense of "logic" logically untenable, but rather conceptually paradoxical because they involve, or imply, radically different ranges of experience from those we in fact have; such ranges of experiences as we have, when they come close to the core of our picture of the world and ourselves, can seem to be inevitable and ineluctable. That is perhaps why Wittgenstein constantly implores us to remind ourselves of our "natural history," of common and deep, and hence easily overlooked facts of experience. To do this is to refresh and resuscitate our conceptual framework, by exposing or reminding us of the very general and pervasive facts upon which it rests.

NOTES

1. See, for example, J. L. Austin, "A Plea for Excuses," in *Philosophical Papers*, Oxford, 1961; A. I. Melden, "Free Action," London, 1961; and G. E. M. Anscombe, "Intention," 2nd ed., Ithaca, 1963.

2. J. L. Austin, "Other Minds," *Proceedings of the Aristotelian Society*, Supp. vol. 20, 1946, p. 135.

3. *Knowledge and Certainty*, Englewood Cliffs, N.J., 1963, pp. 1–57.

4. P. F. Strawson, *Individuals*, London, 1959, p. 105.

5. L. Wittgenstein, *The Blue and Brown Books*, New York, 1960, p. 55.

6. Austin, "Other Minds," p. 141.

7. L. Wittgenstein, *Philosophical Investigations*, New York, 1953, p. 312, which is expanded upon by P. F. Strawson in his review in *Mind*, January, 1954, pp. 87–88.

8. Cf. Austin, "Other Minds," p. 141n., "The educative tautology '*He* feels *his* pain.'"

MY PAINS AND YOURS

ISABEL C. HUNGERLAND

I

I shall be concerned in this paper with the epistemological character of self-ascriptions and other-ascriptions of pain. Like most who write today on these matters, I reject at the outset the two extremes of crude behaviorism (when we seem to be talking about sensations, feelings, and so on, we are "really" only talking about behavior, or physiological events) and of Cartesianism (the only objects of "direct," that is, noninferential knowledge are one's own inner states). However, this rejection leaves open a variety of possible intermediate views. Suppose we accept the Wittgensteinian dictum, "an 'inner process' stands in need of outward criteria" as an expression of an intermediate view. How are we to take "criteria" in the dictum, and just what is the relation between criteria and inner phenomena? For example, one might take criteria as behavior patterns (or physiological processes or states) that are, in some way *correlated* with the inner phenomena, that is, which usually precede, or accompany, or follow the inner phenomena. (This interpretation might, in a very general sense of the word, be called a "causal" one.) But this account of criteria may be developed in at least two quite different ways.

The most familiar mode of development is to leave the concepts of "inner state" synthetically related to the concepts of outer (or public) criteria. Thus my friend, observing my behavior, infers, inductively, that I am elated, the occurrence of the correlated factor giving a certain probability that the inner state occurs, while I "directly confront" the inner state, and so do not need to depend on inference to know that I am elated. My judgment to that effect is, barring purely verbal errors, incorrigible, while my friend's judgment is eminently corrigible.

There are a number of difficulties in this version of the causal interpretation. I mention first two well-known objections that seem to me not at all unanswerable by an exponent of the view in question.

First, the inference has often been alleged to be a very odd one, for though I can observe the correlation of behavior and inner feeling in my own case, I cannot observe it in yours. An exponent of the view, however, can reply that the inference is, indeed a unique one, since the inner-outer phenomena relation is a unique one, but nevertheless has certain analogies to well-established examples of indirect verification, of past events by present happenings, of things which we in one way or another cannot observe, by things we can observe.

Second, it has been objected that the view that when one ascribes, say, elation, to one's self, the statement is incorrigible (except verbally), and that this so-called "Incorrigibility Thesis" is implausible for any kind of statement. The weakness of this objection lies in the fact that the Incorrigibility Thesis (while compatible with the view) is not necessitated by it, does not follow from it. A holder of the view is committed to the difference between direct verification (confrontation) of an inner state, and indirect verification (inference), but he is not committed to the thesis that the only mistakes we can make in direct verification are purely verbal ones. For example, when an oculist tests my eyesight by asking me how letters on a chart look, I might be said to have a "privileged access," based on direct confrontation, to information which he can get only by inference or by asking me. Nonetheless, it is plausible to hold that facts like self-deception, arising from vanity or fear, or inattention, due to fatigue or boredom, might lead me to make mistakes that were not purely verbal, in my report to the oculist. There is no reason why the same sort of factors might not lead to errors of substance in direct verifications of inner states.

The more serious difficulties in the view are, I think, these: The position has an initial implausibility, a counterintuitive character which it does nothing to dissipate. Surely we can all think of innumerable cases in which our knowledge of, say, our friends' elation or depression, seems as direct, as noninferential as our knowledge of our own elation or depression. "I saw that he was elated (or depressed)" we say in ordinary, uncomplicated cases. To analyze these primary or basic cases as instances of an elaborate and curious inference by analogy produces a singularly unconvincing account of the phenomena.

Last, there is the following difficulty of omission. If, as exponents of the view seem to hold, the descriptive content of concepts like that of *elation* is of something wholly inner, and hence wholly distinct from behavior, how is it that the tests for the occurrence of the inner phenomenon refer to something which is wholly outer? Must there not be some connection between the sense (descriptive content) of a concept and methods of testing the presence or occurrence of the sense, or content?

It is this difficulty which another version of the causal interpretation of criteria attempts to answer by making the correlated criteria part of the descriptive content of the concepts of inner states, or processes. Thus, a sensation of a certain quality Q becomes, in the new version, *by definition*, that quality which is correlated with $C_1, C_2 \ldots C_n$. The fact that in unusual cases, for example, in anesthetization or in artificial brain stimulation, the correlation may not hold, can be taken care of by adding a provided clause, or a "normality or usual circumstances" proviso to the definition. I find three main difficulties in this version.

First, if when I ascribe a sensation of quality Q to myself, I ascribe the same predicate (am concerned with the same concept) as when I ascribe a sensation of quality Q to you, and if Q is defined (with a proviso) in terms of outer phenomena, $C_1, C_2 \ldots C_n$, why is it that in self-ascription, verification (or confirmation) is so different from verification (or confirmation) in other-ascription? Even though my judgment that I have a sensation of quality *Q* need not be taken as incorrigible, still I do not seem to have to wait to observe my behavior, or learn about my physiological processes, to know that I have a sensation of quality *Q*.

Second, this version attempts, as it were, to close the gap between "inner" and "outer" implicit in the first version, by placing the "outer" into the definition of the "inner." But the gap has been simply relocated; it still produces puzzles in its new place. The pattern of the proposed definitions is a curious one. It is as though we should (as we well could) propose to define a certain color, *C*, as that color which is (usually) found in such and such flowers. If we accept the definition, it is, indeed, analytic that *C* is (usually) found in such and such flowers. But the analyticity appears to be the result of an arbitrary and unenlightening procedure of definition.

Finally, the second version does not distinguish between two quite different sorts of attempts to analyze or, in a broad sense, define the concepts of ordinary life and language. There is, first, the philosopher's attempt to explicate these concepts by comparing their relationships and workings to relationships and workings of others from the same ordinary life context. Then there is the attempt of the scientist to explain the phenomenal world. In this accomplishment, the ordinary everyday concepts are replaced by scientifically satisfactory ones which are part of a theory. For example, the everyday concept of the color red, as a hue which lies between yellow and purple, is replaced by the concept of light waves of certain measurable properties. The relation between the ordinary concept and the scientific one is that of theoretic, or explanatory, identity, and the scientist might be said to be "defining" the ordinary concepts in terms of "correlated" phenomena. But the philosopher who wants to understand our ordinary concepts, whether of the colors we see or the pains that we have, must proceed in a different fashion. His problems are not solved or dissolved by a simple recourse to the concepts of light waves or physiological processes.

Another possible intermediate view arises from distinguishing criteria for the correct use of certain expressions from criteria in the sense of that *on the basis of which* certain expressions may be employed to make a statement. (I shall call the latter "criteria for support.") Then it can be said that while the criteria for support for self-ascriptions of concepts like that of *pain,* are wholly private and inner and for other-ascriptions wholly public and outer, in both cases the criteria for the correct use of "pain" are wholly public and outer.

This position has the virtue of pointing to the often ignored fact that "criteria" as a technical philosophical term has a variety of interrelated uses. It also has the virtue of directing our attention to what stands in need of philosophical explanation in concepts like that of pain. How is it that when I say truly "I am in pain" and you say truly, "Mrs. H. is in pain," we make the same statement (in the sense of same proposition, of what is true or false) but the support, the ways of confirmation differ strikingly. However, the distinction on which the view is based does not by itself answer the question, and we are left with the same puzzle that the first version of the causal interpretation engendered.

I propose in what follows to attempt to make out a position, intermediate to the rejected extremes of Cartesianism and crude behaviorism, which avoids the difficulties noted above and throws some light on the puzzles that remain. My attempt will be exploratory in character. I shall not try to answer such questions as "Is a private language possible?" or "Is physicalism true?" but will deal with matters which, I think, are preliminary to such questions. I shall start by making out a set of distinctions applicable to the whole field of language use, and then proceed to consider them in their application to the unique case of the relation of inner phenomena to outer, and I shall confine myself to pains, "Mine" and "Yours."[1]

The distinctions I make are not novel, and lines might be drawn, usefully, in different ways. But I find that the distinctions are often only implicit, or are not clearly developed in

discussions of the "outer criteria for inner phenomena" formula.
My drawing of the logical picture is not offered as final, but
only as adequate to the purposes of this essay.

II

The distinction between the sense (descriptive content) of
a statement (proposition) and the way in which the act of
making the statement (claiming truth for the proposition) receives logical support (confirmation, verification) goes back
at least to the early days of Logical Positivism in this century.
But that the distinction is one between two categorically different ways of considering linguistic phenomena is not always
made clear. To consider the sense or content of a statement
(proposition) is to consider abstract entities—identifiable
within speech acts but not to be identified with them—and their
entailment relations. (Speech acts have dates and places, propositions do not.) Thus, if I assert that John Jay Smith is the
father of Tom Jay Smith, or that there are four sheep in my
pasture, or that my pasture is triangular in shape, the sense
of what I am asserting, the content of the abstract entities,
the propositions, is explicated respectively, in entailments of the
form "X is the father of Y" entails "X is the male parent of Y";
"There are four sheep in my pasture" entails "There are
$1 + 1 + 1 + 1$ sheep in my pasture"; "My pasture is triangular
in shape" entails "My pasture is in shape a plane figure bounded
by three straight lines." There are, of course, other ways of
explicating, elucidating the sense of a concept. When we are
concerned with a working, and relatively vague language, the
giving of paradigm cases, and the examination of bizarre and
borderline ones may be a better way of making content clear
than is the offering of definitions and the drawing out of their
consequences.

Now, in considering the basis for my making any of these
claims, and hence the support I would bring forward for so doing, if the truth of what I claim is challenged, we find our-

selves in a different universe of discourse about discourse. For a claim of the form "S is the father of Y" I adduce various observations, testing, records; to support a claim of the form that the number of something is X, I refer to a procedure of counting; and to bolster an assertion like "X has shape Y," I make various measurements. Note that there are no entailment relations between the propositions claimed to be true, and propositions describing the supporting tests or procedures. *That the number of Xs is Y* does not entail *that a certain counting procedure with a certain result has been gone through*, this is not the sense of the proposition. Moreover, acts are not the sort of entities that have entailments, though, of course, descriptions of them can have logical consequences. In brief, what I support, give reasons for, and logically justify is the making of the claim that a given proposition, p is true. A given proposition, p, entails innumerable others, but among them is no proposition about the relevant testing procedures for bolstering the act of asserting that p.

If this account of a distinction often made roughly, but just as often blurred, is to be at all convincing, two questions must be answered. "Why is an obvious and important distinction often ignored?" and "What *is* the relation between the sense or content of propositions and the testing procedures which support claims that they are true?"

There are a number of reasons why the distinction is often lost sight of—only two will concern me here.

First, there is a fairly systematic and in many instances harmless ambiguity of the terms "assertion," "statement," "proposition" with a related ambiguity of the terms "support," "logically justify," "confirm," "verify." The ambiguity is that between a speech act and what can be identified as an abstract linguistic entity expressed in and through the speech act. We speak of "supporting a proposition" or "bolstering an act of assertion." Our logical notation fosters this harmless enough ambiguity, by representing propositions by the sentence forms, "X is Y," that are the conventional linguistic devices for performing an act of asserting that S is Y. I have no objection to the notation or to the ambiguities. I am concerned only when failure to note the distinction obscures the philosophical eluci- dation of a concept.

The second source of the blurring of the distinction is more directly related to the topic of this essay, for it is the source of the confused and confusing use of "criteria" as a tech- nical term in discussions of the relation of inner phenomena to "outer criteria." This source of confusion may be made apparent by considering the following examples.

Suppose I am challenged to support my act of asserting that John Jay Smith is the father of Tom Jay Smith or that there are four sheep in my pasture or that my pasture is trian- gular in shape. (We can put the challenge in this way: the truth of what I claim to be true is doubted, so I am called upon to support, to logically justify my acts of asserting *that* . . . .) Irrelevant and silly answers to the challenges would be "John Jay Smith is the male parent of Tom Jay Smith" or "There are $1 + 1 + 1 + 1$ sheep in my pasture" or "My pasture is in shape a plane figure bounded by three straight lines." In these cases the difference between giving the sense by giving entail- ments based on definitions, and appealing to the results of relevant methods of support, is strikingly clear. But suppose my claim is a bird watcher's one, that there is, say, a Horned Grebe in my pond and that this claim is challenged. Here my answer, without appearing silly, may well be "Yes it is, it does have these ducklike characteristics, and golden ear tufts, black head," and so on. This sort of answer seems to be simply an assertion that the creature in question does have the features listed in the definition of the species. So I seem at once to be giving entailments of my originally asserted proposition (hence, to be giving the criteria for correct use) *and* to be giving my support to my act of asserting *and* to be giving identifying criteria. Since bird-watching or similar examples have been prominent in current discussions of "criteria," it is no wonder that supporting criteria, criteria for correct use of an expression, and the sense of a given concept, have been taken as the same. I propose to sort them out and indicate what my technical uses of the expression "criterion" will be.

Assuming that it is not my knowledge of the definition of a species that is challenged when I assert that there was a bird of species "*F*" in my pond, then my support in the form of "Yes, it did have features T_1, T_2 . . . T_n," if it is a relevant answer, has the force of "Yes, I did observe it to have T_1, T_2 . . . T_n," and the proposition which can be extracted from this is clearly *not* entailed by the proposition that a certain bird is an "*F*." In brief, when the relevant test for supporting an assertion is not a definitely patterned procedure like counting or measuring, but merely looking to see, then it becomes easy to disregard or slur over the difference between elucidating the sense of what is asserted and supporting the act of asserting *that*.

In what follows, I shall, in order to mark the difference, employ "criteria for support" or "supporting criteria" when I am concerned with ways of testing or confirming our acts of assertion. Criteria of this logical sort are requirements which must be satisfied if the speech act in question is to have adequate support. To "satisfy the criteria," then, is to offer a supporting reason for an act of asserting, the reason being of the kind specified in the criteria.[2]

What are "criteria for identification" and "criteria for correct use" and how are they related to sense, or content, and to supporting criteria?

The concept of criteria for identification includes, I think, the defining characteristics of a class of things, but is often wider, including also some usually associated properties, for example, usual habitat in the case of zoological identification. Moreover, when we speak of identifying criteria, we may have in mind mainly either the phenotypical (the visually apparent or "surface") characteristics of a species or the genotypical (usually ascertained by more elaborate techniques, like dissection).

The expression "criteria for correct use" is sometimes employed to call attention to the defining characteristics of something and sometimes to call attention to the relevant criteria of support for an assertion. I might be said not to know the criteria for the correct use of "being four in number" if I didn't know that this entailed "being $1 + 1 + 1 + 1$ in number," but I could also be said not to know the criteria for the correct use of the expression in question if I didn't know that the primary supporting criterion for asserting that a set of objects is four in number was a certain procedure of counting and its results.

The next question to be answered is: "What is the relation between the sense, the descriptive content of what we assert, and the relevant (primary or basic) supporting criteria?"

It is clear that the propositions asserted in sentences of the form "X is red," "X is five feet long," "There are four Xs" do not alone, (that is, without additional premises) entail anything, respectively, about looking (vision), procedures of measurement, or of counting. However, if we examine the logical contexts, the network of definitions within which being X *in color, X in length, X in number,* appear, as definitions employed in describing the world, then the information that the presence of colors is ascertained by vision, that units of length are determined by certain procedures of measurement and that the number of a set of objects is determined by counting, this information becomes, not strictly tautologous, but truistic— extractable, I find, from the most ordinary of dictionaries by one who speaks the language. Accordingly, I shall say that the descriptive content of what we assert to be true, considered as the content of a natural, working language, "indicates" to us the relevant primary criteria of support.

There remain two more technical terms to elucidate. They have reference to speech acts, and the general kinds of distinctions they make have been very widely accepted in contemporary philosophy of language. I draw the lines a little differently from the accepted ways. The justification for this divergence can be found only in the results of working with the technical concepts.

I shall distinguish "normal" from "abnormal" speech acts, and both in turn from "pseudo-speech acts."

Speech acts, as we all know, can "go wrong" in a variety of ways. But only some of these ways of "going wrong" (of failing to satisfy certain requirements) are such that no speech act at all of the specific sort in question, takes place. Other deviations, for example, lying, employing words incorrectly, result in an "abnormal" but genuine speech act. A "normal" speech act fulfills all the relevant requirements.

I shall speak of a "pseudo-speech act" (and "pseudo-proposition") when one of the basic requirements for the *accomplishment* of an act is not satisfied and there is only an unsuccessful attempt to make an assertion. For example, successful reference of the referential terms I employ is essential to my making a genuine assertion.

If I say "My house is in Piedmont" when there is nothing to which "my house" refers, I have not succeeded in making an assertion, in saying something that is true or false. Note that it makes no difference whether my failure was due to ignorance of facts (unknown to me, in my absence, my house was burned down) or to my hallucinating, and so on—in neither kind of case is a proposition asserted.

Finally, the requirement of referential success calls attention to a special class of conditions for accomplishing a speech act, conditions generally called "presuppositions of statements."[3] One way of treating these requirements, however, leads to the awkward notion of statements (propositions) that are neither true nor false. I shall speak of "pre-conditions of asserting" and say that when pre-conditions are not satisfied, the result is a pseudo-act of stating and a pseudo-statement. I shall not attempt here to formally define the class of pre-conditions, but shall merely list two features which together serve to mark them off, roughly, from other requirements. First, they are conditions which a speaker must believe to exist, or hold, or at least somehow take for granted, if he is employing language correctly and is not lying. But, second, pre-conditions are not part of the sense, the content, of what the speaker asserts. For example, should I make the statement that *this student got an A and that student got an F*, pre-conditions for this act of assertion would be that there *are* the two students in question, and that the one referred to by "This" is nearer me (the speaker) than the one referred to by "That." Yet I do not assert that these conditions hold, nor are they entailed by the proposition I do assert.

In what follows, I shall apply the general distinctions developed in this section to our linguistic expressions in ascribing pain to ourselves and to others. I shall employ "pain-ascribings" to talk about our speech acts in this domain, and "pain-ascriptions" when I am concerned with the statements asserted. "$X \ldots P$" will stand for the propositional form displayed when sentences like "I am in pain" and "You are in pain" are used in pain-ascribings.

There are two main conclusions that I hope to establish. First, that the concept of being in pain not only comprehends both inner feeling and outer manifestation, but that these two aspects are so related that no "logical wedge" as the saying goes, can be "driven between them." In other words, I hope to show that the notion of a wholly inner (private) feeling (sensation) properly called "pain" is empty and that the notion of pain-behavior which is not manifesting behavior is equally empty. As a consequence, I shall argue, we cannot take "criteria for correct use," (whether we are talking about sense or supporting criteria) as referring us solely to outer (public) phenomena.

Second, that, though self-ascribings of pain have *somewhat* different supporting criteria than do other-ascribings, the criteria are not wholly different. This conclusion will establish a basis for arguing that the Incorrigibility Thesis has no plausibility whatsoever for self-ascribing of pain, and that in certain cases, you might have better knowledge of my pains than I have.

III

It will be convenient to start by pointing to two often neglected features of our talk about pain.

1. The concept of *being in pain* is a perfectly general one, that is, there is no peculiar logical priority for "*I*" as a value for "*X*" in "*X...P.*" To be sure, all pains are someone's pains just as all skills and abilities are someone's and accordingly, "I" (or "me," "my") are the correct words to employ when a speaker is reporting or describing his own pains, skills, or abilities. And, just as it is impossible for a given speaker's skills, abilities (or for that matter, a state or condition of his body) to literally be, now or later on, the skills and abilities, of another, so it is impossible for a given speaker's pains to literally be, now or later on, those of another. These logical facts do distinguish the way in which, say, property is mine, from the way in which skills, abilities (and states of my body) are mine. But they in no way force me to suppose that only when "I" is used to refer to *me*, Mrs. H., do I get what for me is the uniquely significant value of "*X*" in "*X...P.*"

2. Self-ascribings of pain have as pre-conditions the existence of the speaker's body, or at least of those parts of it essential to life. (Hence, in having the existence of a body as a pre-condition, self-ascribings do not differ in this respect from other-ascribings.) It is curious that this fact, (which even Descartes, in some passages, seems aware of!) should be neglected in some contemporary discussions. Perhaps it is because in concentrating on expressions of the form "*X ... P*" we can forget about the more common "I have a pain in my foot, a headache, a stomach-ache, and so on"; but "unpleasant sensation" is a rough synonym for "pain" and "bodily sensation" is a redundancy. When we hurt or ache "all over" or when our pains are not localized in relatively determinant areas of our bodies, we may well employ the "*X ... P*" form in self-ascribings without reference to a special bodily part. Later, in the course of my argument, I shall discuss further this class of pre-conditions for self-ascribings. Here, I shall content myself with noting that while "I have a pain in my foot" may be employed in a pseudo-stating (my foot has been amputated), it is an apparently contingent fact that "I have a headache" cannot be even thus employed if I have been beheaded. What about "I am in pain, but

have no body"? This, like "I don't exist" or "I am dead" is the
sentential form of the sort of paradox that results when I assert a certain proposition and conjointly deny that the pre-
conditions for asserting it hold.

What, now, is the sense, the descriptive content of "*X*'s
being in pain," whether "*X*" takes as values "my" or "your,"
and whether the body presupposed in pain-ascribings is the
one to which I have, or the one to which you have, the "strange
and intimate" relationship?

No philosophical problems, I think, were ever solved by
consulting a dictionary, but it can be, I think, a useful starting
point for philosophical clarifications of concepts. If we start in
this pedestrian way, what we get is something like "Pains are
extremely unpleasant, or distressing bodily feelings (sensations)." My dictionary rightly notes that the definition of pain
as a sensation "caused by excessive stimulation of nerve-end-
ings, etc." is a technical definition of science (psychology or
physiology), not a definition of ordinary language. The scientific definition concerns microscopic phenomena which are
correlated with the phenomena with which the ordinary concept is concerned, but the ordinary concept, I wish to show, is
not concerned with correlations, or causal laws at all.

Let us start by examining an uncomplicated paradigm example of *being in pain*. The assumptions will be that there is no
repression of pain-behavior, that is, of the natural manifestations of pain, that the subject has normal senses, and the usual
bodily parts (is not, for example, a blind mute or mutilated)
and that there is nothing unusual in the circumstances (he is
not, for example, tightly bound in the dark), and that the pain
is not of a special sort (stabbing, throbbing, and so on) but
just extreme pain, and that it is not very precisely localized.
(If at this point, someone should object "But I can't imagine
your paradigm case unless I am told whether I am to imagine
that the subject is me or someone else," my reply would be
"Imagine it as a novelist, not writing in Hemingway's style,
would imagine it.") The whole experience is something like
this. One has an extraordinarily distressing feeling, located

roughly in a relatively large area of one's body, and one both feels and observes the natural manifestations of distress, of unpleasantness that cannot be avoided or run away from because it is located in our own body. One feels the scream "rising" in one's throat and hears it as one hears another's. One feels and observes the writhing limbs, the flinching torso, and so on. (Note that it is essential to *what we think to be so,* that the limbs we feel and the limbs we observe are the same, that is, that there are not two sets of limbs and two torsos, the felt and the observed.)

Now, imagine the following examples, and ask yourselves whether or not they are examples of *being in pain.*

Imagine a compulsive neurotic or psychotic, in the numbed inner state of which so many of them complain ("I don't *feel* anything") who nonetheless is somehow "compelled" on occasions to go through the motions and make the sounds of pain-behavior. Is he in pain? The answer, I think, is "No" and it is "No" because behavior which is not manifesting (or displaying) behavior, is not pain-behavior.

Suppose now that we encounter a mystic who claims that as a result of intense mental and physical discipline he is able to "contemplate" his pains without distress, that is, without feeling the slightest inclination to display pain-behavior. Does he still have pains? Or imagine the case of one of those physiological oddities who, the doctors report, are unable to feel pain. Suppose one of these tells us that it is his conviction that he does as a matter of fact constantly feel excruciating pain, but is abnormal only in that he has not the slightest tendency to flinch, groan, and so on.

The point of both sorts of examples is briefly this. Not only does the sense of *being in pain* comprehend both inner and outer aspects, (feeling *and* behavior) but these are not synthetically related, not, that is, merely found empirically to be correlated, or causally connected. The reason is this. The notion of the unpleasant, the distressing is not just synthetically connected with the notion of avoidance behavior. (The notion of something which is extremely distressing but attracts every

actual or possibly imagined person, angel, or God, is paradoxical.) Now, pain is distressing but it cannot, since it is in
our bodies, be avoided, and the general features of pain-behavior are those which are appropriate to this sort of situation.

Accordingly, I suggest as a rough, informal expansion of
the sense of *being in pain*, that pain is a distressing bodily
feeling and a distressing bodily feeling is one which is naturally
manifested in the ways just indicated. It follows that when
we are concerned with the sense of being in pain, it is misleading to speak of "criteria of correct use," solely in terms of
outer phenomena, of behavior which is not taken as manifesting an inner state.

Thus far, I have examined the sense of *being in pain* with
only the paradigm, the normal and uncomplicated example in
mind. How does the account given fare when more complicated
cases are considered?

Pain-behavior may be repressed in greater or less degree
for a variety of reasons. Any defining account of pain, then,
which mentions manifesting behavior, must contain some *provided* clauses and also some account of the natural (small-scale)
behavioral features of repression. Note that no definition of a
natural object or phenomenon can be sensibly applied without
a knowledge of the relevant provisos. No competent ornithologist
supposes that if having a red head and a certain skeletal structure are characteristics contained in the definition of a certain
species of bird, then no bird with a white head or different
skeletal structure can be said to belong to the species. Perhaps
the bird is an albino and its frame has been twisted by disease,
or some human agent has altered it. Some writers on provisos
for definitions, make them part of the content. I am inclined
to treat them as rules for operating with the content, but this
matter has no great importance for my purposes here.

What is important for my purposes is that when there is
repression of the natural expression of pain, there may be dis-
plays of behavior that are the result of accepting certain social
conventions (the stiff upper lip, for example) or of personal

idiosyncracies (such as playing a certain piece of music). When this happens, some patterns or features of behavior are indeed just "symptoms" of someone's being in pain, not part of the sense of his being in pain; and from these symptoms, or signs, we make inferences. If these complicated cases are taken as the paradigm, of course, we get the view that pain-behavior only "happens to be" correlated with inner states and that I can only make inductive inferences about your pains. But there is no reason at all why these complicated and derivative cases should be our starting point.

If my account of ascriptions of the form, "$X \ldots P$" is thus far correct, it follows that "criteria for identification" of pain are the same for all instances of "$X \ldots P$," since the sense is the same.

The next main question to be answered is: how does the sense of pain-ascriptions "indicate" to users of the language, through a series of truistic moves, what the relevant criteria for support are? The answer reveals a unique logical feature of pain-ascribings (which they share with all ascribings of inner states), namely, that the criteria for support for self-ascribings are somewhat different, not exactly the same as the criteria for other-ascribings, although the sense of what is ascribed is the same. This is exactly what should be expected.

Pain-ascriptions are part of our common language and hence should be expected to share some features of all forms of ascription. I have shown this to be so in showing that propositions of the form "$X \ldots P$" have the same sense, no matter what appropriate value is substituted for "X." However, that sense, as I have attempted to elucidate it, does lead to the conclusion that the act of self-ascribing has some striking differences from the act of other-absorbing. For self-ascribings there is, as I made out in the paradigm case, as a basis for support, both "having" the feeling and feeling the manifestations, as well as observing them. In other-ascribing, there is and could be only observing of manifestations. Again, this conclusion is exactly what should be expected, for the inner-outer (private-public) relationship *is* unique, at least in certain ways. The conclusion appears paradoxical only if one overlooks the following points. When "criteria for correct use" are employed in connection not with sense, but with criteria for support, both you and I, as in the former case, have *exactly the same criteria for correct use*. We agree on what are the supporting criteria when "I" is substituted for "*X*" in ascriptions of the form "*X . . . P*" and also on what they are when "you" is substituted. It follows, of course from this general agreement that when the "I" happens to refer to *me,* Mrs. H., then the criteria for support my speech act differs partly from the relevant criteria when I, Mrs. H., substitute "you" for "*X*."

Should someone, at this point, object "But the concept of *being in pain* is fully exemplified for me only in my own case —how can I know that there are any other instances?" the reply runs as follows.

According to the account given, it would be *impossible* for *anyone* who understands the sense of being in pain in his own case, and what the related criteria for support are, in his own case, without understanding (a) the sense of the concept in other-ascriptions (for the sense is the same), and without knowing (b) what would be adequate logical support for his ascribing pain to another (for the criteria in his own case make plain that for others the criteria are and have to be patterns of pain-behavior), and (c) what would be adequate logical support for another's ascribing pain to him (for this information is also extractable from the criteria in his own case).

At this point, the question may arise "How does the Cartesian wedge get driven in between inner and outer phenomena?" It lies far beyond the scope of this paper to consider the sort of skepticism which results from supposing that if we can be mistaken in a given case of alleged knowledge of the pains of others, then we (probably) are mistaken in all, or the kind of skepticism resulting from a phenomenalistic and solipistic account of the concept of bodies. I shall have to confine myself to brief remarks about the special sort of skepticism which does not question that we have knowledge, acquired through observation and inference, about bodies, but supposes that, while we have a peculiar certainty in self-knowledge of states like pain, our alleged knowledge of the pains, and so on, of others has extremely shaky foundations, if foundations at all. Some of the main sources of this sort of skepticism are, I think, these. (1) A confusion of the sense of *being in pain,* with one part of the criteria for support in self-ascribing, namely, the having the feeling and feeling the manifestations. (2) Taking as the paradigm cases of self-ascribing of pain, those in which it would, indeed, be foolish to suppose that anything at all had gone wrong with the speech act, and where observation of one's own behavior need not be appealed to. (3) Taking as the paradigm cases of other-ascribings of pain, those in which inference rather than observation enters into the support, and which are imagined to be such that it would not be foolish to suppose that we are mistaken. (4) Forgetting that in the case of *any* empirical proposition, it is possible that, though we have adequate reasons for support of an act of assertion, (the criteria for support are satisfied) we still *might,* as a logical possibility be wrong. (To put the matter more formally: the statement "The criteria for support for asserting that p are satisfied" entails "p" only on the following vacuous definition of "satisfying the criteria for support": "The criteria for support for asserting that p are satisfied if and only if p.")

These remarks bring me to the topic of the Incorrigibility Thesis for self-ascribings of pain. I propose to argue for a Corrigibility Thesis for self-ascribings as well as for other-ascribings of pain.

Consider the wide variety of ways in which the speech act of self-ascribing of pain can go wrong.

First, the matter of "merely" verbal mistakes is far more complicated and serious than those holders of the thesis who admit their possibility seem aware of. We can with pains, provided they are not excruciating, get into the same sort of situation we do with the eye-doctor, hounding us to say how this or that letter looks to us, and we might decide in instance after instance that we did or might have "used the wrong word." Imagine a dentist, searching for defective tooth roots, tapping on one tooth after the other, asking "Is this painful?" In my efforts to reply "correctly," to give him the reports only of an "attentive and unclouded mind," I may find myself saying, "Well, it's partly pleasant, partly not, it hurts a little, slightly uncomfortable, but I wouldn't call it painful" and so on.

Then there are the reports made when our "mind" is inattentive and clouded, whether because of fatigue, boredom, or vanity that breeds self-deception, reports wherein mistakes that are not "just verbal" may occur. Imagine a patient with a mildly painful chronic disease. In the sort of circumstances indicated, a doctor with a good knowledge of the patient's personality and physiological state, might make a more correct report than the patient, might have more knowledge of the patient's pains than the patient has; and the patient might, having recovered an "attentive and unclouded mind" agree that he had been mistaken.

Consider next the familiar phenomena of "phantom limbs." A man, waking from the anesthetic after a left foot amputation may claim that he has a pain or ache in his left foot. He will have to resort to observation to learn that his speech act has gone badly wrong, for a pre-condition of his making the assertion he did, is that he have a left foot.[4]

I do not have to argue for the Corrigibility Thesis in the case of other-ascribing of pain, but rather to show that such ascribing can receive as adequate support as any other asserting of an empirical proposition. If there is no reason for me to believe that a man is abnormal physiologically or that he is acting, and I observe him displaying certain kinds of behavior under conditions that we would commonly call "torture," then there is no more reason for doubt than in any other example of alleged empirical knowledge.

As I said at the outset, this paper is exploratory in character and deals with matters preliminary to debates on the possibility of private languages or the merits of Physicalism. But in conclusion, I should like to point out that the account I have given does seem to lead to certain conclusions, both about the theories of private phenomena that lead to theories of private languages for reporting them, and about the general position of Physicalism.

There are at least two versions of the privacy of the inner. (1) "Y is a private phenomenon if and only if there is exactly one person X such that it is logically impossible that X should be ignorant of or mistaken about the occurrence of Y," and (2) "Y is a private phenomenon if and only if there is exactly one person X such that as a matter of fact X is never ignorant of or mistaken about the occurrence of Y." The first version is not indeed nonsensical and is, at least prima facie, not inconsistent; but is for beings like us empty. The second, while it outlines a concept of the inner which is not the one we actually employ, does, I think, have some "filling." From certain sorts of cases of pain, we might imagine, not human beings, but beings of a superior disembodied order, living in a world of basically different structure, to whom this version might apply. But it is not us and not our world and is wrongly offered as an analysis of its features.

As for Physicalism, my account of what it is to be in pain is in no way opposed to the thesis that "inner states" have a theoretic, explanatory identity with states of my body. The account, however, does suggest that a *physiological* account of pain must be an account of states or conditions that are behavior-initiating states or conditions. For the physiological concept is a theoretic substitute for the ordinary one, and the ordinary one is not of a simple, complete-in-itself inner entity. Also, the account suggests that a *behavioral* psychological account of pain is still close to the ordinary concept and will have to admit introspective reports as legitimate sources of information.

Finally, the unique logical feature of pain-ascribings, namely that the criteria for support are somewhat different for self-ascribings than they are for other-ascribings, points to the need for some kind of physicalist substitute, in explanatory theories, for the ordinary concept of pain. That concept does not meet a strict interpretation of the requirement of intersubjectivity for the testing of truth-claims. Perhaps, however, that requirement will have to be modified in some way for a behavioral psychology.

NOTES

1. Restricting myself to this example will restrict the applicability of my account. However, if my account of pain (in general, without reference to special qualities like "stabbing" and so on) is correct, it should be applicable, with appropriate changes, to other concepts of the same general family.

2. It is clear that the specification of criteria will not, in general, give us a precise, complete list of requirements. Provisos concerning normal circumstances will often be needed, and in some instances, reference to normal observers. Standards for normality will have to be decided on within the particular context of acts of assertion.

3. Following P. F. Strawson's well-known account.

4. One could add to this list situations where, waking from a dream of being tortured, we do not, for a moment at least, know whether or not we are in pain.

THE PRIVACY OF EXPERIENCE

NORMAN MALCOLM

I

In writings on the topic of "the privacy of experience" two themes can often be discerned, one of which I shall call "the privacy of observability," the other "the privacy of ownership." The first means that I can *observe* (or perceive, or be aware of, or know) something that no one else *can* observe (or perceive, or be aware of, or know). The second theme means that I *have* something that no one else *can* have.

The first theme is illustrated by Bertrand Russell's book *The Analysis of Mind.*[1] He asks:

> Can we observe anything about ourselves which we cannot observe about other people, or is everything we can observe public, in the sense that another could also observe it if suitably placed?

Russell gives the answer that at least bodily sensations and mental images are "private": that is, "each is only observable by one observer."[2] Russell is saying that only *I* can observe or perceive *my* sensations and images: the emphasis is on the idea that there are objects that only one person can *observe*.

In other writers the emphasis is on the privacy of *ownership*. For example, Professor A. J. Ayer, in his *Language, Truth and Logic*,[3] has the theory that a *self* is nothing but a series of sense-experiences; and he says that "it is logically impossible for a sense-experience to belong to the sense-history of more than a single self";[4] or, as he also puts it, "all sense-experiences, and the sense-contents which form part of them, are private to a single self."[5] In his book *The Foundations of*

129

Empirical Knowledge[6] he retains the theory that a self is a series of experiences, and he repeats that "it is impossible that the same experience should be part of the history of two separate selves."

Ayer was stating, in those books, the theme of the privacy of *ownership*. His idea may have been (this is only a conjecture) that since, on his theory, my experiences *make up* what I am, therefore you and I cannot *have* the same experiences, because then there would be only *one* of us, not two.

Some writers would not see any difference between the privacy of observability and the privacy of ownership. For example, Ayer in a later book, *Philosophical Essays*,[7] says:

> The warrant for saying that I can have direct knowledge of my own experiences but not anybody else's is just that my experiences are exclusively my own. The reason why I cannot directly know the experiences of another person is simply that I cannot have them.

It is not clear whether Ayer is thinking here that there is a difference between the privacy of what I directly know (i.e., the privacy of observability) and the privacy of what I have (i.e., the privacy of ownership), or whether his view is that there is only one fact that is being expressed in two different ways. Many philosophers would incline toward this latter view. For they would say that what only I can be aware of only I can have, and what only I can have only I can be aware of: to speak of the privacy of what is observed and of the privacy of what is owned is to speak of the same thing. It is likely that the following remarks by Professor W. T. Stace reflect this view:

> I cannot experience anything except *my own* experience. I can see my red, but I can never see yours. I can feel a pain in my leg. But I can never feel the pain in your leg. I can feel my emotion, but not yours. Even if your anger infects me, so that I feel it in sympathy with you, it is yet, in so far as I feel it, *my* anger, not yours. I can never be you, nor

you me. I cannot see through your eyes, nor you through mine. Even if you can telepathically transfer a mental state, say an image, from your mind to mine, yet, when I become aware of it, it is then *my* image and not yours. Even if, as some think, I can directly perceive your mind, without having to infer it from your body, still this perception of your mind will then be to me *my* perception, *my* experience.[8]

Stace seems to be saying that there is a class of things that only I can *perceive* (or experience, or be aware of), and a class of things that only I can *have,* and that these two classes coincide.

But some writers would think that there is an important difference between the privacy of observability and the privacy of ownership. For example, consider the view stated in a recent paper by Mr. D. Locke.[9] He makes a distinction between what he calls "logical privacy" and what he calls "mental privacy." Something is "logically private" if it cannot be "owned by or shared with others."[10] This is what I called "privacy of ownership." Something is "mentally private," according to Mr. Locke, "if only one person can perceive it."[11] This is my "privacy of observability." It should be noted that Locke regards feeling a pain as *perception:* "I use 'perceive' in the wide but not extravagant sense in which feeling a pain is a species of perceiving."[12]

Locke holds that these two forms of privacy are *not* equivalent. In respect of the example of pain, he thinks that the privacy of *ownership* is a necessary truth: it is logically impossible for anyone else to *have* this pain I have. But the privacy of *observability,* he thinks, is merely a contingent truth. At the present time it is impossible for you to feel a pain of mine; but someday technological advance may make it possible for one person to feel another's pain.

Let us ask what the difference would be between my feeling *my* pain and my feeling *your* pain? Locke ought to believe that there is some criterion for distinguishing, from among the pains I might feel, those that would be *mine* from those that would be *yours.* And indeed Locke does believe there is such a criterion, and that it is *location.* "Identity of location," he says, is a necessary condition for the identity of bodily sensations;[13] by "identity of location" he means identity of location in physical space. Since the headache that one man feels is in a different location in physical space, namely, in a different head, than is the headache another feels, therefore they are different headaches. The criterion of *mine* and *yours* with regard to headaches, according to Locke, is that the headache *in my head* is mine, and the headache *in your head* is yours. At the present time it is not possible for me to feel your headache or toothache. But some future scientific development might make it possible, says Locke, for our respective nervous systems to be so connected that I should be able to feel the toothache in your tooth, i.e., I should be able to feel *your* toothache. We could "plug into" another's nervous system "in order to feel his pain."[14]

I want to ask whether there is any difference between *owning* bodily sensations and *observing* or *perceiving* them. As I understand it, "owning sensations" is to mean having sensations. But how are "perceiving" and "observing" to be understood? It is suspiciously unnatural to speak of "perceiving" a sensation. Let us assume that "perceiving" a sensation will mean just the same as *feeling* it. What about "observing" a sensation? This expression, too, has an odd ring. But we do speak of being aware of, or conscious of, or noticing, or paying attention to, a sensation. Let us assume that "observing" a sensation will mean some or all of these things. I will ask two questions: First, whether there is any difference between having and feeling a bodily sensation; Second, whether there is any difference between having a sensation and being aware of it, or being conscious of it, or noticing it, or paying attention to it.

Considering the first question, it seems clear that there is no distinction, except verbal, between *having* and *feeling* bodily sensations. The questions, "Does he still have those twinges?" and "Does he still feel those twinges?" are used interchangably. The doctor asks, "Are you in pain?", "Do you have pain?", "Do you feel pain?" It doesn't matter to us which set of words is used. The verification that someone has pain is identical with the verification that he feels pain. To verify that he has pain we must observe some response or reaction of his, some movement or utterance, that shows he is in pain. This same movement or utterance will also show that he *feels* pain. We cannot find out that he has pain without finding out that he feels it; and we cannot find out that he feels it without finding out that he has it. This identity of verification is one aspect of the complete identity in use of such expressions as "having a burning sensation" and "feeling a burning sensation." In applying those expressions to myself and to others, I do not know how to make a difference in my use of them.

Turning to the second question, it should be observed that a person can pay *more or less attention* to a sensation he has: he can be more or less conscious of it or aware of it. If someone is strenuously complaining of a toothache, he is sometimes admonished or advised in the following ways: "Don't think so much about it!"; "Try to take your mind off it"; "Don't pay so much attention to it." Sometimes the advice is effective: he really does succeed to some extent in taking his mind off the pain. Does it follow that he feels *less* pain? This is an interesting and difficult question which I will not pursue.

But even if it is true that the less attention a man pays to pain the less pain he feels, it does not follow that if he is not conscious of any pain then he feels no pain. We can think of cases in which we should be inclined to say that a man felt a sensation without being conscious of it. For example, a soundly sleeping man is jabbed in the leg with a sharp object: the leg is drawn back violently and he gasps: but his state of heavy sleep is resumed, and when he is awakened a minute or two later he has no recollection of pain. This case makes us feel pushed toward saying both that the jab *pained* him, but also that he was not *conscious* of pain. The violent movement and the gasp, together with the fact that here was a normal cause of pain, provide a criterion for saying that the jab *pained* him, i.e., he *felt* pain. His continuing state of sleep, and his negative testimony on awaking, provide a criterion for saying that he was not *conscious* of pain. There is a genuine difference

in the nature of the two criteria, and therefore a reasonable
basis for making this distinction. It can be employed not only in
regard to animals (especially lower animals) but also in regard
to human beings when they are in unconscious or semiconscious
states, or are heavily distracted.

What bearing does this discussion have on the supposed
distinction between the privacy of ownership and the privacy
of observability? I think it is relevant only in the sense of
showing what philosophers have *not* meant by this distinction.
When Russell, in *The Analysis of Mind*, speaks of "observing"
one's own bodily sensations, he only means *feeling* them.[15]
He is not concerned, for example, with the phenomenon of
paying more or less attention to a sensation, nor with the
difference between feeling a sensation and being conscious of it.
When Locke, too, speaks of "perceiving" pain he simply means,
as already noted, feeling pain. But we have seen that there is
no difference between having and feeling a bodily sensation.
If the philosophical distinction between the "ownership" and
the "perception" of sensation is meant to be a distinction between *having* and *feeling* sensations, then it is a distinction
without a difference. Thus the themes of the privacy of ownership and the privacy of observability seem to be identical. For
the remainder of this paper I will assume that these two verbally different themes of privacy do come to the same thing.

II

I return now to Mr. Locke's conception of the supposed
distinction between the ownership and the perception of pain.
On his own view this would be a distinction between having
and feeling pain; but since there is no real distinction here,
he is wrong from the start. A more interesting problem is provoked by his claim that the criterion of the ownership of pain
(i.e., the criterion of *who* has pain) is the *location* of pain. I
will contend that the ownership of pain is determined, not by
location, but by *who expresses pain*. Wittgenstein remarks:
"Pain-behavior can point to a painful place—but the suffering

person is the one who expresses pain."[16] The one who expresses pain, either by natural pain-behavior or by words, is the one who is in pain. If you were informed that there is a person nearby who is in pain, but you did not know which person, you would find out by finding out which one expresses pain in movements, actions, or speech.

The view that which person has pain is to be settled by finding where the pain is located, puts the cart before the horse. Our discovery of where pain (other than our own) is located, presupposes that we know who the subject of pain is. Knowing that *this* person is in pain, we can be guided by his pain-behavior (his flinching, limping, caressing, pointing, exclaiming) to the location of the painful area. His expressive behavior *defines*, for others, the location of the pain. The knowledge of who is in pain is logically prior to the knowledge of the location of pain. It cannot be true, as Locke thinks, that the ownership of pain is determined by the location of pain. This would make a mystery of how the location of pain is itself determined.

The fact that the ownership of pain is not fixed by its location is also proved by the empirical fact that sometimes people locate pains outside their bodies. The most familiar phenomenon under this heading, known for centuries, is the so-called "phantom limb." A person who has had a limb amputated may, for some months after, feel pains in the place where the limb used to be. He points to a place not occupied by a part of his body and declares that he feels the pain *there*. We cannot get around this phenomenon by holding that the man is not really in pain but only (mistakenly) believes he is, or by holding that the pain is not where he (mistakenly) believes it is but in some other place. I think we have to accept at face value his indication of the painful place. His pain really is located in a place that is not occupied by flesh, bone, or nerves.

One may feel doubtful about this view for the following reason. The locating of pain in empty space has the disadvantage that much of the behavior that can be directed toward a painful place will necessarily be missing. The man who feels pain in a phantom limb cannot caress, protect, or favor the painful place; the pain cannot be intensified by probing that place; and so on. A substantial amount of the behavior commonly serving to identify the location of pain will be impossible. This may seem to prevent it from being *completely correct* to say that the pain is where the man points, even though he is not making any sort of *mistake*.

Against this objection it needs to be pointed out that there is *no conflict of criteria* in this case. The facts are *not* these: that although the man sincerely declares he feels pain in his leg, he does not limp, does not flinch when the leg is probed, and so on. Such facts might give the result that there was *no right thing to say*. There would be a conflict between his words, and the rest of his nonverbal behavior. In the actual phantom-limb case, his declaration in words and his nonverbal behavior of pointing are in agreement: and there is no nonverbal behavior in disagreement. The facts are not that he has the leg but does not limp with it, flinch when it is probed, etc. Adequate criteria for the location of pain (both his statement and his pointing) are satisfied. No countervailing criterion is satisfied. I do not see any sound basis for the inclination to feel that it is not entirely correct to say that the pain is where the man indicates.[17] This inclination may arise partly from the assumption that the location of a pain is the location of a *cause* of the pain (and empty space can contain no cause of pain). I will proceed to this point immediately.

It is interesting that there is a strong inclination to take the phantom-limb case as proving that a person's pointing, limping, favoring, protecting, and other pain-behavior, does *not* define for us the location of his pain. For example, Professor Kurt Baier says the following:

> The facts of the phantom limb clearly demonstrate that by "the place of a pain" we cannot mean the place to which we have a disposition to point. When he learns of his misfortune, the legless soldier withdraws his claim that he has a pain in his foot, although he was and still is inclined to point to the same spot, namely, the spot where the foot would be if he still had one. It is clear why the soldier withdraws this claim.

It is because, as a matter of empirical fact, the history, the fate, the life of the pain no longer depend on what happens to his foot. The doctor can move about, cut, squeeze, burn the amputated foot without thereby in any way affecting the person's pain. The pain is therefore no more "in" his foot than it is in the blanket occupying the spot where it would be if it were still his, or anywhere else. To claim that the pain is *in* the foot is therefore to imply that, causally speaking, "the key to the pain" lies in the foot. Therefore, the pain cannot be *in* the place to which the legless soldier is disposed to point. For whatever is in that place, whether his amputated foot, the bed in which he lies, or the blankets covering his body, is not "the key to the pain," not the object whose fate determines the fate of the pain. Hence we do not say that the pain is *in it*. The place to which we are disposed to point, when we have a pain, is merely the place where we believe, *rightly or wrongly*, that the pain is. The disposition to manifest "directed pain behavior" is tied to our *belief* about where the pain is, not to where the pain is. Since this belief may be erroneous, as the facts of the phantom limb show, we cannot identify the place of a pain with the place to which we are disposed to point when we have a pain.[18]

It is true that the amputated soldier may feel it a bit awkward to say that the pain is in his left foot when he knows that he has no left foot. But this is trivial. The important fact is that he will still say that the pain is *here* (pointing at a place not presently occupied by a part of his body); and Baier admits this. Baier goes wrong, I believe, in supposing that the reason the soldier will be reluctant to say that the pain is in his foot is that he no longer believes that "the fate of the pain," as Baier puts it, depends on what happens to his foot (or what used to be his foot). Baier thinks that the notion of the location of a pain involves the notion of the location of the *cause* of the pain. He says: "To claim that the pain is *in* the foot is therefore to imply that, *causally speaking*, 'the key to the pain' lies in the foot."[19]

It is true that in a huge number of cases the bodily cause of a pain has the same location as the pain. But there are

familiar cases in which this is not so. The "key" to a headache is sometimes a nerve in the neck; and the so-called "referred" pains of angina are located in the shoulder rather than
in the heart where the bodily damage is. Even if we ignore
these empirical facts, we can see that it is wrong to think that
locating pain is the same as locating the (or a) bodily cause
of pain. These are different concepts. A man may give us the
location of his pain without having any beliefs at all about the
location of its bodily cause. He need not even assume that it
has a bodily cause. (He might think it was "psychosomatic.")
The notion of the location of the bodily cause of pain is a good
deal more sophisticated than is the notion of the location of
pain. The first notion relies on past experience and experiment;
the second notion does not.[20]

III

To summarize our progress thus far: (1) Feeling a sensation and having it are the same. (2) Which person has pain
(the problem of ownership) is not defined by the location of
pain, but instead the location of pain is defined by the directed
pain-behavior (verbal and nonverbal) of the person who is
in pain. (3) The concepts of cause of, and location of, pain
must not be confused.

I turn now to the question of the "privacy" of pain. This
is the idea that it is impossible that two people should have
(or feel) the *same* pain. I believe this idea is pure illusion. In
the *Investigations* there occurs this remark: "In so far as it
makes *sense* to say that my pain is the same as his, it is also
possible for us both to have the same pain."[21] Wittgenstein is
implying that there is *not* some sense of the expression "same
pain," such that you and I *cannot* have the same pain. This
goes counter to what many philosophers think. They think that
there is *a* sense in which you and I cannot have the same pain.
They will say that there is an ambiguity in the expression "same
pain." On the one hand, this may mean "qualitative similarity"

or "exact similarity": on the other hand, it may mean "numerical identity." It is in this latter sense of "same pain," they say, that it is impossible for you and me to have the same pain.

Ayer takes this view in his *Philosophical Essays*.[22] He allows that two people may "share" the same fear. But, he adds: "To say that the feeling is shared is to say that the two feelings are qualitatively similar and that they have the same ostensible object: it is not to say that they are numerically identical." He admits there is some difficulty about how we are to *count* the feelings. But he declares that it is simply a convention "that we are to say that there are two feelings and not one, just because there are two persons."[23]

In Ayer's *The Problem of Knowledge*,[24] he says: "It is true that one does quite frequently speak of different persons sharing the same thoughts or feelings, but it would generally be held that what is meant by this is that these thoughts or feelings are similar, or proceed from similar causes, not that they are literally the same." And in his book *The Concept of a Person*,[25] Ayer says: "Headaches are private: it does not make sense to say that several people are feeling the same headache."

Mr. Peter Strawson, in his *Individuals*,[26] holds that with regard to "states of consciousness" there is a "logically nontransferable kind of ownership." He says that if we consider "the requirements of identifying reference in speech to *particular* states of consciousness, or private experiences, we see that such particulars cannot be thus identifyingly referred to except as the states or experiences *of* some identified *person*. States, or experiences, one might say, *owe* their identity as particulars to the identity of the person whose states or experiences they are." And he declares that it follows from this "that it is logically impossible that a particular state or experience in fact possessed by someone should have been possessed by someone else."

Let us consider the distinction between "exact similarity" and "numerical identity" to which these philosophers allude. We can certainly think of cases in which we want to make use of this distinction, or something like it. With cigars, for example. If it were said that after dinner Petersen and Hansen smoked the same cigar, the remark could be ambiguous. It could mean that the cigar Hansen smoked was not distinguishable in respect to size, shape, color, or brand, from the cigar Petersen smoked. We could express this, in ordinary speech, by saying that they smoked "the identical cigar." We say, for example, that "Six ladies at the ball were wearing the identical dress." What these remarks tend to mean is that *two* cigars were being smoked by Petersen and Hansen, and that neither cigar had any feature that distinguished it from the other: and among the dresses at the ball there were *six* that were indistinguishable— "You could not tell them apart."

But one could mean something different by saying that the two men smoked the same ("the identical") cigar: namely, that all together only one cigar was being smoked by them: (they passed it back and forth like a peace pipe). The expression "numerical identity" is supposed to take care of this case. We are to say that the two men smoked "numerically the same" cigar. I suspect that this phrase is not actually used in ordinary speech, but has been invented by philosophers. Still, this does not prevent it from being a useful phrase. If you have told me that *A* and *B* are smoking the same cigar at the dinner table, and I ask "Numerically the same?", you could understand me to be asking how many cigars, all together, are being smoked by *A* and *B*.

The fact that there is a distinction between exact similarity and numerical identity that can be made in regard to cigars and dresses, does not imply that it can be made in regard to anything whatever. You can say that two people have the same ("the identical") *style* in playing tennis: but what if I asked whether you meant that *A*'s style is exactly like *B*'s style or that *A* and *B* have numerically the same style? You would not understand this question. You informed me that *A* and *B* have exactly the same style of play: there cannot be a *further* question as to whether *A*'s style is numerically identical with *B*'s style. With the cigars and dresses there can be this further question: *A* and *B* appeared in the same dress at different times during the evening, but was it numerically the same dress?

Thus a question of the form "*x* and *y* are exactly alike, but is *x* numerically the same as *y*?" makes sense with some values for *x* and *y*, but not for others. If we substitute "*A*'s cigar" for "*x*" and "*B*'s cigar" for "*y*," we obtain a sensible question. We understand how it might turn out that *A* and *B* had only one cigar all together, or that they had two. In regard to some other sorts of things, e.g., tennis style, this further question is meaningless.

Let us consider whether this further question has any meaning with respect to *colors*. Surface *A* and surface *B* have exactly the same color, i.e., they are "identical" or "indistinguishable" in color. Can there be a further question as to whether the color of *A* is numerically identical with the color of *B*? What would it mean? Given that the color of one area is indistinguishable from the color of another area, what more can be asked? Despite what we are tempted to think, there is not a sense of "same color" such that the color of one place *cannot* be the same as the color of another place. It is one of the most truistic of truisms that the very same shade of color can be many places at the same time. In such cases there are numerically different colored areas colored the same shade.

Let us turn to the psychological realm, considering first *opinions*. Two people can be of the same opinion, e.g., that a summer in the mountains would be more enjoyable than a summer at the seashore. But once you know that *A* and *B* have the same opinion, would you know what it meant to further find out whether *A*'s opinion was numerically the same as or different from *B*'s? You would not. In this respect opinions are different from cigars and dresses, and are more like styles and colors.

What about *sudden thoughts?* Surely a sudden thought is a "mental event," if anything is. Two people might have the same sudden thought at the same time, e.g., the thought that the stove has not been turned off. Is there now a further question as to whether all together they have *two* thoughts, exactly alike, or just *one* thought? What would be the difference?

My suddenly thinking that the stove has not been turned off is a different occurrence, or event, from *your* suddenly thinking the same thing. But it does not follow that I *have* something which you do not have. It cannot be said, for example, that I had my having the thought that *p*, whereas you did not. To say, "I had my having the thought that *p*," is to speak gibberish. It is no better to say, "I had my thinking the thought that *p*, but you did not have it." What can be said is, "I had the sudden thought that *p*": but then you could have had the same.

Let us turn to *bodily sensations*. Here the temptation is great (indeed, overwhelming) to suppose that there is a sense of "same sensation" in which two people *cannot* have the same. But the case is really no different from that of styles, colors, opinions, and sudden thoughts. If the description of my back-ache is the same as the description of yours, then you and I have the same backache. This is how the expression "same backache" is used. If your backache answers to a different description then it is different. There is no other sense of "same" and "different" in regard to sensations. There is no sense of "different sensation" such that my sensation and your sensation *must* be different: just as there is no sense of "different color" such that the color of two areas *must* be different.

It is worth noting that descriptions of sensations can be impersonal. A sensation might be described as "a throbbing pain in the shoulder." Personal pronouns do not have to enter into verbal descriptions of sensations. The descriptions of sensations in a medical book would not say *whose* sensations they were, yet they could be complete descriptions.

By "a description of a sensation" I mean what is ordinarily meant. In describing a bodily sensation one would mention whether it was dull or sharp or throbbing, whether the intensity of it waxed and waned, what its location was, and so on. Many things that were *true of* a sensation (e.g., that I had it on February 22nd, in the afternoon) would *not* belong to a *description* of it.

There is an inclination to think that *A*'s sensation and *B*'s sensation must have different descriptions: for *A* says, "The ache is in my shoulder," and although *B* utters the same words, he refers to a shoulder that is numerically different from the shoulder referred to by *A*. Thus *A* and *B* give *different locations* to their sensations; and so they describe them differently.

This is wrong. Giving the location of one's sensation is not locating it in the space of physics or astronomy, but in a space of sensations that has one's own body as its frame of reference. If *A* locates a sensation in his space of sensation (e.g., in his right shoulder), and *B* locates a sensation in the *corresponding* place in *B*'s space of sensation (e.g., in *his* right shoulder), then *B*'s sensation is in the *same* place as *A*'s sensation. If *B* located his sensation in a *non*-corresponding place (e.g., his right foot), then *B*'s sensation would be in a *different* place from *A*'s. *This is how we use* the expressions "same place," "different place," in regard to sensations. Therefore, *A* and *B* are *not* giving different descriptions when each says, "in my shoulder."

Descriptions of sensations provide the criteria of identity for sensations.[27] Since your sensation can have the same description as mine, you and I can have the same sensation. Contrary to Strawson's view, the identity of sensations does not depend on the identity of the persons who have them.[28] It is not a characterizing feature of a sensation that *I* have it. As Wittgenstein remarks, "In pain I distinguish intensity, location, etc., but no owner."[29]

If being *mine* were a characterizing feature of a sensation I have, then I ought to be able to say, "I have a pain that is mine"; just as I can say, "I have a pain that is throbbing." But actually the first remark means no more than that I have a pain—which has yet to be described.[30] The first remark ought to be a contribution to the description of the sensation: but it is not.

Thus we make a senseless move when we assert, "Another

person cannot have *my* sensation." If we were to provide a
description of the sensation (e.g., "a throbbing pain in the
shoulder") it would be plainly false that another person cannot have *that*. If no description is provided, or in the offing,
then we have not said anything.

So it is a mistake to think that if you and I have the
same sensation this can only mean that your sensation is exactly
like mine, not that it is *numerically* the same. In so far as we
understand the concept, "exactly alike but numerically different," it has no application to sensations.[31] Nor to any other
"contents of consciousness," such as images, feelings, or emotions. Given that the description of your image, feeling, or
emotion is the same as mine, there cannot be a *further* question
as to whether yours is *different* from mine. One could express
the point by saying that contents of consciousness have only
generic identity and not *numerical* identity.

I hope it will not be thought insulting if I say that all of
us are influenced by very *crude* imagery. We tend to think
of a *mind* as an intangible volume of space, and of the *contents*
of that mind as located inside that volume of space. Another
mind is a different volume of space, and its contents are
numerically different from the contents of any other mind
because they are located in a different space. I believe our
strong temptation to assume that one person's thoughts, feelings, and "experiences," cannot be "numerically" the same as
another's, springs in part from this imagery—although that is
not the whole story.

The assumption that your sensation and mine must be
numerically different is a *bad* mistake, philosophically speaking,
because it embodies the idea that the contents of your mind
(your thoughts, feelings, sensations) are hidden from me. Thus
it puts us on the road to skepticism about other minds, and
even to solipsism.

Of course it is often impossible for me to find out another's thoughts or feelings. This might be because the other
person does not trust me or is afraid of me, or because he has
greater intelligence, sensitivity or depth than I have. It is not

because the contents of his mind are "numerically different" from mine.

If the distinction between "the same" and "numerically the same" *were* to be given an application to sensations, then we should have to *make up* criteria for it. Our ordinary speech contains none. It is interesting that we are drawn in different directions when it comes to stipulating criteria for the numerical identity of sensations. This comes out plainly enough in the imaginary case of the Siamese twins who share a common limb, e.g., a hand. Suppose that each of them complained of a pain in exactly the same spot in their common hand, each giving the same description of the pain he felt. Would there be one or two pains in that hand? Now there is some inclination to count the number of pains by counting the number of spatial locations of pain. By this rule there would be *one* pain felt by two people. On the other hand, there is some inclination to count the number of pains by counting the number of persons in pain. By this rule there would be *two* pains in the same spot in that hand. Which rule is the right one? Neither. Our ordinary concept of pain does not embody either rule. And if it came to adopting one of these rules, in order to solve the problem of the Siamese twins, it would be as arbitrary to choose the one as the other.

Despite the mountain of confusion on the subject I hope my discussion has shown that our ordinary concept of pain embodies the following features: (1) Having and feeling pain are the same; (2) the criterion of which person has pain is which person expresses pain, and not where the pain is located; (3) there is no sense of the expression "same pain" such that it is impossible for two people to have the same pain.[32]

IV

I wish to raise the question of what it is that gives rise to the illusion of the *privacy* of pain, i.e., to the mistaken inclination to assume that you and I cannot have the same. The persistent strength of this illusion is something that needs to be explained. I believe it is provoked by certain features of our use of the word "pain." In Wittgenstein's metaphors, they are features of the "grammar" of the word, or of the "language-game," with the word. I think the facts that give rise to the illusion of privacy, would be the following: (a) You can be *in doubt* as to whether I am in pain, but I cannot; (b) You can *find out* whether I am in pain, but I cannot; and (c) You can be *mistaken* as to whether I am in pain, but I cannot.

The most surprising thing about this set of facts is what *I* cannot do. *I* cannot be in doubt, or find out, or be mistaken as to whether *I* am in pain. Of course, someone could fail to understand the English word "pain," but that is of no interest. Wittgenstein remarks that if someone said, "Oh, I know what the word 'pain' means; what I don't know is whether *this,* that I have now, is pain," we should be at a loss to understand him.[33] This remark of Wittgenstein's is a little misleading, since it can actually be informative for a person to say, "I don't know whether this is pain." It shows us that his sensation is *hard to classify.* He might be telling us that his sensation lies in the borderland between a pain and a tickle, say, or a pain and an ache. His remarks would be a partial characterization of his sensation. It would be a contribution to the description of his sensation.

To appreciate Wittgenstein's point, let us make the following two assumptions: First, that the speaker understands the use of the word "pain"; second, that he is not characterizing his sensation as borderline. Given these assumptions, "that expression of doubt does not belong to the language-game," as Wittgenstein puts it.[34]

Notice that "the expression of doubt," to which he refers, is a speaker's expression of doubt about *his own case.* If a speaker is referring to someone else, there is no problem: "I don't know if he has pain" is not prima facie a logically troubling remark. Furthermore, as we saw earlier, there can even be cases in which we should be *inclined* to say something of the following sort: "The jab pained him but he was not conscious of the pain, or was not aware that he felt pain, or did not know that he felt pain." This implies that there can be cases in which we should be *inclined* to say: "He is not aware (does not know) that he has pain." I think it is not definitely settled that such a remark is excluded from language.

But what is true is that a person, who understands the language, cannot himself express doubt, or ignorance, as to whether he has pain. One is not permitted to say, "I do not know if I have pain" (unless one is characterizing a sensation as border-line). A genuine expression of doubt is not allowed.

This is a striking and important fact; and I interpret Wittgenstein as pointing it out. If a man understands the word "influenza," and even if he has influenza, he is allowed to express a doubt as to whether he has influenza. But he is not allowed to express a doubt as to whether he has pain. He is not permitted to say "I don't know if I have pain," or "I believe I have pain but I may be wrong," or "I intend to find out whether I have pain." Why is this?

V

It leaves us discontented to be told that the expression of doubt does not belong to the language-game with the word "pain." We should like an explanaion of *why* this is so. It is my conjecture that the philosophers who espouse the thesis of the privacy of pain are wanting to *explain* why it is that the expression of doubt about one's own case is missing from the game with the word "pain." The *reason* for this, they want to say, is that when a person is in pain, he has direct and immediate *knowledge* that he is in pain. This is why he cannot be in doubt, cannot be mistaken, and cannot find out: for as soon as he is in pain he *knows* it.

This explanation is unsatisfactory. The utterance "I know I am in pain" is just as queer as the utterance "I don't know if I am in pain." To be sure, we can think of cases in which it would be quite natural to say "I know I have a toothache."

This might be an emphatic way of stating that I have a toothache (a sort of rhetorical flourish). And there is the case where the dentist has injected more than a normal amount of novocain, but you still complain of pain, and he asks "Are you *sure* it still hurts?": to which you reply, "I *know* it still hurts." Possibly he suspected that you were pretending or exaggerating, and your reply assured him you were not. Or perhaps your reply just meant, "Don't talk nonsense!"; in which case it was a logical or philosophical comment; and an appropriate one!

When the phrase "I know" is prefixed to a sentence it is normally a *useful* prefix. It does a job. One job it can do is to inform the auditor that the speaker has *grounds* for asserting that *p*, and is not making his claim from mere prejudice or unsupported rumor. Another job it can do is to inform the auditor that the speaker is an *authority* on the general subject matter of the statement *p*. ('I know his agreement to purchase is illegal." "How do you know?" "I am a lawyer.") Or this prefix can inform the auditor that the speaker is in a *privileged position* to say whether *p* is true. ("I know the lady snores." "How do you know?" "She is my wife.")

I think everyone feels that the sentence "I know I am in pain" is a rather queer thing to say; and some would hold that it is senseless. I wish to argue that it *is* senseless. But I do not mean that I perceive, as it were, a clash of meanings in my mind when I say the words. I mean that in this case the prefix, "I know," cannot do any of its normal jobs. Thus there is a good and sufficient reason for excluding the combination of words, "I know I am in pain" from language.[35] For the prefix does no work.

None of the previously mentioned jobs can be done by this prefix when it is attached to the sentence "I have pain." It cannot serve the purpose of informing you that I have *grounds* for saying I have pain. For what could the grounds be, other than that I *feel* pain? There is, however, no distinction of meaning between "I feel pain" and "I have pain." Thus it would be a redundancy for me to put forward the fact that I feel pain, as my grounds for saying I have pain. The only plausible "grounds," therefore, are not *grounds*.[36]

Nor can my use of the I-know prefix inform you that I am an *authority* on the question of whether I have pain. An authority can be *proved* to be an authority. His answers can be checked out, independently of his say-so, and it can be determined that he does not make mistakes, or hardly ever, in his subject (e.g., the history of the Civil War). But since we do not know what it means for a person, who understands English, to *believe mistakenly* that he has pain,[37] the notion of a person's proving an authority on this question is also meaningless.

For the same reason a person cannot be said to be in a *privileged position* with regard to the question of whether he is in pain. Generally speaking, a husband is in a privileged position with regard to the question of whether his wife snores. Yet we can easily understand, in various ways, how he might be wrong. This is what we do not understand in the case of one's own pain. So the notion of being in a privileged position really has no application here.

Ayer admits that prefixing "I am in pain" with "I know" makes an otherwise "respectable" sentence "appear somewhat ridiculous."[38] He goes on to say: "But the reason for this, surely, is not that the claim to knowledge is inapplicable in these cases, but rather it is superfluous. We find it silly for someone to tell us that he knows that he is in pain, because if he is in pain we take it for granted that he knows it."[39]

Well, we really do take it for granted that the people we have dealings with in daily life *know their own names*. Experience teaches us that it is the normal thing for an adult person to be able to say that his name is so-and-so and to be *right.*. So I do take it for granted that the people riding with me in the bus know their names. I am justified in making this assumption. I do not make it in the case of small children, and sometimes it goes wrong in the case of grown-ups. This shows that Ayer has not given a correct explanation of the "ridiculous" appearance of the sentence "I know I'm in pain." We do not "take for granted" that if a man is in pain he knows it. Experience could not justify this "assumption": for we do not know what it would mean for a person who understands the words to be *wrong* when he says "I am in pain."[40]

This utterance should not be thought of as the report of an observation of something whose ontological status is completely independent of the utterance. The utterance is itself an expression of sensation, just as flinchings, grimaces, and outcries are expressions of sensation. If the occurrence of this utterance is an expression of sensation then it serves as a criterion of sensation, just as does natural pain-behavior.[41] But then, to produce a case of a man's mistakenly believing he feels pain will not be possible. The nearest approach to this would be a *conflict* between his utterance ("I'm in pain") and his other behavior (a conflict of criteria), producing a case where it would be neither right nor wrong to say he feels pain. This would fall short of providing a case in which he was *mistaken*. Thus there cannot be a consistent criterion of the latter.

When "I know" is prefixed to "I have pain" it cannot do any of the jobs that this prefix normally does in speech. It really is a knob that does not turn anything.[42] The fundamental reason for this is that it is not a genuine possibility that a person, who understands the words, should be in error when he says he has pain. This prevents the prefix from fulfilling its normal purpose. I would apply here a remark from the *Tractatus:* "Signs that serve no purpose are logically meaningless."[43]

Yet, when we philosophize about sensation, we have a strong desire to assert, "If I am in pain I *must know* it." Why is this? I think we are trying to point out the unacceptability of the supposition that a man who either definitely does have pain, or definitely does not have pain, and who understands the words, should truthfully declare, "I don't know if I have pain." We are not going to accept this as a possibility. If that is *all* we mean when we assert, "If I have pain I *must know* it," then I do not want to make any objection to this use of the sentence. We are expressing a logical or philosophical observation that embodies a correct appreciation of the concept of sensation.[44]

It will be recalled that the proponent of the privacy of

experience was going to *explain* why the expression of doubt, "I don't know if I have pain," is not in the language-game. His explanation consisted in asserting, "If I am in pain I *must know* it." But we see that the only true thing he can mean is that the expression of doubt is ruled out. If this is what his assertion comes to, then he is not explaining why the expression of doubt is excluded from the language of sensation. He is merely saying over again that it is excluded.

The theme of the privacy of pain may also be thought to explain why it is that you can be in doubt, can be mistaken, and can find out, that I have pain, whereas *I* cannot. This would be because you cannot have, or feel, *my* sensation. You cannot have "direct" knowledge of my sensation, but only "indirect" knowledge by way of my behavior and words. This attempt at explanation is as unsatisfactory as the previous one. As we saw, you can have, and feel, the very sensation I have. (Do not protest, "But I can't feel your feeling of it"; for what could that mean?) Also we saw that in the sentence, "I know I have pain," the "I know" does not serve any purpose: consequently, I cannot say that I know "directly" that I have pain; and so you cannot say, in contrast, that you know "*only* indirectly" that I have pain.

In addition, this attempt at explanation embodies a picture of my sensations as *hidden* from you. But then it undermines itself. For part of what it was going to explain is how it is that you can *find out* what my sensations are, whereas *I* cannot. But the picture it carries seems to say that you *cannot* find out my sensations.

VI

The philosophical theme of the privacy of sensation is a complete failure if conceived as an explanation of the grammar of sensation. But can there be no explanation at all? I confess that I, too, feel some discontent with the statement that this is simply how the game is played. What I conceive to be a kind of explanation, and one that satisfies me, is to see what the consequences would be for our concept of a *person,* if the grammar of sensation (or of thinking or intending) were different in the respect that the expression of doubt, which has no place in the language-game, *were* to have a place in it.

What I am trying to imagine is that I could be in doubt or mistaken as to whether *I* have pain, just as you can be; and also that I could find out whether *I* have pain, in the same way that you can. In short, I am trying to imagine that I should be in the same position as you are with regard to the question of whether *I* have pain. I want to see what the results would be if the asymmetry of our positions should be abolished. Your position is that you observe my behavior and listen to my words in order to find out if I have pain. So I will imagine that I too will observe my own behavior and listen to my own words, to find out if I have pain. If I cannot observe my behavior or hear my words, I shall be in doubt, just as you would be. In the present language-game, if another wants to know whether I have pain, he will ask me. So I will imagine that, in the projected game, I shall sometimes ask myself, "Does it hurt?" If I reply, "Yes, it does," then I shall know that I have pain, my evidence being *that I myself said so!* As things are, others sometimes question my sincerity. So I shall question my own sincerity. I shall dispute with myself, and I may or may not convince myself. Suppose I believe I am a liar: then, on the one hand, I shall say I have pain, but, on the other hand, deny it. Imagine the possibility that some- one, noticing my exclamations and gestures of pain, should hurry to my aid, but I should inform him that in my opinion I do not have pain at all, or at least I am probably exaggerat- ing; and I should urge him not to be concerned about me— yet at the same time I should continue to groan and writhe and implore him to help me!

It is clear enough that these would be bewildering phe- nomena. At best it would be a split personality—two persons, as it were, inhabiting one body.[45] At worst, it would be com- plete lunacy. It is evident, furthermore, that our concepts of sensation would have no application to such a case. If I behaved in this weird way it would not be right to say I was in pain, nor right to say the opposite. Nor even right to say that I was *in doubt* as to whether I was in pain. This behavior would diverge too far from the normal. Our concepts of sensation and emotion, of belief and doubt, grow out of certain regular patterns of behavior and circumstances that are frequently repeated in human life. Our concepts are taught, and mastered, by reference to those patterns. The concepts can be extended gradually to new patterns that resemble the old. But they could not be extended to cover the phenomena we have been imagining. Those phenomena would not be coherent expressions of anything.

I have been trying to explain why we do not have the concepts of doubting, being mistaken, or finding out, whether *oneself* has pain. It is an odd sort of "explanation," and one may be reluctant to call it by that name. Whatever we call it, it provides a kind of clarification that is often required in philosophy, namely, to make a perplexing fact less perplexing by pointing out the part it plays in supporting a familiar structure. In the present case, the clarification comes to the following: If we try to imagine what it would be like if doubting, making a mistake, and finding out, concerning one's own sensations, were to occur (and I do not mean merely that, for example, the words "I don't know if I have pain" should be uttered, but also that there should occur both the spontaneous behavior and deliberate actions by which doubt is expressed, and the inquiries, observations, assurances, by which doubt is removed)—if we try to imagine such behavior, we see that it could not be accommodated under the headings we use in describing the attitudes and feelings of people.

We have tried to imagine what it would be like if the expression of doubt did belong to the grammar of sensation. Similar results will be obtained with the grammar of *intention*. Imagine someone learning from his own present movements and speech, what his intentions are! If he put forth a statement about his present intention, based on such observations, would you have learned his intention? Does he *have* an intention?

Or imagine trying to carry on a conversation with someone who continuously infers from his own words and gestures what he *means!* Or picture someone who watches his own bodily movements to find out what he *wants!*

A person expresses feelings, beliefs, intentions, by action and by word. We look to him for information about his thoughts and intentions. He is our primary source of information about himself. (But only if his disclosures are *not* based on his observations of his own words and movements.) His behavior and utterances reveal to us his experiences, wishes and aims (insofar as they are revealed). And accordingly, we respond with sympathy, or reproach, or indignation, or encouragement. We concert our own plans with his, or we seek to frustrate him. These are ways in which we respond to people and engage with them.

If some human-like creature exhibited behavior of the sort we have imagined, his movements and utterances would not reveal to us any experiences, intentions, or sensations. And they would not provide a foundation for any human attitude toward him—of sympathy or annoyance, of reliance or distrust, of agreement or disagreement. To the extent that he exhibited behavior approximating the behavior of being in doubt as to whether he himself feels pain (or wants or intends something), and the connected behavior of trying to remove the doubt by observing his own movements and utterances, he could not appear to us as a person! This shows that it is essential to the concept of a person that the expression of doubt should not occur.

Thus the explanation of why the expression of doubt is excluded from language is not that each person has something, or feels or knows something, that another person cannot have, feel, or know—the explanation is not that experience is "private." The explanation is that the expression of doubt could not fit coherently into the structure of our concept of a person. The excluding of it from working language is no superficial point of grammar or semantics, but a matter of deep philosophical importance. For it is an aspect of the asymmetry between your position and mine, with respect to the question of what *I* feel or think or intend. This asymmetry is a necessary feature of the concept of a person.

NOTES

1. New York, 1921, p. 117.
2. *Ibid.*, p. 118.
3. London, 1936; second edition, London, 1946.
4. *Ibid.*, p. 125.
5. *Ibid.*, p. 128.
6. New York, 1940, p. 139.
7. New York, 1954, p. 194.
8. *The Theory of Knowledge and Existence*, Oxford, 1932, p. 67.
9. "The Privacy of Pain," *Analysis*, March, 1964.
10. *Ibid.*, p. 148.
11. *Loc. cit.*
12. *Loc. cit.*
13. *Ibid.*, p. 149.
14. *Loc. cit.*
15. E.g., *op. cit.*, p. 118.
16. L. Wittgenstein, *Philosophical Investigations*, New York, 1953, sec. 302.
17. For thoughts on this problem I am indebted both to Professor David Sachs and to Miss Ann Wilbur.
18. Kurt Baier, "The Place of A Pain," *Philosophical Quarterly*, April, 1964, p. 140.
19. *Ibid.*, my italics. There is a similarity, and also a dissimilarity, between Baier's view and the view of Thomas Reid. According to Reid, pain, being a *sensation*, can exist only "in the mind," not in the body. When the ordinary man says he has pain in his toe, he is making a complex assertion, one part of which is that he feels pain, and the other part is that the *cause* of the pain is in the toe. "When we consider the sensation of pain by itself, without any respect to its cause, we cannot say with propriety, that the toe is either the place or the subject of it. But it ought to be remembered that, when we speak of pain in the toe, the sensation is combined in our thought, with the cause of it, which really is in the toe." (Thomas Reid, *Works*, W. Hamilton, ed., Edinburgh, 1858, *Essays on the Intellectual Powers*, Essay II, chap. 18, pp. 319–320.) Baier does not hold that we cannot say, "with propriety," that our sensations are located in our bodies. But he does hold, with Reid, that when I say I have pain in my toe, part of what I assert is that the (or a) *cause* of the pain is in my toe. If this part of my assertion turned out to be mistaken, then I would have a mistaken belief that I have pain in my toe.

20. One could be misled by the fact that sometimes we probe a painful area in order to discover the point of maximum tenderness, i.e., the "center" of the painful area. Sometimes we call this center of pain the "source" of the pain. Since the word "source" commonly has a causal meaning, this way of speaking might give a philosopher the idea that what the probing determines is the bodily cause (i.e., the "source") of that pain. In reality what has been determined is merely "where it hurts the most."

21. *Op. cit.*, sec. 253.

22. *Op. cit.*, p. 194.

23. *Ibid.*, p. 195.

24. New York, 1956, p. 226.

25. New York, 1963, p. 50.

26. London, 1959, p. 97.

27. It might be objected that there are indescribable sensations. And indeed we do want to say, sometimes, that a sensation is "indescribable." But still a lot can be said about the sensation: for one thing, what it is *not*; and also that it is "indescribable."

28. Strawson, *op. cit.*, p. 97.

29. L. Wittgenstein, *Philosophische Bemerkungen*, Frankfurt am Main, 1964, p. 94.

30. Cf. Wittgenstein, *ibid.*, p. 91.

31. I am not holding that there are no cases at all in which the question "Numerically the same?" will have application to sensations. Suppose, for example, that a doctor tells me that each time Petersen and his wife come to see him, "they complain of the same sensation." I might ask "Numerically the same?" What I might want to know is whether there is a sensation that only *one* of them has and of which both of them complain; or whether there is a sensation *both* of them have and of which both of them complain. My question is a request for information as to whether one or both of them have the sensation to which the doctor refers; and this is an intelligible question. (I owe this example to Professor John Cook.) One can easily think of still other cases in which those words would express an intelligible question. The philosophically interesting case, as far as the problem of privacy is concerned, is the one where I *know* (i.e., it is given) that *A* has a sensation of a certain description and *B* has one of the same description. It is in *this* case that my question "Do they have numerically the same or numerically different sensations?" is unintelligible—despite our metaphysical conviction that it *must* be intelligible and indeed that we know the answer. To think that because there are two people there must be two sensations is exactly like thinking that because there are two areas colored a certain shade there must be two colors.

32. This remark may not be *literally* true. We do speak of "occurrences," "instances," or "cases" of headache. The criteria of identity for instances, occurrences, or cases of headache, would include the identity of the owners. If two people each had headache of description ϕ, then there would be two *cases* of headache ϕ, i.e., numerically different cases of the same headache. Your case of headache would, necessarily, be numerically different from my case of headache.

It is possible that economy of language sometimes leads us to use the expression "different headache" when what we mean is *different case of the same headache:* and also to say "same headache" when what we mean is *same case of the same headache.* Whether or not we actually do this, we *could* do it. I shall call this a "secondary" sense of the expressions "different headache" and "same headache." Within the phrase "different case of the same headache," the expression "same headache" occurs in its primary sense. In this primary sense, the criteria of identity for headaches include location, intensity, etc., but not the identity of the owners. In the secondary sense, the criteria of identity do include the identity of the owners.

I am confident that when Ayer says "Headaches are private: several people cannot feel the same headache" (*The Concept of A Person*, p. 50), he *wants* to be speaking of "same headache" in the primary sense. If we construed his remark as being about the secondary sense of "same headache," we should be entitled to translate it as follows: "Several people cannot feel the same case of headache." But then we should want to object to speaking of feeling a *case* of headache. What does it mean? It isn't even English. The same holds for "feel an instance of headache," or "feel an occurrence of headache." Thus if we are going to understand Ayer's remark, we should interpret it as using "same headache" in the *primary* sense of the expression. But then the remark that "several people cannot feel the same headache," although good English, is not true. In the primary sense of "same headache" several people can feel the same headache.

33. *Investigations,* sec. 288.

34. *Loc. cit.*

35. "To say, 'This combination of words makes no sense' excludes it from the sphere of language and thereby bounds the domain of language. But when one draws a boundary it may be for various kinds of reason." (*Ibid.,* sec. 499.)

36. Compare with this case: My grounds for saying I have a hole in my tooth are that I *feel* a hole in my tooth. There is no redundancy here.

37. In the case of the sleeper who was jabbed in the leg, our inclination was to say that he was not conscious of pain he felt. It was not a case of his believing (mistakenly) that he did not feel pain.

38. Ayer, *The Concept of A Person*, p. 59.

39. *Ibid.* I have also heard it said that the reason we do not say "I know I'm in pain" is that it *is so easy to tell* whether one is in pain: it is as easy as remembering one's name—perhaps even easier.

40. Ayer gives the following "proof" that if we are in pain we know it, namely, that one can tell lies about one's sensations. For "to tell a lie is not just to make a false statement: it is to make a statement that one knows to be false; and this implies denying what one knows to be true." (*Ibid.,* p. 60.) I should take this as a proof that telling a lie is not, in all cases, stating what one knows to be false. The word "lying," like the word "game," is applied over a broad range of diverse cases.

41. Cf. my *Knowledge and Certainty*, Englewood Cliffs, N.J.: 1963, p. 140.

42. Wittgenstein, *Investigations,* secs. 270, 271.

43. Wittgenstein, *Tractatus Logico-Philosophicus,* trans. Pears & Mc-Guiness, New York, 1961, #5.47321.

44. In actual practice our meaning tends not to be so pure. Mixed in with this true perception of the "grammar" of sensation, there will be the temptation to think one has grounds, or is an authority, or has an unobstructed view of one's sensation, and so on. I suspect that the phrase "privileged access" usually indicates such a mixture.

45. Cf. Wittgenstein's remark: "If I listened to the words of my mouth, I might say that someone else was speaking out of my mouth"; and also: "My relation to my own words is wholly different from other peoples." (*Investigations,* p. 192.)

3

SAYING, BELIEVING, STATEMENTS

COMMENTS ON SAYING AND BELIEVING

HENRY A. ALEXANDER, JR.

You and I are taking a walk in the country. There are no special reasons for taking our walk. We just want some fresh air and a little exercise. As we walk along, engaged in no particular prolonged conversation or discussion, you happen to notice some odd-looking mushrooms two or three yards over on your right underneath some bushes. You call my attention to them, but since I may be even less enlightened on such matters than you are, you don't expect anything more than my acknowledgement that they are unusual-looking things. I look at them, however, and lo and behold I recognize what they are and say, "Bless my soul, those are morels!"

Reflecting on my remark in such circumstances, we may be led via our philosophical interests to speculate upon the connections between saying what I say (as in the above circumstances) and my state of mind, or my thoughts or what I believe. What we state or assert or affirm seems to need securing, to need orientation, to need anchoring. Anchoring to what? To the firm rock of belief! Or to the system of our real attitudes, dispositions, inclinations, expectations, beliefs, and knowledge. And if what we say isn't secured by what we believe, then what? Well, one isn't talking sincerely; one isn't being truthful; one isn't honest; one could be hypocritical or even deceptive; one could even be a liar! We could all be liars! And then what would become of rational communication?

How can you know when I say, "those are morels" that
what I say is truthful? How do you know that I'm not deceiving you? How do you know that I'm not trying to play
some joke on you? How do you know that I'm not lying? How
do you know I really believe what I say?

After all you have heard tell of the Cretans and there
must be some tribe somewhere which considers "successful
lying . . . as an art in itself . . ." You know about little children and most of all you may have a good opinion of your
own lying ability, an opinion which, by the way, many of us
probably have and in which we may also take pride.

Well, there we are walking in the country. I've just said,
"those are morels." But am I telling the truth? Do I believe
what I say? Do I believe that those are morels? Isn't it important for you to find out? You can't be taken in! How can
you be sure that what I say is at least a reflection of what
I believe?

What reason have you, what reason has any man, for
believing that another man's words are "signs of [his] thoughts"
(as it has sometimes been expressed)? Traditional philosophers
have spoken of "a propensity to speak truth" or of a "principle of veracity" to the effect that "truth is always uppermost
and is the natural issue of he mind."[1] But contemporary philosophers have put it somewhat differently.

When I say during the course of our walk, "those are
morels," my saying this implies that at the time of speaking
at least I believe that those are morels.[2] Even if I were lying,
still I would be implying that I believe that those are morels.
And anyone who hears me will in general take me to believe
what I say.

Of course, if my saying that those are morels *implies* that
I believe that they are, the use of "implies" is different from
that of entailment. That is, that I believe those are morels does
not *follow from* anything that I say. It could be true both that
those are morels and that I don't believe they are. Here is no
inconsistency. Furthermore, what is implied, namely, that I

believe that those are morels, is not the same or any part of my assertion that they are. If it were, then in order to determine whether they really are morels you would have to determine whether when I say they are, I believe that they are. And this is "clearly not the case."[3]

Some examples: I wake up one morning and hear a resounding noise all around me—the kind of noise you hear in the tropics during a torrential rain. (But I'm not in the tropics.) My wife is half awake. Our bedroom draperies are drawn together. As I get up my wife asks, "What's all that noise?" Well, I stumble over to the most accessible window, draw aside the drapery, and after taking a careful survey of the situation I say, "it's raining" because in fact, it is raining cats and dogs! According to the account I've just given, my saying "it's raining" implies that I believe it is. Of course, I'm not saying or asserting "I believe it's raining"; nor is my belief that it's raining a necessary condition for my saying truly that it is: it may be raining even though I don't believe it.

You and I are discussing the President's murder:

> You say: "It's a fact that the suspect could easily have fired three bullets with considerable accuracy in the time available."
>
> I say: "But were there only three shots? What about those two witnesses who were closer than anybody else to the President? And what did they hear?"
>
> You say: "Well, the FBI says they have three shells and there were three wounds."
>
> I say: "All right! Yet if more than three shots were fired, then the suspect was not alone and unaided!"[4]

According to the account we considered, by making my last remark I imply that I believe that if more than three shots were fired, then the suspect was not alone and unaided.

I'm at a party. I bump into a person I haven't seen since we were in high school. We get into the usual kind of filling-in-blank-spaces-conversation during which he asks, "Are you married?" I say, "Yes." He asks, "Where's your wife? Is she here?" I reply, gesturing, "Certainly, she's over there by the desk talking to that woman with the pink and green feathers." Accordingly, by asserting this, I imply that I believe that my wife is over there by the desk talking to that woman.

I'm down in the basement looking for something or other. My wife has been shopping; she returns and calls out: "Yoohoo, where are you?" and I answer, "I'm down in the basement." By saying this, I imply that I believe that I'm down in the basement.

I have a headache, one of that throbbing kind. I lie down. My wife gives me two or three aspirins. After a half hour or so she asks, "How do you feel?" I say, "Pretty bad, my head is still aching." So saying, I imply that I believe that my head is still aching.

I want to register to vote. So I go up to one of those little old ladies who sit behind a desk in a grocery store or some such place, and she asks, "What's your name?" I answer, "My name is Henry Alexander." By so answering I imply that I believe that my name is Henry Alexander.

Let's take the first example, that in which I look out the window, see that it's raining and tell my wife that it is. She might say then, "Oh!" and turn over and go back to sleep. She might say, "Really!" in surprise (since it hadn't rained in several months). But let us suppose she says, "Really? The weatherman didn't predict it," indicating doubt, and follows this up with, "Do you believe it?" Well, there I am, I've just gotten up and I'm still holding the drapery aside looking out the window! And my wife asks, "Do you believe it?" What am I to say? What do you think I should say? Is she asking me to make sure? (After all, I've just woken up. But I *am* looking out the window; what else am I to do?) Perhaps she's asking whether I have my glasses on? (But I've already put them on.) Is she really asking, "Do I believe that it's raining?" (Perhaps she remembers my telling her that I read somewhere that by my saying that it's raining, I imply that I believe it and she

may now wonder whether in these circumstances I remember it
too.) But the matter at hand is this: What am I to say?

Do I believe it's raining? Of course not! Then I don't
believe it's raining? Heavens NO! But my wife has asked,
"Do I believe it's raining?" What am I to do? What am I to
say? I haven't the slightest idea! Probably in order to get
myself off the hook and to get her back to sleep (she needs
it!) I would say, "Yes, dear, I believe it's raining," hoping
that that would terminate our early morning dialogue. But
notice that if I should say this, my remark has the function of
extracting me from a difficult situation. It doesn't function as
a report of any kind of belief-commitment to the proposition,
"it's raining."[5]

Situations of this sort are very common. And what I've
wanted to bring out is an uneasiness I have in looking for
connections between saying and believing. I suspect there are
more occasions than many philosophers are willing to admit
in which communication carries on its business efficiently and
smoothly without tuning in on the belief circuits either of the
speaker or the hearer. This is not to say that connections or
lines don't arise between saying and believing. But the determined effort to discover such connections may have an over-
powering effect. Why must we suppose in the circumstances outlined and in response to a question, my asserting "it's raining"
implies I believe it? Or why should my remark entitle my wife
to infer that I believe it? Or why under just these circumstances
would my wife or anyone else for that matter feel entitled to
ask concerning my remark, "do you say that from the heart or
not?" "are you saying that with feeling or not?" "are you
saying that with conviction or not?" "are you being truthful
or not?" "are you sincere or not?" "do you believe it?" To
suppose that such questions are always, inevitably, or even
for the most part applicable, appropriate, or relevant is gratui-
tous, at least so it seems to me.

Let's consider our discussion of the President's murder.
We left the discussion when I had said: "If more than three
shots were fired, then the suspect was not alone and unaided."

You say: "Look, three cartridges were found in and around the place from which the suspect had allegedly fired his rifle. And the Warren Commission, as everyone knows, states that 'the most convincing evidence relating to the number of shots' is the number of shells found in and around that place. What else would you ask for?"

I say: "Only this: that the statements of various witnesses should be reasonably accounted for. One witness said, for example, that she heard at least four shots, if not more. And then an FBI agent informs her that perhaps she had heard firecrackers or echoes! Isn't this a little too cavalier?"

But this sort of discussion can go on and on, covering any number of different factors and circumstances surrounding the murder in question. But consider this: do I by saying "she heard at least four shots, if not more" imply that I believe this? Here we are discussing what the Warren Commission reports about the President's murder: neither of us is joking or teasing or pretending or deceiving or lying. Do I by my remarks imply that I believe them? Do you by your remarks imply that you believe them? Is there any question as to the manner in which we make these remarks? Of course, I've drawn out the situation in a very sketchy manner; even so, there is no reason, at least so far in the discussion, to suspect anyone's truthfulness or honesty or sincerity. Do you discern any intent to deceive? That either one or both of us may be prejudiced in one way or another might even be expected; that either one or both of us may slip in our reasoning isn't surprising; that either one or both of us may abuse or even misuse language may be regrettable; and that either one or both of us may lack common sense, may be bad judges of human nature or may generally be prone to errors in judgment is depressingly sad. Let these possibilities apply to our discussion: still would either of us have reason to suspect the honesty or truthfulness or sincerity of the other? So what's at stake when it's maintained, as it so often is, that by my saying or asserting "she heard at least four shots," I imply that I believe it? What's the point?

This is something that puzzles me. Why is it important or necessary or helpful or whatever, to push this kind of connection between saying something and believing it? Why is it here necessary to haul up this special sense of "imply" and then try to show, as some have done, that there is "nothing mysterious" about it and that it is about as plain as the nose on my face? The philosopher says: ". . . anyone who states *p*, whether or not he believes it, *does* imply that he believes it."[6] I've gotten myself into the frame of mind in which I'm utterly baffled and I can't see what such a remark is getting at. And in this, I'm sure I must be wrong!

Let's begin again: when I say in our discussion "one witness said she heard at least four shots," does my saying this entitle you to infer or license you to assume or give you to understand that I believe that one witness said she heard at least four shots? Strange as it may be, I can't see it! Nor can I see that my saying what I say entitles you to infer that I don't believe it! We're talking about a murder, the Warren Commission's report, and the testimony of at least one witness. I don't see how matters of your or my belief enter into it. After we've thoroughly beat the subject to death, after we've disputed over, say, the weapon, its identification, the description of the suspect, the testimony of witnesses as to his whereabouts at the time of the murder, the results of tests of one sort and another, the testimony of physicians, and so on and so on and so on, after all this, you might say: "Well, it's quite obvious that you believe the Warren Commission as well as local law enforcement officers have failed to do their duty. You really believe," you would continue, "that all those fine citizens have in some manner deceived the public!" And I would respond, "Yes, I certainly do believe it"; and then I might add, "I believe the entire proceeding was a deliberate, unmitigated sham!" From here on the discussion can become quite uncontrollable but we won't pursue it. I've reached this point in it because I think a feature of such discussions comes out which is relevant here.

There may come a stage in which the discussion takes on

a different character; a turning point is reached and a new direction is found. When you say, "Well, it's obvious you believe . . ." you indicate perhaps not only that you get the drift of my interests and arguments but also that our line of discussion has been, as far as you are concerned, exhausted. In matters of disagreement, as in the present case, no doubt some annoyance may be felt on both sides. Your annoyance may reveal itself in this ". . . you believe . . ." kind of expression. At this point your use of such an expression can indeed imply that you believe something quite different from what I believe. My annoyance finds expression in wholesale affirmation of belief sprinkled with a considerable helping of hyperbole. If the discussion continues, it is easy to imagine that its next stage may become a full-fledged, hot-headed quarrel, particularly if each of us thinks there are private interests or so-called ultimate considerations at stake.

The feature to which I call attention is this: when we reach this stage in the discussion, the exchanges may well be affirmations of belief. Disputants may consciously argue from matters of belief and nothing else. Whether this is either desirable or profitable is not in question. Nevertheless, the reference point so to speak for each disputant will be what he thinks of as his "system of beliefs" or what he holds dear. And in such a quarrel perhaps we could say that by saying whatever he says, each disputant implies that he believes it; and even if he in fact doesn't, he will still imply that he does. This, incidentally, is quite a convenience since in such quarrels we are very apt not only to discover many things we have believed that we have never before thought of but also to adopt whatever other beliefs happily flow from the original ones.

An observation about this stage of the discussion might well be in order at this point. We quarrel and in ill-disguised anger we do little else than exchange and exhibit beliefs. In such circumstances, it becomes very strange—so it seems to me—to say that by saying whatever I do, I imply that I believe it; "imply," that is, in such a manner that I entitle you to infer or give you to understand that I believe what I say.[7]

In order to show why I think this is strange, let us consider two more examples.

(1) My wife has asked me to go to the greengrocer to buy some watercress. So when I get there I ask for two bunches. He replies: "Very sorry, but today's shipment is late." When I return home, my wife is surprised and annoyed to see me empty-handed. "Surely," she says peevishly, "the grocer wasn't out of watercress at this time of year!" Feeling quite guilty that I've failed to come through, I say: "But he gave me to understand that he had none." Of course, I neglected to say that strictly speaking the greengrocer didn't tell me anything of the kind; and that I just forgot to pressure him into selling me the watercress he always keeps on ice for his more regular and affluent customers. (By the way, I certainly don't want to give anyone to understand that this example exhibits the only use of such a phrase as, "he gave me to understand that so and so." But it is, I think, a characteristic use.)

(2) My wife and I are about to employ a painting contractor. There are only two who seem to be viable candidates for the job. They've submitted estimates; we have interviewed them and examined their references. Andrews is one and Donaldson is the other. Their estimates are about the same, but each set of references requires a considerable amount of reading-between-the-lines. It is obviously going to be a risky business. My wife wants us to make a choice and so she opens the discussion with "Do you think it prudent to give the job to Donaldson?" I reply, "Well, I really believe Andrews will do the faster job, and that, you know, is of prime importance."

Now what I want you to note here is that it would be strange for my wife to say: "So you give me to understand that you believe Andrews will do the faster job. . . ." I've done nothing of the sort! I've stated my opinion about Andrews. And for the purposes of the situation at hand I've been sufficiently explicit. I haven't left anything unsaid. And she doesn't have to make a kind of conceptual leap by saying, "So you're giving me to understand . . . ." I've *told* her at least what my initial opinion is and our discussion will go on from there.

Back now to the quarrel which began with all that talk about the President's murder. Does my saying what I say imply that I believe it? And does the same apply to you? In other words, by my saying that I believe the entire proceeding was a deliberate, unmitigated sham, do I really give you to understand that I believe it? What have I left unsaid because of which you must conceptually hop, skip, and jump to the assertion, "So you're giving me to understand . . ."? In our quarrel we are throwing beliefs at each other right and left. What's the sense of your saying that I'm giving you to understand or of my saying the same of you? For all practical purposes aren't we both *telling* each other what we believe? Can we be said to be giving each other to understand what the other believes?

Let's take an example of a conversation that is unquestionably about a man's beliefs. A younger and an older man are talking about the older man's beliefs. The older man is the English chairman of an international publishing group controlling more than two hundred various kinds of publications.

Harris: Have you any fundamental causes in which you believe, and for which you deliberately create space in your papers?

King: What sort of causes? I am really interested myself, deep down, in the under-dog. I would do anything I can through my newspapers to see that the under-dog of whatever kind gets a break.

Harris: Give . . . some examples of the kind of under-dog that you try to do something for.

King: . . . I think the elderly and old . . . get a raw deal. I think that they are not properly provided for; financially they are at the bottom of the heap; they are desperately lonely. I think that we all ought to do far more than we do. I take that very seriously. I also feel that those people who are poor, ignorant, should be less poor, less ignorant. I have a great feeling for coloured people, who I think have been very badly treated by our country in the past, and I would like to do what I can during my time to level that up.

> *Harris*: Why do you do this? Why should you care about Africans—why should you care about old people? Is there anything in you that leads you to an interest in these particular problems you have mentioned? Are you a religious man, for instance; do you have religious principles which point in this direction?
>
> *King*: I think I am religious but I don't think most people would agree: I don't go to church, but I am very conscious of an Almighty, which I think makes one humble and makes one feel that one is here to play a part which one tries to discover. And when one has discovered it one plays it to the best of one's ability.
>
> *Harris*: I mean—is your religion a kind of Christian religion? Do you believe in charity, for instance, and mercy and suffering?
>
> *King*: And all that—yes.[8]

Would we want to say that Mr. King gives us to understand that he is a kind of religious man? That he is a kind of Christian? Does he *entitle us to infer* that he believes in charity? If you say "Yes" to these questions, I become very puzzled because it seems to me that he has clearly and positively stated that he is religious (although most people might not agree), that he is a kind of Christian, and that he believes in charity. By saying "yes," you've discouraged me from saying what I should have thought King did entitle us to infer. For example, he certainly entitles us to infer that he believes in God. In addition, remember that Mr. King said his "Almighty" makes him feel "humble." Now in a later part of the discussion Mr. King says he is going to do a lot to change the unconverted vote into a Labour Party vote. When asked what exactly he's going to do, Mr. King said: "Ah, if you could spare threepence a day somewhere from about October 1, I think you'll possibly find yourself being converted. The only thing I can mention is that I have ordered a red flag for my Rolls-Royce, with 'Vote Labour' on it." By his remarks we are given to understand that humility is *not* one of Mr. King's outstanding virtues.

During the discussion, Mr. King agreed that he understood "what the young and the up and coming people want." This in connection with his "deep down" feeling for the various kinds of "under-dog" he mentions does entitle us to infer that Mr. King certainly plays quite well the part that his "Almighty" has assigned to him.

Earlier Mr. King had said: "I try to publish in a simplified form the news that I think my readers should have at their disposal." This taken in conjunction with his "liking to do what [he] can . . . to level . . ." things up gives us to understand in what sort of way Mr. King is doing his "leveling," a matter, by the way, which he doesn't mention.

So much for the private views of the yellow press! But I hope there is no question that I have entitled you to infer that I think Mr. King is a humbug. However, should I state this, I would not entitle you to infer it. By so stating, neither have I given you to understand, nor have I given you reason to presuppose, nor have I licensed you to assume, that I think Mr. King is a humbug. I have in fact stated that he is! And by so doing I give you my authority (if that is needed), to quote me (if for some wild reason you would want to), or perhaps to include my name as a possible subscriber to an anti-Cecil King campaign.

I want at this point to recall the examples I mentioned earlier. Each of them requires careful study, but I shall not take time for it. However, I hope that by recalling them now, you'll come to see how strange it is to maintain the philosophical thesis that by saying what I say, I imply that I believe it.

There's the party incident: meeting an old friend and pointing out my wife to him, saying, "She's over there by the desk talking to the woman with the pink and green feathers." Does my friend recall that I have a bad memory? Does he want reassurance that I now remember who my wife is and what she looks like?

There's the time when my wife returns home, wants to find out where I am, and I call out, "I'm down in the basement." Does my wife think that I don't really know where I am (perhaps I'm lost or I'm sleepwalking or I'm senile)? "He's so absentminded, he never knows where he is!"

There's the headache situation in which to a query I answer, "my head is still aching." I always have extreme difficulty in knowing whether I'm in pain. However, my wife can usually tell me. This time, however, she herself doesn't know what to tell me; but still she wonders whether I know what I'm talking about.

And finally, to the vote registration question, "What's your name?" I say, "My name is Henry Alexander."

Take the last situation: by saying my name is H. A., I imply I believe it, meaning by this that I am entitling you to infer that I believe it! Do I believe that my name is H. A.? Am I unprepared to say for sure? Do I lack confidence that my name is H. A.? Or is it perhaps that I don't really know but merely believe my name is H. A.? Just what am I doing when I'm implying I believe my name is H. A.?

The emphasis, you may say, is not quite right, for by implying that you believe what you say, you really are entitling a listener to infer that you believe what you say. All right! If we stick to the case at hand, why in heaven's name would the little old lady behind the desk, who is doing her part for vote registration, give even a feeble thought to whether I believe my name is H. A.? Why should she care? After all, if I sign under oath whatever it is I'm supposed to sign and my name is *not* H. A., my goose is cooked! So what's it to her?

"Well," you say, "this business of signing under oath distorts the situation for the purposes of our investigation!" All right! All right! Suddenly I recognize who the little old lady behind the desk is. "Why! Miss Hinkelberry!" say I, "you don't remember me! I was in your kindergarten class thirty-four years ago. No, you wouldn't remember; it's been too long. My name is H. A." By saying this I have entitled Miss Hinkelberry to infer that I believe my name is H. A. Of course, Miss Hinkelberry isn't worried about this now, since she is trying to remember the class that she taught thirty-four years ago.

Maybe she does remember that first day of school long ago, asking a child, "Well, little man, can you tell me your name?" And maybe she remembers the answer, "My name . . . is . . . H. A." And then she might have said, "My! what a fine lad you are!" Miss Hinkelberry, having been engrossed in memories, suddenly wakes up to the fact that I'm still standing before her and she asks: "What did you say your name is?" I say: "My name is H. A." (thereby entitling her to infer that I believe it). Of course, this time she doesn't reply by saying what a fine lad I am—both Miss Hinkelberry and I are, after all, growing old. But you can imagine Miss Hinkelberry thinking to herself: "Well, well, after all these years he still believes it! Isn't that nice?"

This isn't the right attitude! One should be more serious and certainly more respectful of Miss Hinkelberry. So let's get down to business. Miss Hinkelberry is going to register me so I can vote. She must write my name down on the registration book and then she must make out a receipt in triplicate. Now Miss Hinkelberry has been instructed that she is not to write anyone's name down in the registration book until she knows that the person whose name she is about to write believes that his name is the name that he tells her to write down, that is, until she knows he's truthful. (You see, it is very important that there should be no duplication!) So here I am in front of the desk and I say again, "My name is H. A." Miss Hinkelberry looks up, for by my saying what I say, I entitle her to make the inference that I believe it. She looks up just because she wants to double-check by also looking into my eyes. (You can tell whether a man is truthful if he looks you straight in the eye.) This extra precaution shows her good sense. After all she can write my name down only on the condition that I believe it is my name. But she can know this only if I imply it—i.e., entitle her to infer it. Is it any easier for her to know when I say "My name is H. A." that I imply that I believe my name is H. A. than for her to know that my name is H. A.? Are the criteria for determining whether by saying what I do, I imply I believe my name is H. A. any easier to fulfil than those for knowing that my name is H. A.? But if Miss Hinkelberry is going to write my name down, she must first know that in saying "my name is H. A." I believe it. But in order to know this, she would need to know much more (or know what is no less difficult) than is required for knowing my name. What is required for Miss Hinkelberry to know that by saying what I do I imply that I believe my name is H. A.? Amongst many things, she must know that I am not testing microphones* or practising elocution* or rehearsing a speech or recording one; she must know that I am not playacting* or storytelling* or talking in my sleep or under hypnotic influences or possessed by evil spirits; she must also know that I am not a liar.*[9] No wonder she looks into my eyes—but, unfortunately, she won't find any solution to her difficulties there. For looking into my eyes will not give her the knowledge that my name is H. A. any more than determining whether I imply that I believe my name is H. A. will give her that knowledge. Looking into my eyes and determining whether I imply that I believe . . . are comparable; one is as easy or as difficult as the other. And neither are of any help to Miss Hinkelberry who only wants to write my name down in a voters' registration book.

When philosophers try to formulate rational connections between saying and believing, they sometimes tell us: "anyone who states *p*, whether or not he believes it, *does* imply that he believes it."[10] Miss Hinkelberry no doubt has great sympathy for them. The philosophers' position is somewhat similar to hers. She can't write my name down for voters' registration unless she knows that by my saying my name is H. A. I imply I believe it. Philosophers say rational communication is impossible unless by our sayings we imply we believe those sayings. Fortunately for everybody, including Miss Hinkelberry and the philosophers, voter registration and rational communication give no signs of decline, although for each there are many perils of different kinds.

Let's move to an entirely fresh example.

My automobile is getting along in years. It is beginning to use a lot of oil; my gasoline bill is getting bigger; repairs are on the increase and generally, I'm beginning to lose confidence in its performance. Should I dump it or is it worth a complete and thorough overhaul which may add a year or two to its use? I go to the garage down the street where Jim is the service manager. Ours is a long-standing relationship, friendly and straightforward. "Jim," say I, "you know that work you did on my clutch day before yesterday didn't help a bit!" "Really!" says Jim. "Yep," say I. "Still have that trouble getting into second." "Well, I'll have another look at it. Can you leave it for awhile?" I reply dejectedly, "Jim, I paid $17.82 for that work the other day." According to the account I've been considering, in saying to Jim "I paid $17.82 for that work the other day," I imply that I believe it.

But look at it this way: Jim knows about my car and my indecision about it. He has made a few suggestions, but after all, he is no oracle and he knows it. I've got to make the decision sooner or later. Jim is a very sympathetic guy and, more importantly, he's honest. When Jim hears me say, "I paid $17.82 for that work the other day" he doesn't need to wonder whether I believe it. He doesn't even have to remind me that if the work that was supposd to have been done the other day was not in fact done or not done as it should have been done, or was not completed, I will not have to make a second payment of $17.82 for the same job. I know this; it is a policy that Jim uniformly follows without question and many people who know Jim have had the unusual pleasure of knowing that this is his policy. So in saying what I do I'm distinctly not implying that I have this work coming to me since I have already paid for it.

No! In saying "I paid $17.82 . . ." Jim rightly understands that I'm alluding to my general indecision regarding my automobile. But less implicitly and more to the point, he understands me as requesting his precaution in making any additional repairs that will add considerably to the increasing expense of upkeep. What I imply or refer to by my remark is some aspect of the situation with which both Jim and I are acquainted. It might be added that if I hadn't made the remark as I did, i.e., in a thoroughly dejected and discouraged tone of voice (Jim knows not only my automobile's symptoms but also mine), he might not have seen the point of my remark. And then he might have asked, "What do you mean?" or he might feel he had to remind me of his general policy. But this is only to say that sometimes our remarks just don't come off and we try again.

The mailman has just come to the door. I answer it. He wants seven cents for a postage-due stamp. "Do you have any change?" I ask my wife. She replies: "There's some in the left-hand drawer of the hall cabinet." What possible light does it throw on this situation to say that in saying this, my wife implies she believes it? Suppose that my wife is a penny collector and the only money in the left-hand drawer are eleven pennies which she has just collected because they are particularly interesting specimens. Would she then say: "There's some change in the left-hand drawer of the hall cabinet"? One might say if one wanted to that she believes it, but she *certainly* wouldn't tell me, because quite naturally she doesn't want the postman to have those valuable pennies. Yet in fact she does tell me that there is change in that left-hand drawer! And the point of her remark—which she does not need to state—is to give me leave to use the change in that left-hand drawer to pay the postman. (Suppose after handing the postman seven cents, my wife said, "But I didn't say you could give it to the postman." What am I to do or say then?)

Let's go back to the morel case. Can it really be that in saying, "Bless my soul, those are morels!" I'm implying that I believe it? That is, entitling you to infer that I believe it? You don't know anything about morels; you've never seen them before! Naturally, you're going to ask me about them—i.e., if you can catch up with me as I dash off to grab as many of them as I can! In this situation, I'd be delighted if you don't infer that I believe it; if you don't believe anything I say about them; if you should be one of those people who thinks that every wild mushroom is sheer poison! After all, I could then without a pang of conscience keep them all for myself. As it is, it's a situation in which you don't think I'm lying or play-acting or talking in my sleep or any other silly thing. So un-fortunately, after I've answered your questions and told you what I know about morels, I'll have to divide them up with you.

Why do philosophers tell us "anyone who states p, . . . implies that he believes it"? Let's go back a bit. I commented earlier that philosophical speculations may lead us to consider the connections between our sayings and our states of mind. Often the connections sought for are those supposedly reflected in "communal assumptions" or "rules of rational discourse" or "norms of truthfulness," "necessary background conditions," or "primary conceptual connexions" or "circumstances in which human communication takes place." The aim is to formulate such assumptions, rules, norms, or whatever. Contextual impli-cation is formulated to supply one such assumption or rule. "Anyone who states p, . . . implies that he believes it." Or, "to say 'p' is to imply that one believes that p." But what do these accounts tell us? I don't want to say that there are no con-nections between saying and believing. Why shouldn't there be? But why this one? If philosophers want to determine assump-tions or rules that are involved in human communication, what help are we given, what point is made, when we're told that "anyone who states p, . . . implies that he believes it"?

I've indicated some considerations that have led to my bafflement. The following remarks, mostly questions, may sum it up.

There are a great number of things that come under the rubric of our sayings and statings and equally diverse are the attitudes, postures, or frames of reference we may adopt to-ward what we say. Why, then, should we want to maintain that some attitude even toward characteristically normal and prosaic statements is "implied" by our making those state-ments? And then, why would we want to say that the specific state of mind is one of believing? What logical perspective do we attain when we're told that statement-making occasions are conceptually so connected with particular beliefs of speakers on those occasions that we can know in advance of the circumstances and individual features of such occasions that the speakers will have those beliefs? Why should we suppose that by saying what we say we imply *any* attitude, *any* posture, *any* frame of mind? Why should their beliefs, for example, be more germane to the purposes of communication than the implicit background, manifest foreground, or intended development of whatever exercises those speakers and their listeners? It isn't false that by their sayings, speakers imply they believe so-and-so. But what is understood in claiming its truth? What would such a claim come to?

Further, I don't understand what considerations would prevail so that, even in efforts to study assumptions, rules, or norms operating in communication, we produce philosophical legislation which narrows or programs what by our sayings we imply or what we entitle others to infer. Imagine finding areas in communication and understanding to which rules apply. Perhaps to such areas as convention, style, usage. Would we then be encouraged to find rules that cover what speakers imply or what their hearers are entitled to infer? Why in ongoing and live communication and understanding would anyone think that independent of knowing his intonation, gesture, facial expression, emphases, choice of words, situation, purposes—yes, even independent of knowing to whom he speaks —the account, "in saying *p*, a speaker implies he believes it" has a point? If it does, what is it? And to what clearer comprehension of conversation and discussion does it lead us? Could it be that by remarking about morels, as well as rain, or three shots, or where his wife is, where he is, how he feels, his name, or the price for car repairs, or change in the hall cabinet, a rational speaker in each and every case uniformly implies that he believes what he says? Is this the verve, the reach, the life of dialogue?

NOTES

1. Thomas Reid, *Works*, ed. W. Hamilton, Edinburgh, 1858, p. 196.
2. As Crawshay-Williams puts it: "It is axiomatically understood

...that, if anyone asserts a proposition, he wishes to be interpreted as believing it to be true (or probable or acceptable in some sense). In other words, we almost invariably base our discussions upon an unstated agreement to adopt as one of our premises the double implication: 'A says that p' implies 'A asserts that p,' and this in turn implies 'A believes or holds that p.' " *Methods and Criteria of Reasoning*, p. 183.

3. See G. E. Moore, *The Philosophy of G. E. Moore*, pp. 541–543; *Philosophical Papers*, p. 176; and J. L. Austin, *How to Do Things With Words*, Lecture IV.

4. Suggested by remarks from the *National Observer*, October 24, 1964, p. 16.

5. The same considerations would apply to the question, "Do you know it?" In this sort of situation, in these circumstances, I don't see how either this or the above question has any place.

6. Nowell-Smith, "Contextual Implication and Ethical Theory," *PAS*, vol. 36, 1962, p. 9.

7. Nowell-Smith makes an even stronger claim by the use of these expressions. For example, he says: "In saying 'no foxes eat hens' [a speaker] gives me to understand both that no foxes eat hens and also that he believes this." (*Ibid.*, p. 10.) I am not concerned with the former part of this claim.

8. From "Encounter with Cecil King," *The Listener*, August 27, 1964, p. 297.

9. Conditions marked by an asterisk are those mentioned by Nowell-Smith in "Contextual Implication and Ethical Theory," *op. cit.*, pp. 7–8.

10. *Ibid.*, p. 9.

STATEMENTS

AVRUM STROLL

1. "What are statements?" The question is clearly well formed and perfectly proper, if somewhat uncommon in everyday speech. I cannot myself recall anyone except philosophers ever having asked it, but it is easy to imagine circumstances in which it might naturally arise. A new, very raw office assistant asking it of an accountant; a child asking it of his teacher; an adult foreigner asking it of a native speaker of English. In answering it, the accountant will explain the nature and purpose of accounts rendered. The teacher will describe certain uses to which language is put. The native speaker will search for a synonym or a characterizing phrase in his language or in that of the foreigner. Each query thus demands and receives a different response, a response determined in part by the experience and background of the questioner and in part by the circumstances in which the question arises. What the adult foreigner wishes to know is not what the child wishes to know, and what either of them wishes to know is not what the new assistant wishes to know. That this is so might be brought out more sharply by contrasting the question, "What are statements?" with the question, "What does the word 'statement' mean?" This latter question is also well formed and somewhat uncommon in everyday speech. Yet it is very likely the question the foreigner had in mind when he asked, "What are statements?" It is also possible, but less likely, that this is what the child had in mind; and it is very unlikely indeed that this is what the new assistant had in mind in asking her question.

In thinking about these cases, one is tempted to say that the question arose because each of the speakers lacked a certain bit (piece or kind) of information. One is also tempted

179

to say that the answers were diverse because each of them lacked a *different* bit (piece or kind) of information. But is what one is tempted to say also true to say about these cases? The issue is an intriguing one and we shall want to explore it in some detail in what follows. Nevertheless, apart from its intrinsic interest, we have other reasons for wanting to deal with it here, and these may be elaborated on as follows:

2. The situation in philosophy resembles, yet differs from, the sorts of situations we have described above. The philosopher, like the assistant, the foreigner, and the child, also asks the question, "What are statements?" But in philosophy it is a common question—so common that we tend to overlook the fact that it may also arise only in special circumstances. What are these circumstances? Are they the same, or similar, to those which give rise to the question for the assistant, the foreigner, and the child? Does the question arise for the philosopher because he lacks some bit (piece or kind) or information? If so, is it the same bit (piece or kind) of information as that lacked by the assistant, the foreigner, and the child? If it is not, does the philosopher lack a *different* bit (piece or kind) of information from that which they lack—and if so, what is it? Or does the question arise even though he lacks no information at all? And why should the answers to his question be so diverse?

It is these queries which form the main concern of this paper; in attempting to answer them, let us begin by looking more deeply into the cases we have described above.

The Case of the New Assistant

The new office assistant's problem arises from circumstances such as these. She has been told by someone that all statements must be mailed out by the twenty-fifth of the month. New at the job, and with no previous office training, she asks, "What are statements?" In answering, the accountant does a number of different things. He may begin with some comments about normal business practice, about the extension of credit, the need for keeping tax records, and so forth. He may then turn to billing procedures in particular, pointing out that they involve the mailing out of abstracts of accounts at regular intervals; and he may say that such abstracts are called "statements." His initial description of statements may thus be very general and may be insufficient to enable the new assistant to identify particular examples of statements or to produce new examples of them. In order to overcome this deficiency, he may show the new assistant samples of the kinds of statements his company sends out.

The new assistant's question was thus more complex than it appeared to be. It demanded a variety of answers. But in essence it was a technical question, whose answer required the possession of technical information she did not possess. And because it required such technical information, it is possible (though unusual) for an ordinary person, even a native speaker of English, not to have been exposed to the training, experience and background necessary to answer it. This was indeed the case with our young assistant.

In asking his question, "What are statements?" the philosopher will not be satisfied with the answer the accountant gives the new assistant. The philosopher is likely to express his dissatisfaction by saying that he does not want to know what statements are "in that sense of 'statement.'" He is likely to add that "in that sense of the term, he already knows what statements are." The piece of information he wants, if any, is thus not the piece of information the new assistant wants. What motivates his question is, accordingly, not what motivates hers.

But is it equally clear that he is not looking for the same *kind* of information she is looking for? Is he not, after all, looking for a bit or piece of technical information? The answer, I should say, is "No." There are, of course, such technical questions in philosophy. An existentialist may wonder what the deduction theorem is. The answer requires that he obtain some technical information about logic; and he may do this in a variety of ways—by asking a logician or even by looking up the term in a philosophical dictionary. But "statement" is not a technical term in this sense. There is no specialist to whom the philosopher can appeal for an answer—indeed, is he not himself the philosophical specialist looking for an answer? And if he looks up the term in a philosophical dictionary, he will find that he already knows what the dictionary tells him. His concern is thus not a technical concern. But if it is not, what then is the bit (piece or kind) of information which he lacks in asking his question? Or does it arise even though no such bit (piece or kind) of information is lacking to him?

The Case of the Adult Foreigner

The foreigner, as we have seen, is an adult, and accordingly, presumably a person with some education and some experience of life. His question is, therefore, not like the child's question in stemming from a lack of education and a paucity of experience. The example also is set up to exclude his being a professional philosopher, asking the philosopher's sophisticated question. Under what circumstances, then, will the question arise for such a person? It might arise because he has come across an English word whose meaning he does not know; and in asking his question, "What are statements?" he wishes to find out what this word means. But means in what sense? The answer is determined by the sort of reply he would find acceptable; and we have already indicated what sort of answer that would be. If he is German, for example, he wants the native speaker of English to inform him that "statement" means the same as "Ausserung." Such a response would constitute an ideal answer. However, a native speaker of English may not be in a position to provide it, for he may not know enough German to do so. But there may be other things he can do. If the foreigner knows some English, a native speaker of English may answer the question by supplying him with an English word, or an English phrase, or a set of English words which means the same, or approximately the same, as "statement." In doing this, he thus supplies the foreigner with a "translation within" English, and in this way answers his question. If this account is correct, it seems the foreigner lacked a piece of information in asking his question; and that the piece of information he lacked was either that "statement" means the same as "Ausserung" or that "statement" means the same as some specific word (e.g., "assertion") or some specific set of words in English.

Now if all this is so, it seems equally clear that the philosopher's problem is not the foreigner's problem. The philosopher is not in the position of being unfamiliar with English. His question does not arise because he does not know what the word "statement" means in the way in which the foreigner does not know what it means. He is not looking, ideally, for a translation of this word into some other langugae which he speaks better than English. Being a native speaker of English, he speaks English as well as he can be expected to speak any language. Nor does his query arise because he fails to know what word or set of words would count as a synonym for "statement" in English. The piece of information he lacks, if any, is thus not the piece of information which the foreigner lacks.

But if he does not lack the *piece* of information the foreigner lacks, does he lack the *kind* of information the foreigner lacks? Once again, it is clear that he does not. The foreigner's problem in this respect resembles the assistant's in being, as it were, a technical question about the English language. A certain kind of expertise was required in order to answer it. Such technical questions confront the native speaker, too. Even though he is wholly fluent in the language, a native speaker may nevertheless not know what "gerund" means, for example. This is because "gerund" is a word which appears only in special, technical contexts, and even a native speaker may lack the sort of training which will familiarize him with its use in such contexts. "Statement" is a word which differs importantly from "gerund" in having both technical and non-technical uses. Among the former, as we have seen, are those which occur in business contexts, and there are others as well.

But as we have also seen, it was not the philosopher's unfamiliarity with the use of the word in such contexts that gave rise to his question. The philosopher is concerned with the ordinary, nontechnical use or uses of the word "statement" and not its use or uses in such special contexts. His problem is not a technical problem about the English language in the way in which the foreigner's problem is. It therefore seems that the *kind* of information which the philosopher lacks is not like that which the foreigner lacks when he asks his question.[1]

The Case of the Child

And, finally, what about the child? What is it that he wishes to know when he asks his teacher, "What are statements?" The problem may arise for him as it does for the foreigner. He may hear or read the word for the first time and not recognize it; or even having heard or seen it a number of times, he may still not know what it means. His question is designed to find out what statements are by finding out what the word "statement" means. But means in what sense? What sort of answer should the teacher supply?

Although the child is unquestionably familiar with a large number of the multifarious uses to which language is commonly put, what he knows in this familiar way may be latent and unarticulated. If asked, he may not be able to describe the difference between making a statement and issuing advice,—even though he may be quite capable of knowingly disputing the claims advanced in the statement and of knowingly disregarding the advice. Part of the teacher's answer consists in articulating for him that which he is already familiar with. She instructs him in what "statement" means by helping him to distinguish between statements, orders, advice, commands, questions, and so on.

But this is not the only sense in which he may not understand what "statement" means. He may also fail to know what names grammarians traditionally assign to the items we employ in our everyday use of language. To find out what "statement" means in this sense is to come to understand to what items this name is traditionally applied.

What he wishes from the teacher, therefore, is not only a more articulate account of some of the uses to which language is put, and how they differ from one another, but also an account which will enable him accurately to assign the commonly used designations for the items so employed. The teacher meets these needs in part by generalized talk about language, in part by giving him "rules of thumb" for recognizing and distinguishing statements from commands, questions, etc., and in part by producing examples of statements, commands, etc., naming these so that the student can pick out new examples of them. The child's problem is thus to some extent a technical problem—one of learning the names used by grammarians for these items, of learning certain mnemonic devices for recognizing them, and so on. In this respect, it resembles the problems facing the new assistant and the foreigner. But his case differs from theirs in certain ways, too. The new assistant's problem consisted in learning to identify an item she was wholly unfamiliar with, while the child in knowing how to operate with statements was in some sense already familiar with them. The pedagogic devices he learns enable him to explain and make articulate what he only "knew latently" (i.e., enable him to explain his practice) and thus enable him with greater accuracy to recognize statements when they occur and to distinguish them from other things with which they might be confused. The foreigner also knew what statements are (but not latently); what he did not know is also partly what the child did not know, i.e., the English name for them.

3. Now it is clear that such specific items of information and such expertise are not what the philosopher lacks. Having been to school, he already knows what names are traditionally assigned to such items as statements, commands, etc. He knows how to distinguish these items from one another and to pick out examples of each. But even if these are not the specific

bits and pieces of information he lacks in order to answer the question, "What are statements?" it is still not evident that he does not lack bits and pieces like them.

Many writers describe the philosopher's predicament in such a way as to suggest that this is in fact the case. As they portray it, his situation is not unlike the child's. Like the child, the philosopher is in the position of wanting to identify that which in a certain sense is "obvious" and familiar to him— and yet which, curiously enough, he tends to confuse with other things that he is also familiar with, such as sentences and utterances. These concluding passages from a recent paper by Professor Richard Cartwright give admirable expression to just this point of view. He writes:

> And with this we may return, finally, to the question which generated these technicalities—the question: What was that to which B referred and of which he predicated truth? The answer is surely obvious: the subject of B's predication of truth was (i) the statement that A made. This, indeed, was evident enough at the outset and nothing subsequently said should be taken as an effort to *prove* it. The advantage gained so far as the question is concerned is simply the protection we now have against confusing (i) with any of (ii) through (ix).
>
> But I think that we are thereby better equipped, also, to deal with the general question as to the proper subjects of predications of truth and falsity. Statements, or assertions, are surely to be counted as at least *some* amongst these. This, too, might well have been said at the outset. For what could be more obvious than that something asserted—something put forward as true, can properly be said to be true? Still, the frequency with which sentences—or their meanings, or their utterances—are claimed to be the *sole* bearers of truth suggests that, unless the obvious is often overlooked, statements are all too easily mis-identified.
>
> Still, protection against these mis-identifications is by no means the whole story so far as this general question is concerned. For one thing, there may well be things other than statements that can equally qualify as truths or falsehoods. And more importantly, perhaps, to say what statements are

not is not to say what they *are*. To distinguish them from other things is not by itself to provide either means for their detection or rules for distinguishing one of them from another. There is thus an important sense in which it remains to be said *what* it is that is susceptible of truth or falsity.[2]

But why should that which is "obvious" be so readily confused with these other things? In going on to assert that "statements are all too easily mis-identified," Professor Cartwright implies that there is some special difficulty about making such identifications; that the task is not one which any educated native speaker can automatically be expected to carry out successfully. And in these passages he offers hints why this is so. His suggestion appears to be that the problem of identifying statements is at least to some degree a technical problem, requiring some expertise for its solution. He writes that the question "generated these technicalities," and implies that the "technicalities" assist the philosopher in distinguishing statements from these other things. He avers, beyond this, that one must develop "means" for the "detection" of statements. Such remarks build up a picture in which the problem of identifying statements is seen to be remarkably like that which faced the child, and yet different, too. Professor Cartwright does not suggest or imply that the philosopher is looking for the same bit of information which the child seeks; nor does he imply that he is looking for that bit of expertise which will give him the ability to apply the names grammarians assign to these items; nor does he intimate that the "rules" he seeks are those easily memorized rules of thumb which the teacher employs in order to assist the child in distinguishing statements from commands, advice, etc. But it is clear that he is nevertheless suggesting that the philosopher seeks the same kind (if not the same piece or pieces) of information as that which the child seeks, and the possession of which will enable him to avoid conflating statements with such things as sentences and utterances.

4. I have quoted Professor Cartwright's remarks in order

to show how natural they are, how neatly they point up the analogy between the philosopher's situation and those in which the ordinary man sometimes finds himself. They also suggest that one reason why the philosopher may think of himself as looking for special bits (pieces or kinds) of information is that he tends to assimilate his question, "What are statements?" to questions which are verbally indistinguishable from it and which are asked by ordinary people in the sorts of situations we have described. Because the questions asked by such ordinary people do elicit answers which supply them with bits (pieces or kinds) of information—some of it of a technical sort—the philosopher is disposed to believe that his question should do so as well. It seems fair to say that he is induced to believe that only a certain kind of answer will be appropriate by the very form of the question itself.

And yet the analogy between his situation and theirs is strangely incomplete. For as we have seen, it is easy to specify the bits (pieces or kinds) of information the assistant, the foreigner, and the child lack in asking, "What are statements?", whereas it is not at all easy to specify what it is that the philosopher lacks in asking his question. What corresponds to the kind of information the teacher supplies the child; and where is such information to be obtained? It is this very lack of specificity which at once makes it persuasive that he lacks information but also makes it puzzling as to what it might be. There is thus a prima facie difference between his case and theirs.

We might bring this out in yet another way. "What are statements?" resembles other questions a person might naturally ask—for example, "What are mangoes?" This latter question is again a technical question, requiring some special bit (piece or kind) of information for its resolution. Now where might one find such information? Of course, one might ask it of persons he knows, but if the answer is not forthcoming, then an obvious place to look for it would be in a dictionary. *The American College Dictionary* in fact informs us that a mango is "a yellowish red tropical fruit with a firm skin, hard central stone, and a juicy, aromatic subacid pulp."[3] What could be clearer or more helpful? If we now adopt an analogous procedure in attempting to find an answer to the question, "What are statements?" what do we discover? The same dictionary gives us, under the heading "Statement," the following bits of information:

> *n.* 1. Something stated. 2. A communication or declaration in speech or writing setting forth facts, particulars, etc. 3. *Com.* an abstract of an account, as one rendered to show the balance due. 4. Act or manner of stating something.[4]

Other answers in other dictionaries look remarkably like this one. *Webster's Seventh New Collegiate Dictionary* (1963), for instance, supplies the following information:

> **state·ment** \'stāt-mənt\ *n* **1 :** the act or process of stating or presenting orally or on paper **2 :** something stated: as **a :** a report of facts or opinions **b :** a single declaration or remark **: ASSERTION** **3 : PROPOSITION** 2a **4 :** the enunciation of a theme in a musical composition **5 :** a summary of a financial account showing the balance due

> By permission. From *Webster's Seventh New Collegiate Dictionary*, copyright 1965 by G. & C. Merriam Company, Publishers of the Merriam-Webster Dictionaries.

The philosopher who consults dictionaries such as these is likely to be disappointed in the information he obtains from them. The trouble is not that they are bad dictionaries, incomplete or inaccurate; even the best won't do. The trouble is of another sort. If one knows, for example, that the word "statement" means—as the dictionary informs us—the same as "something stated," one may still wish to know what that something is which is stated; or if one is told that a statement is a "communication or declaration in speech or writing setting forth facts," one may still wish to know what a communication is; what a declaration is; and what it is to set forth facts. Or if one is told that a statement is the "act or manner of stating something," one may still want to know what sort of act it is; how it differs from other kinds of acts, and in particular how such acts differ from the kinds of "statements" which are "something stated." In brief, after receiving dictionary answers to his question, "What are statements?" a philosopher may still feel that he has not received the bit (piece or kind) of information which he seeks—information which will give him the expertise he needs in order to identify statements and to distinguish them from other things with which they may be confused. It is as if the dictionary *almost* supplies the information he needs, but falls short at the last moment; as if the dictionary, instead of assisting him to make articulate what he is obviously familiar with, has perversely contributed to concealing, by failing to mention it, just that bit (piece or kind) of information which would give him the answer he is looking for. It thus seems natural to suppose that such information exists, but exists tantalizingly beyond the dictionary level, and accordingly that one must probe more deeply for it.

And yet, as I have said, though it may be natural to view the philosopher's predicament in this way there is something puzzling about it, too. Why should the dictionary be able to answer his question about mangoes and yet not be able to answer his question about statements, if both questions are technical questions, fundamentally similar in requiring some bit (piece or kind) of information for their resolution? Or is there something wrong with this picture? Is the philosopher's question not like the question about mangoes? Is it not like the question the assistant, the child, and the foreigner ask in spite of the verbal similarities between them? Is it importantly different—and if so, in what way?

5. One begins to suspect that the similarities between the philosopher's question and these other questions is more apparent than real; that the philosopher is not looking for pieces of technical information at all, and accordingly that what he is really doing is not what he claims, or even believes himself, to be doing. One suspects this on a variety of grounds—don't all of us with a reasonable amount of education and experience in living know what a communication is; what a declaration is; what it is to set forth facts; and don't we know what sentences are; and how to distinguish them from utterances and

indeed from statements? What else could one be expected to know in order to answer the question, "What are statements?" Why won't what we ordinarily say about these things, based upon such experience, satisfy the philosopher's need? Is it because the philosopher is not really looking for information at all, let alone technical information?

I believe this is the case. We begin to develop some insight into what motivates the philosopher and what perplexes him, too, when we notice that he comes to the inquiry—to what he describes as a search for special bits (pieces or kinds) of information—with a certain conception about statements already in mind. This conception colors and prejudges the nature of his "search" in very special ways. We can see this to be so by re-examining the terminal paragraph in Professor Cartwright's paper. He writes there:

> Still, protection against these mis-identifications is by no means the whole story so far as this general question is concerned. For one thing, there may well be things other than statements that can equally qualify as truths or falsehoods. And more importantly, perhaps, to say what statements are *not* is not to say what they *are*. To distinguish them from other things is not by itself to provide either means for their detection or rules for distinguishing one of them from another. There is thus an important sense in which it remains to be said *what* it is that is susceptible of truth or falsity.[5]

These remarks are characteristically philosophical. They exude an air of mystery about things not easily identifiable—but unmistakably there, even if hidden from the ordinary eye by a welter of items (sentences, utterances and the rest) with which they are only too readily confused. Such things must be "detected" by "means" not available to the native speaker, or even to the intelligent, reflective nonspecialist. They must be uncovered and distinguished from one another by "rules" which the philosopher must devise. Is there not behind such talk the image of the philosopher as a kind of scientist, going beyond the common sense of the school boy and the ordinary man, to search for that piece of information or those "rules" which will cause the world to give up its secrets? Is the philosopher, as so conceived, not a kind of Dr. Ehrlich, looking for the secret formula (the information) which will enable him to discover the magic bullet (the statement) which is there if he can but find it?

If statements are conceived of as mysterious, hidden things of this kind then the philosopher's perplexity about them becomes comprehensible. It also becomes comprehensible that the ordinary sources of information are no longer open to him in his effort to find out what statements are. And his search for special bits (pieces or kinds) of information now makes sense, too; for it is only by possessing such special bits of information that he is able to "detect" these esoteric things. And finally, it enables us to understand why he believes such things are readily confused with things which are immediately accessible—for being hidden amidst them, as it were, they are difficult to discern and these other things can easily be mistaken for them.

6. But now we must ask a deeper question: Why should philosophers think of statements as things to be "detected," as esoteric entities not immediately discernible to the ordinary eye?

The question has many answers. I cannot hope to deal with all of them here; instead, I should like to concentrate on one which goes to the heart of the matter and illuminates what it finds there. As I see it, the philosopher is gripped by a certain model: he is, as Wittgenstein puts it, "held captive by a picture." This model is very compelling; it not only arises in a natural way, but its explanatory powers seem very great to one who sees the world through its eyes. Let us call this model the "vehicle-content" model. In its simplest, most literal form it arises from distinguishing between such things as automobiles and their occupants, between coal cars and the coal, between things which carry something and that which they carry. The power of such a model lies in its apparent universal applicability to a wide range of things. One wants to say that it fits, with nothing left over, and that is why it is a good description of what is the case. As Wittgenstein remarks in the *Investigations*,[6] "The picture is *there;* and I do not dispute its *correctness.* But *what* is its application? . . . In numberless cases we exert ourselves to find a picture and once it is found the application as it were comes about of itself. In this case we already have a picture which forces itself on us at every turn —but does not help us out of the difficulty, which only begins here."

The vehicle-content model is a picture of this sort; it seems not only to apply to automobiles and their passengers, but to letters and their contents, to translations and what is translated, to a sentence (or an utterance) and its content—the message it carries.[7] But philosophical difficulties arise just because the model is not universally applicable; because it does not fit equally well such cases as a letter and its contents, a sentence and the statement it is used to make.

Among those who accept the model and who wonder what statements are, vehicles are distinguished from one another in a variety of ways; and all such vehicles are distinguished from their contents. The contents are themselves distinguished from one another in a variety of ways, as well as being discriminated from the vehicles which convey (carry or express) them. J. L. Austin, for example, distinguishes sentences per se from the utterances of sentences on particular occasions; and distinguishes words per se from the words as used by a certain person on a certain occasion.[8] Cartwright carries these distinctions even further, separating off (i) what *A* asserted, namely, that *p* (the statement) from (ii) *A*'s asserting on that occasion that *p*; (iii) asserting that *p*; (iv) *A*'s predicating something of the person he was speaking about; (v) what *A* uttered, namely, the words "Botvinnik uses it"; (vi) *A*'s uttering those words on that occasion; and (vii) uttering those words. Austin and other writers, Cartwright among them, distinguish a variety of contents from one another—statements from propositions, statements from the meaning of sentences, statements from thoughts, and so on.[9]

Now the distinction between a vehicle and its contents when applied to sentences (words, utterances, etc.) and the statements they are used to make seems natural enough. Certain ordinary considerations directly give rise to it. It seems natural to distinguish between the words a German utters when he says "Es regnet" and the words an Englishman utters when he says (on the same occasion) "It is raining." Obviously the words they use are different; therefore, the vehicles they use are different; yet both vehicles have been employed in those circumstances to make the same statement. Accordingly, it seems to follow that the statement the speakers make in using the vehicles they do must be different from the vehicles they employ. Cartwright describes this situation by saying that the "arithmetics of statements and sentences are different," and therefore that the entities in question must be different from one another.

Other common considerations lead to the same conclusion. When we translate from a foreign language into English, or into another foreign language, there is something we translate and which, when the translation is correct, remains invariant under such transformations. This something is the content to be translated, to be rendered from one language into another. Not all such contents are statements, of course (we translate things other than statements), but it is commonly held that statements are among such contents; that they are among the things we render from one body of discourse into another. The picture here is thus like transferring a load of coal from one coal car into another. And since it is the same content which is thus transferred, while the vehicles which convey it are different, it seems to follow that the statemental content in such cases differs from the vehicles used to carry (convey, transfer, express) it.

Or, to take an example from Cartwright, "Clearly in order to assert that *p*, it is not necessary to utter exactly those words: the words 'Botvinnik uses the French Defense' and 'It is used by Botvinnik' would do as well—as would a host of others." If the vehicles used in making the same statement can be this different is it not the case that the statement they are used to make must be distinguished from the vehicles which are used in making it?

7. So it would seem; yet there is a fly—perhaps a host of flies—in the ointment. The trouble with this model is that it breaks down when we attempt to give an independent description of the statement a person makes in such circumstances or when we attempt to identify the statement in contradistinction to the vehicle conveying it. For instance, what statement was it the German made? If we ask him or another German, we are likely to be given "Es regnet" as an answer. But "Es regnet" is an expression in German. This was the vehicle he employed in making his statement. Our question is, "What statement did he make?" not "What vehicle did he employ?" How does the statement he made differ from the words he used on that occasion? If we ask a Japanese who knows German what the speaker said, he will reply that he said, "Ame ga futte imasu." But once again he has produced the vehicle, this time in Japanese. A favorite device used by those who espouse the model is to suggest that it is possible to identify the statement a speaker makes by referring to it in the so-called material mode of speech. Thus, it is said that the statement the speaker made is that it is raining. This is not likely to be helpful; it merely shifts the issue to the material mode of speech.[10] This can be seen if we ask a German what our speaker said and he replies in the material mode, "Er hat gesagt, dass es regnet." Like the unquoted words in English, the vehicle this time consists of unquoted words in German. Yet the sets of unquoted words are different from one another. What then remains invariant under these transformations?

The model requires that there must be an independent way of characterizing both the vehicle and its content. It is clearly possible to do this for the vehicle. It is invariably a word or group of words belonging to some given language, and is easily describable. But how is one to characterize the statement which a person uses these words to make if the statement is different from them? It seems that any attempt to do so only leads to the production or description of another vehicle belonging to a given language. We thus seem to be in the position of attempting to characterize the content conveyed by the vehicle by either describing the vehicle itself or some other vehicle belonging to a different language—something which *ex hypothesi* is different from its statemental component. The model thus differs importantly from its prototypes. I can give independent descriptions of the coal car and the coal it carries; I can give independent descriptions of the automobile and its passengers; but I cannot give independent descriptions of the vehicles which convey statements and the statements they convey.[11]

It now becomes clear why statements appear to have such odd properties to those who accept the model; why they are at once things one is familiar with and yet are difficult to detect. For in terms of this conceptual model statements become shadows of the vehicles which convey them; as shadows they become difficult to discern, except by special "means." And it now becomes clear why they are easily confused with sentences and utterances, for being shadows of them, never appearing independently of the sentences which convey them, it is easy to mistake the one type of thing for the other.[12]

8. What is interesting about such philosophical models is that they tend to mislead those who reject them as well as those who accept them. We see this with the inward-state, outward-sign model in the Other Minds Problem, where the alternatives seem to be restricted either to opting for the mind as a mysterious entity, "known only to one"—as Wisdom puts it— or opting for the mind as a species of outward behavior. And since neither alternative is really viable, one seems confronted with an irresolvable dilemma.

The same situation is to be found in discussions of statements. Those who reject the vehicle-content model are likely to opt for things which are not mysterious, things which are readily accessible, as the bearers of such properties as truth or falsity. We thus begin to see why the answers philosophers have given to the question, "What are statements?" are so

diverse. Such diversity does not arise because they lack different pieces (or kinds) of information, but because they react
differently to the same model. In a recent book on logic, for
example, Benson Mates writes:

> Another matter deserving attention is our decision to take
> *sentences* as the objects with which logic deals. To some
> ears it sounds odd to say that sentences are true or false
> and throughout the history of the subject there have been
> proposals to talk instead about statements, propositions,
> thoughts or judgments. As described by their advocates, how-
> ever, these latter items appear on sober consideration to share
> a rather serious drawback, which, to put it in the most
> severe manner, is this: they do not exist.[13]

Mates, of course, does not believe that the word "statement" has no use (or uses) in English. Nor does he believe
that its uses are the same as those of "sentence." And therefore
he does not really believe that statements do not exist. What
he does not believe, as he says, is that there are entities of the
sort described by those who accept the vehicle-content model.
What he wishes to emphasize by putting his point in so paradoxical a way is that it is impossible to give an independent
description of statements, to identify them independently of
the vehicles which presumably convey them. His remarks thus
stem from a temper of mind which is on the whole admirable
—tough-minded and antimetaphysical.

But in resisting the lures of the metaphysical trap, in
reacting against the model, he has overreacted against it. He
wishes so strongly to dispense with shadowy entities that he
seizes on those things which are obvious and accessible to the
ordinary eye, on things which are tangible and malleable—on
marks on paper and spoken words. He says in this connection:

> Propositions, we are told, are the senses or meanings of
> sentences. They are so-called abstract entities and, as such,
> are said to occupy no space, reflect no light, have no begin-
> ning or end, and so forth. At the same time, each proposition
> is regarded as having a *structure* upon which its logical

properties essentially depend. If we were to study logic from this point of view, therefore, it would be imperative to have a way of finding out in given cases what that structure is. Unfortunately no simple method is ever given. Since everyone agrees that sentences of wholly different shapes and structures may have the same meaning, the structures of propositions must not be confused with those of their corresponding sentences; yet a perusal of the literature leaves little doubt that just this sort of confusion frequently takes place. Sometimes, to be sure, one is advised not to rely upon sensory perception at all, but instead to look directly upon the proposition by means of the "mind's eye." Whoever admits that he is unable to do this leaves himself open to an obvious and uncomplimentary diagnosis traditionally employed in such cases. But, when all the rhetoric has been expended, we are left once again with the problem of how in practice to ascertain the structure of propositions expressed by given sentences.

Like difficulties are involved in talk about statements . . . . Thus, as with propositions, the structure of a statement cannot be determined simply by looking at the sentence that is used in "making" it. Yet the friends of statements do not hesitate to classify them as singular, general, or existential, as conjunctive, hypothetical, affirmative, negative, necessary, contingent, etc., or to say that they are of "subject-predicate" form, or that some of them "have the same form" as others, or that they "contain descriptions" and so on.[14]

In reacting for these reasons against the model, Mates goes on to "reduce" statements to sentences, to identify the one type of thing with the other. The only alternative to opting for statements as he sees it, is to opt for sentences. But in doing this he is in effect accepting the framework in question, accepting the model—only not all of it, but merely a part of it. This is not to reject the model entirely, but only a special feature of it. He thus fails to see that the very sorts of philosophical difficulties he wishes to avoid stem from adherence to the model in any form.

Such a posture serves to contribute to the deadlocks which are characteristic of philosophical activity. The proponents of the model opt for it because they recognize the defects and limitations of the position Mates is advancing. Part of their motivation is to be found in their desire to eliminate the disposition to identify statements with sentences or utterances. The two positions when thus juxtaposed lead to an antinomy, a seemingly irresolvable confrontation. What neither side seems to realize is that the source of the antinomy is to be located in a framework they both accept. It is the model which must be rejected if one is to achieve a perspicuous view of the role statements play in everyday discourse—that is, if one is to achieve a perspicuous view of what statements are.

9. But if statements are not identical with sentences or with the utterances of sentences, and if they are not mysterious, ineluctable entities different from sentences and utterances, then what are they? The answer is that they are both identical with sentences (utterances, words, etc.) and yet different from them— and the problem which faces one who advances such an answer is to provide an explanation showing how these apparently incompatible things can be so. In particular, one who advances such an explanation must show that (a) statements and sentences have "different arithmetics," (b) that in human communication nothing is uttered except words, (c) that words per se are not the bearers of such logical properties as truth and falsity, and (d) that it is possible to give an independent description of statements.

Is it possible to produce an explanation satisfying these conditions? The answer is yes. In providing such an explanation one must appeal to a variety of devices—analogies, examples, and specific cases. So far as I know, there is no word in the language which covers all the devices which may be used for this purpose. Each of these devices differs from the others not only in the kind of device it is, but also in its power to illuminate the nature of statements—and because this is so, the power each of them has to illuminate the role played by statements can only be appreciated by developing each of them in detail. Let us now do this with a specific case.

In working up such a case, one must put emphasis upon the circumstances in which language is used. We may do this in terms of the concept of "counting as." Sentences per se, or the utterances of sentences or words, do not automatically "count as" statements. But when something does "count as" a statement nothing more happens than that a person has uttered a sentence or a string of words. A statement is thus nothing more than a sentence or a string of words uttered in certain circumstances. But what then makes such a sentence or string of words "count as" a statement? The answer is that it will depend on what the circumstances are—and this answer may be expanded and illuminated by the use of certain analogies which point up how the circumstances enable the words as so used to "count as" a statement.[15]

Consider the case of a man who makes those movements which are called "practice swings" in golf. What is the difference between the movements he makes when he takes a practice swing and the movements he makes when he does something which counts as a stroke? Is he doing something different in the two cases? In a sense he is and in a sense he is not. If he is a trained golfer, he will make exactly the same movements in both cases. Why, then, does one of them count as a stroke but not the other? The answer is to be found in the circumstances in which he makes the gestures he does. One takes a practice swing according to the rules of golf when one does not "address" the ball while making a certain movement. One makes the same movement when one "addresses" the ball—only in these circumstances it counts as a stroke. What it is to "address" the ball is determined by the rules of golf— and hence what makes a certain movement count as a stroke is determined by the rules which describe the circumstances necessary for having such a gesture count as a stroke. In taking a practice swing and in making a stroke one does not do two things—first make a certain gesture and then make a stroke. One does one thing—but in certain circumstances what one does counts as a stroke while in other circumstances it does not. Pursuing this analogy, we may say that certain movements stand to what counts as a "stroke" as a sentence (or the utterance of certain words) does to the statement it is used to make. Words uttered in certain circumstances count as statements—the same words uttered in different circumstances do not. But when they do count as statements, one has not done two things: first uttered some words and then made a statement. In uttering those words in those circumstances, one has made a statement.

The analogy is far from perfect—but this is what we may expect from each of the analogies we employ in giving such an explanation. Better examples may be found—as I have indicated, there is a gamut of such explanatory devices: and it is a matter to be explored in detail to see which of them best serves to characterize the circumstances in which language is used for making statements. But the particular analogy I have employed here brings out certain central features which all such explanatory devices will possess. It illustrates, for one thing, that the relation between the words one uses and the statement one makes in using them is not to be accounted for only in terms of the vehicle-content model. A movement per se (a swing) is not a vehicle, nor is the stroke one makes in performing such a movement the "content" of the swing. And this enables us to see that the words one uses are not a vehicle conveying some statemental content. More than that, the analogy enables us to show how a stroke may be something different from a swing (it is something described by the rules of golf) and yet be nothing different from a swing. And this in turn enables us to show how statements may be the same as, and yet different from, sentences—without one of them being a shadowy counterpart of the other. The analogy also allows us to indicate how strokes may be described independently of those physical gestures which count as practice swings, and in this way, we can come to see how statements may be differently described from the words one employs in making them. Far from perfect though it may be, such a device enables us to see that it is not impossible to develop explanations which satisfy all the conditions we have enumerated above. It thus enables us in a less misleading way than the vehicle-content model to illuminate the roles which statements play in every-day discourse.

1. We must avoid the following red herring in accepting this con-clusion. Some have contended that the philosopher is looking for that which would also satisfy the foreigner: a word, or set of words, in English which means the same, or approximately the same, as "state-ment"—but which has the merit of "being better understood." Of course, the *particular* word or set of words which the philosopher is seeking will not be those which the foreigner is seeking—so that the philosopher is looking for a different *piece* of information. But the point of the contention is that it is the same *kind* of information that both seek.

To deal fully with this objection would require more space than we have at our disposal. Broadly speaking, the contention rests upon a con-ception of philosophical explanation and understanding which is no longer acceptable. The reasons why this is so are at once too extensive and too familiar to be expanded upon here. But it may be worth men-tioning that the most celebrated case of thinking of philosophical activity as if it supplied this kind of information is to be found in Russell's Theory of Descriptions: or more accurately, in an extension of that theory which applied its techniques of analysis to words like "statement" as well as to descriptive phrases. Because of the many compelling reasons which underlie the rejection of this mode of philosophizing, we obviously cannot fall back upon it here as providing a plausible account of the *kind* of answer philosophers of a more modern vintage are looking for in asking the question, "What are statements?" In any case, as we shall see, there are additional grounds for thinking this kind of a "translation" is not what the philosopher seeks in asking this question.

2. Richard Cartwright, "Propositions," in *Analytical Philosophy*, ed. R. J. Butler, New York, 1962, p. 103.

3. Reprinted from *The American College Dictionary*, Copyright 1947, © Copyright 1966, by permission of Random House, Inc.

4. *Ibid.*

5. *Op. cit.*, p. 103.

6. L. Wittgenstein, *Philosophical Investigations*, New York, 1953, pp. 424, 425.

7. The form this may take in philosophy may consist in attempting to distinguish between the act of stating something and that which is stated. Cartwright says, for instance, "It is equally clear that what is asserted by someone on some given occasion is not to be identified with his asserting it on that occasion." *Op. cit.*, pp. 84 ff.

8. J. L. Austin, "Truth," in *Philosophical Papers*, New York, 1961. p. 8.

9. Cartwright, *op. cit.*, pp. 92 ff.

10. It is instructive to see the devices employed by Cartwright and

others for concealing this difficulty. Cartwright often refers to a statement made by a person *A* by the locution, "What *A* asserted, namely that *p*." The expression "that *p*" covertly suggests that it is possible to give an independent description of the statement *A* made without also referring to the vehicle he used. But "that *p*" is hardly the statement *A* made—what then was it? There is also a confusion in Cartwright's paper between taking "that *p*" instead of "*p*" as the variable to be replaced by a statement. See *op. cit.*, pp. 85, 87, 88.

11. It is clear that the philosopher imposes this model on the facts, rather than looking, as Wittgenstein urges we do, at what people do when they, say, translate from one body of discourse into another. Translation does not involve "detecting" and isolating" a statement and then rendering it in a different body of discourse. It consists in pairing pieces of discourse with other pieces. The model suggests irresistibly that such pairing can only take place if the pieces can be compared with a third thing, the "statement." But this is not what we in fact do. We simply juggle the pieces until they fit.

12. The model of shadow and substance also depends for its plausibility upon ignoring some of the things we say about statements in ordinary speech, e.g., "He read a lengthy statement to them." Although some shadows are longer than others, it is difficult to believe that a lengthy speech has a lengthy shadow—a shadow invariably just as "long" as the body of words making up the speech.

13. Benson Mates, *Elementary Logic*, New York, 1965, p. 8.

14. *Op. cit.*, pp. 9–10.

15. I am indebted to Leonard Geddes and Ron Kirkby for some helpful suggestions about this part of the paper.

4

REASONS, CAUSES, ACTIONS

ARE REASONS FOR ACTIONS CAUSES?

DAVID PEARS

It is notoriously difficult to assess the thesis that the reasons for action are causes. One source of the difficulty is that the thesis may be taken either as a contingent statement or as a statement about the meaning of the phrase "reasons for actions." For it might be argued that, though it is true that all reasons for actions are causes, it is not a conceptual truth. So anyone who tried to establish the thesis would have to make it clear whether he was arguing for this version of it or for the more ambitious conclusion that it is a conceptual truth. However, I am not going to try to establish the thesis in either of its two versions. I am only going to cast doubt on several well-known arguments which have been used against it. I shall pit these arguments against the ambitious version of the thesis because it is both more interesting and more vulnerable.

Another source of the difficulty of assessing the thesis is that it is not clear on the fact of it what exactly is supposed to cause actions. Sometimes a person explains his action by saying what he wanted to achieve, and in such a case it would be claimed that his desire was the cause of his action. But it is not always so easy to convert the phrases which people use when they state their reasons for their actions into phrases denoting causes. For the agent may confine himself to stating a fact about his situation, which will usually be some obviously relevant feature of it, and it would not do to say that the fact was the cause of his action, because in some cases, when his factual statement was mistaken, this would be saying too much, and because it would omit his belief, so that from this point of view it would in all cases be saying too little. Perhaps then it would be maintained that his belief is the cause of his action. But is "belief" always the appropriate word? Even if it is, will it always be possible to draw a line between the contributions of desire and belief? Such a division would sometimes be a rationalization of a much more confused situation. It might also be unrealistic to say that the agent's stated reason always includes both an element of desire and an element of belief, because in many cases one or the other is not mentioned, but taken for granted. These questions and doubts are important, but I shall not pursue them, because they lead away from the area which I want to investigate. I shall evade them by assuming, very schematically, that according to the thesis, when an action is performed for a reason, it is caused by the agent's desire and information, and that, if he gave his reason in full, what he said would entail that it was caused by that desire and that information. The question whether this entailment would be taken to exhaust what he meant is a question which will be left open. A complete analysis of statements of reasons would have to settle this question. But the thesis that I am going to examine offers an analysis which may not be complete.

A third source of the difficulty of assessing the thesis is the multiformity of the concept of causation. Here the most important point to be settled is whether singular causal statements entail general statements. Now it may be that some singular causal statements, carry no such general entailment. But those who reject the thesis find it unacceptable largely because statements of reasons are interpreted as singular causal statements which do carry a general entailment. This is not the only thing that leads them to reject it, but it is one of the most important things. The thesis would be less interesting and less vulnerable if it invoked singular causal statements which carried no general entailment. So the arguments that

I am going to examine will be pitted against the version which gives its singular causal statements general entailments.

In choosing this protagonist I do not mean to imply that there are no other features of the concept of causation which might lead to the rejection of the thesis. It may well be that the actual use of the word "cause" in the explanation of an action suggests some irrationality in the performance, or in what led up to it. But, if there is this suggestion, it could not provide a very strong ground for rejecting the thesis. For its supporters are not committed to saying that their analysis is complete, and so could be substituted for ordinary statements of reasons without any change in what would be conveyed. That would be a rash and unnecessary claim. It would be enough for them to claim that their analysis of statements of reasons gives the central core of their meaning. According to them, this would always consist in a singular causal statement with the usual general entailment. They could then explain our discrimination in the actual use of the word "cause" by drawing a distinction between causation which is involved in rational deliberation and causation which is involved in cases in which rational deliberation is disturbed. It is easily understandable that in everyday life the word "cause" should be felt to be especially appropriate to cases of disturbance. If a machine which usually works, works on a given occasion, we do not ask what caused it to work on that occasion. No doubt, people are unlike machines, but the dissimilarity is not to be found at this point.

There is, however, another feature which is sometimes ascribed to the concept of causation by those who reject the thesis. It is sometimes argued that a cause always forces its effect to occur, whereas desire and information do not force a person to perform an action. But there is a familiar answer to this argument. If the statement that a cause always forces its effect to occur implies that an action cannot be caused unless it is performed whether the agent wants to perform it or not, it is false. No doubt the requirement that the action be performed willy-nilly is fulfilled when it issues from a cause which does not include the agent's desire. But it is absurd to require that it should be fulfilled before allowing that a state of the agent which does include his desire might be the cause of his action. If, on the other hand, the statement that a cause always forces its effect to occur only means that it makes the effect inevitable, then, although this is certainly not true of most of the things that are called "causes," it might well be interpreted as a definition of the limiting case. At the extreme limit a cause would be a condition which was absolutely, but not logically sufficient. Now does this damage the thesis? Why should its supporters not admit that this concept of causation is out of their reach? Would it not be enough if they could establish that the concept of causation which they used was no further from the limit than the concept used outside human affairs?

But perhaps they cannot succeed in establishing this. There is a very simple argument designed to show that they cannot succeed. It is contended that any general statement which supporters of the thesis might suggest as the entailment of a singular statement of a reason could turn out to be false, and yet it would not follow that the singular statement of the reason was false. There is here an implied comparison with singular causal statements which are not about human actions. The idea is that in that area the limiting case is attainable, or at least that it can be approached more closely than it can ever be approached in the area of human action. This is an important argument, and it is one of three which will be examined in this paper.

The second argument which will be examined is the contention that cause and effect must be conceptually distinct from one another, but that the desire to perform an action is not conceptually distinct from the performance of it. This is a rather cryptic contention, and it will need elucidation. The third argument is clearer. According to it, causal statements are hypotheses, but statements of reasons for actions in the first person singular are not hypotheses, since the agent himself knows immediately whether they are true or not. This is not to say that he is infallible, but only that his knowledge is not inductive.

Before these three arguments are examined there are two more preliminary points that need to be made. First, it might be suggested that supporters of the thesis ought to tell us whether they take the agent's desire and information to be a necessary condition of his action as well as a sufficient condition. For when people state their reasons for their actions, they often say that they would not have performed the action unless they had wanted this or that, or believed that such and such was the case. However, it is not really necessary to formulate this part of the thesis before examining the three arguments. For the doubts that I am going to cast on them may be taken as doubts about their validity as objections to the thesis that a statement of a reason for an action entails that the agent's desire and information were a sufficient condition of the action. Naturally, the desire and information will often also be necessary, because they could not drop out and leave the action unaffected unless there were some other change as well. But this is not always so, since some actions are performed for reasons which are stronger than they need be in order to produce the performance.

Secondly, it might be suggested that the words "desire" and "want" are too narrow for the thesis. For in the field of action these words are used in contrast with words like "obligation" or "interest," so that their inclusion in the thesis would immediately prevent it from covering the whole field. But the words "desire" and "want" are not always used in this special way. They are sometimes used more generally to cover any favorable attitude to a project and that is how they will be used in this paper.

What is the strategic situation of supporters of the thesis? According to the first argument, it is impossible to produce a general statement whose falsification would necessarily lead to the retraction of a singular statement of a reason for an action. This is a challenge which they have to try to meet. But, if they succeed in meeting it, they are immediately faced by the third argument, that a statement of a reason in the first person singular cannot be regarded as a causal statement because the agent is not putting forward an hypothesis. Now, in general, it may be possible to rebut this argument by showing that singular causal statements are not necessarily hypotheses for all speakers, but it is particularly difficult for supporters of the thesis to make this form of rebuttal work. For, according to them, what the agent knows immediately is that his state caused his action, and this singular causal statement is supposed to carry a general entailment. How then can he know it immediately? Is it just that he is so accustomed to the effect of desire and information? But that does not seem to be an adequate explanation of the immediacy of his knowledge. Perhaps, then, there is a conceptual connection between his state and his action. Indeed, there are strong reasons for thinking that desire and action must be conceptually connected. But this does not seem to make the task of supporters of the thesis any easier. For, according to the second argument, if desire is conceptually connected with action, it cannot cause it.

In spite of the likelihood that any attempt to defend the thesis against the third argument will immediately expose it to the full force of the second argument, I shall take the third argument first. Supporters of the thesis have to explain the immediacy of the agent's knowledge of the reason for his action in a way that is compatible with their view that what he knows is at least that a singular causal statement is true. Now, in order to secure such an explanation, it is necessary to account for the fact that, before he acts, he knows immediately what he wants to do, how much, and under what description he wants to do it, and how his desire to do it compares with his desires to do the things which compete with it. But this is only part of their task. For they must also explain the immediacy of the agent's knowledge of the singular statement connecting his desire with his action, which, according to them, is a causal statement. The explanation cannot be that he is accustomed to the effect of desire in much the same way that he is accustomed to the effect of physical impact. For if he is in a practical predicament, he will be aware of his desire under a description which is in some way relational, because in some way it connects his desire with his future action. Now it might be maintained that the connection is not that the action will follow, but only that the desire is a desire to perform the action. But though this is how such desires are identified by the agent—generically, as desires, and, specifically, as desires to perform particular actions—this method of identification could not be used in any cases, unless in some cases somebody used a different method of identification which relied on the sequel. This puts a gap between a concept like desire to act and a concept like impact. The difference must not be exaggerated, because it is arguable that the concept of impact in some way includes such usual effects as movement and fragmentation. But, even if these effects were universally ignored, there would still be enough left to enable people to identify all impacts both generically and specifically. That is not so with desires to act. For though some desires can be identified independently of the actual occurrence of the sequel, it would be impossible to identify all of them in that way, because the concept could not survive in such isolation.

Perhaps this difference between the two concepts can be used to explain the special immediacy of the agent's knowledge of his reason for his action in a way that is compatible with the thesis. The general form of the explanation would be that, if the agent is in a practical predicament, he will be immediately aware of his desire under the description "desire to carry out a certain project." But the application of this description to his desire implies the application of another description, viz., the description "desire which will be followed by the execution of the project." So he is immediately aware of his desire under one description which implies that it comes under another description which may be, and, according to the thesis, actually is causal.

That is the general form of the explanation. Quite apart from the fact that it exposes the thesis to the second argument, there are three questions about it which need to be answered. Obviously, the second description, "desire which will be followed by the execution of the project," is oversimplified, and needs to be recast so as to include various alternatives to the actual execution of the project. The first question is what the alternatives are. The second question is about the nature and strength of the implication which links the first description to the second. The third question is about the application of this general form of explanation to the various facts that need to be explained. The explanation may work in a fairly straightforward way if it is applied to a practical predicament, in which there is only one desire operating, and the agent's question is whether that desire, which is not opposed by any other desire, is strong enough to lead him to perform the action. But how will it work in more complicated cases in which the project appears under various descriptions, each connected with its own desire, so that a more elaborate account is required?

In order to answer the first of these three questions, it is best to take a simple predicament in which there is only one desire operating, and the agent only asks himself whether it reaches the threshold required for action. If he says that it does, this statement of his has a certain logical connection (whose nature and strength can be left unspecified for the moment) with a statement about his future action. Now the statement about his future action is not the statement that he would perform it at that moment if he suddenly discovered that it was the appropriate moment. It is only the statement that in that case he would perform the action if it were, and were believed by him to be feasible. If the moment for action is deferred, the statement about his future action says even less than this. For in the interval the circumstances might change in a way that reduced his desire, or, even if there were no change in the circumstances, his desire might decrease spontaneously. This gives us a short list of alternatives which should be included in a disjunctive description of his desire which can now be substituted for the original oversimplified description. The list of alternatives is not complete, but it is long enough to give a good idea of the sort of description that is needed to put us in communication with one another about our desires to act.

The second question was about the nature and strength of the implication linking the agent's statement that his desire comes up to the required threshold with the more elaborate disjunctive statement about the sequel, which I have just sketched. It is obvious that, if we never insisted on the truth of the disjunctive statement before allowing that a person really did want to perform the action, we could never establish communication with one another about our desires to act. It is not even clear that we could succeed in establishing communication about idle wishes through signs of satisfaction. For how would we know what counted as a sign of satisfaction? It is only because we use the sequel and insist, at least often, on the truth of the disjunctive statement that communication about desires to act can be established. However, this familiar point is not quite enough to explain how communication is established about desires to act. For one of the disjuncts mentions something which seems to be unusable before communication has been established, viz., spontaneous decrease of desire or change of mind. A large part of the solution of this difficulty seems to be that, when we try to establish communication about desires to act, we rely on cases in which the moment for action is not deferred. But again I wish to avoid involvement in details. It is sufficient for my purpose to suggest that successful communication about desires to act requires that the disjunction should nearly always be true when the agent states that his desire comes up to the threshold. It is in this way that his statement implies the disjunction. I shall call this kind of implication "presupposition": *p* presupposes *q* if *p* mentions something about which we could not establish communication unless *p* were very seldom true when *q* was false. Needless to say, the word "presupposition" has not always been used in this way.

There may be a stronger logical relationship between the agent's statement that his desire comes up to the threshold and the disjunction. For it is arguable that his statement entails the disjunction. This is a very different possibility. If the relationship really is entailment, the situation will be not merely that there can be few cases in which the agent's statement is true and the disjunction false: it will be that there can be none. If this is so, it will be possible to use the sequel as a decisive check on the truth of his statement. But the question whether this is so can be deferred for the moment.

Meanwhile there is the third question: how the explanation of the immediacy of the agent's knowledge of his reason for his action will work in a complicated case. In a simple case, in which there is only one desire operating, the matter is fairly straightforward. He knows immediately that he acted with a desire to secure a certain result, and this description of his desire at least presupposes the application of the disjunctive description which supporters of the thesis interpret causally. He also has and is, of course, aware that he has the requisite factual information. But in a more complicated case, in which several desires are operating, he has to distinguish between the various descriptions of the project under which each desire attaches itself positively or negatively to it. In one way this does not introduce anything new, but merely multiplies factors of the kind that were at work in the simple case. But in another way it does introduce something new. For the agent now has to assess the positive contribution of each of the desires which are included in his reason, and he has to balance the total against the negative contribution of any desires that there may happen to be on the other side. This is a very different matter, because he will not merely be judging that a single desire came up to the required threshold as he did in the simple case. He will be making a series of assessments which are tested together on this occasion, and each one of them, if it is ever going to be tested in different company, will have to be tested on another occasion.

Of course, particular desires can also be weighed against one another without the test of action. But the assessment of their contributions when they are included in a complex reason is to a considerable extent inferential. It would be difficult to

estimate the volumes of a set of cubes, if you used an opaque
vessel containing water which did not come up to its brim,
and if your method was to drop them into it one by one until
the water was overflowing. If you could also tell which cube
in any pair was the larger, the task would be less difficult. But
against this there is the fact that on a second occasion it is
easier to tell that you have the same cube again than that you
have the same desire again. However, the discussion of these
difficulties may be deferred until later.

All that I have given is a rough sketch of a way of recon-
ciling the thesis with the special immediacy of the agent's
knowledge of his reason for his action. But since this recon-
ciliation obviously exposes the thesis to the full force of the
second argument, it would be best to leave it incomplete, and
move to the defence of the thesis on that new front.

What exactly is the force of the second argument? In
order to appreciate its force, it is necessary to remove some
of the obscurity in the contention that a desire cannot cause
an action if it is conceptually connected with it This conten-
ion might be meant in a very ambitious way. The idea might
be that, if a desire cannot be identified except under a description which connects it in some way with the action, it cannot
cause the action. But this can be dismissed immediately. For
fairy stories, which treat wishes as causes and describe a wish
simply as concentrated willing that such and such should
happen, may be incredible but they are not conceptually incoherent. There is no conceptual incoherence even if a wish
cannot be identified except under such a description. Perhaps,
however, it might be thought that this counterexample tacitly
relies on an independent method of identifying wishes. For in
most stories there is a ritual of wishing, like touching a ring.
But a general ritual would not make it possible to identify a
wish specifically. That requires a description which connects
the wish with its object. What the counterexample shows is that
such a description introduces no conceptual incoherence into
the supposition that this object is its effect.

So the contention ought to be less ambitious. It ought to

be not that a cause must be identifiable under a description which does not connect it in any way with its supposed effect, but, rather, that it must be identifiable under a description which does not connect it causally with its supposed effect. This contention is much more plausible, because the suggestion that an event is caused by whatever caused it is not even mythological. It is also clear that this version still makes a real impact on the proposed defense of the thesis against the third argumuent. For if supporters of the thesis are never in a position to identify a specific desire except under the description "desire to perform a certain action," and if the application of this description presupposes the application of the disjunctive description, which they interpret causally, it is obvoius that they face a dilemma. Either they must show that in spite of this presupposition a desire which can only be identified as a desire to perform a certain action can be regarded as the cause of the action, or they must appeal to the possibility that new descriptions of desires which are not conceptually connected with the sequel will one day be discovered. Thirdly, of course, they could admit defeat.

Now it may well be possible to break the second horn of this dilemma. At least it would be wrong to assume that physicalism is false. Although we do not know any specific physical descriptions of states of desire, it would be rash to assume that there are no such descriptions waiting to be discovered. It would also be wrong to suggest that we have no idea of the kind of descriptions they would be. Those who use the second argument would be exaggerating if they claimed that a supporter of the thesis is reduced to saying that an action is caused by whatever caused it. For he can propose a general form for his descriptions of the agent's states of desire. He can say, for example, that they will be neurological, and, when he is challenged to produce a description of a particular state of desire which would identify it specifically, he can say that he is not yet in a position to do so. His opponents are simply assuming that he ought to be able to do so immediately. But why can they not wait for a description of an alleged

cause which would identify it specifically in a way that did
not connect it with its alleged effect? It is not absurd to suggest that a disease is caused by a specific virus before the
virus has been identified.

However, though it may be possible to break the second
horn of the dilemma by asking for time, I shall not explore
that possibility. For I think that it may be possible to break
its first horn using material all of which is already available.
This would be achieved if it could be shown that a desire
to perform a certain action may cause that action, in spite of
the fact that the application of this description to the desire
presupposes the application of the disjunctive description to it.
Of course, supporters of the thesis have to show that the application of the first of these two descriptions does only presuppose
the application of the second, and does not entail it. If it did
entail it, the situation would be quite different, and it might
be impossible to break the first horn of the dilemma using
material that is already available.

The presupposition does not give supporters of the thesis
much difficulty. For all that this relationship requires is that
there should be very few cases in which a desire comes under
the description "desire to perform a certain action" but does
not come under the disjunctive description. This requirement
is backed by the argument that, if there were many cases,
communication about desires to act could never be established.
The more extreme requirement that there should be no cases
which came under the first description without also coming
under the second, would be more than is necessary to achieve
this result. So the statement that a desire is the desire to perform a certain action will only entail that it is a desire to
act of the kind to which the disjunctive description nearly
always applies. It is possible for the agent to be aware that
his desire is of this kind without waiting to see whether it
actually does come under the disjunctive description. When I
say this, I am not implying that he recognizes his desire under
the description "desire of the kind to which the disjunctive de-
cription nearly always applies." For he does not recognize his

desire as he would recognize an airplane, and in any case this description is not one that would occur to him. The point is, rather, that the application of this description is entailed by the application of the descripion which would occur to him, viz., "desire to perform that action." That is all that supporters of the thesis need claim.

If this is right, it seems to overcome the difficulty created by the presupposition. For it allows a desire to act to be identified under a description which does not entail the application of the disjunctive description. Admittedly, the description, whose application it does entail, viz., "the kind of desire to which the disjunctive description nearly always applies," is a derivative description, and so it might be objected that this line of defense does not really succeed in breaking the first horn of the dilemma, on the ground that this derivative description is not conceptually independent of the disjunctive description. The answer to this is that, of course, it is not conceptually independent of the disjunctive description, but the conceptual dependence is not the kind of dependence that can be used against the thesis. For in a particular case the derivative description can apply, and can be known to apply to a desire even if it turns out that the disjunctive description does not apply to it.

But perhaps the application of the description "desire to perform a certain action" actually entails the application of the disjunctive description to the desire. If so, it would seem to be impossible to break the first horn of the dilemma using material that is already available. But is the relation between these two descriptions really entailment? We certainly use the disjunctive description as a check on the truth of a person's statement that his desire to perform a particular action comes up to the threshold, or, to put this in plain English, that he really wants to perform it. But is the check decisive? Suppose that it is you yourself who make the statement with sincerity which you at least can not doubt. If the disjunctive description turned out not to apply to your desire, would you be forced to admit that you had not really wanted to perform the action?

But this quesion is still not posed in a sharp enough form. The point is that when you really are sure of the sincerity of a person who has the concept of desire to act—and, of course, the sincerity can be doubted if the person is not yourself— this is a considerable counterweight to the falsity of the disjunctive statement. But the question still needs to be sharpened because, if there is an interval before the moment of action arrives, there is always the possibility either of a definite change of mind, or of the kind of evaporation of enthusiasm which sometimes makes people say that they must have changed their minds. So let us suppose that, immediately after you have made the statement, you are told, to your surprise, that now is the moment for action, and you do not perform it, and none of the other disjuncts applies. Would you be forced to admit that you had not really wanted to perform it? If so, the relation between the two descriptions really is entailment.

But unfortunately it is not so easy to answer this crucial question. Much of the difficulty of answering it is produced by the probability that in such a conceptual crisis our anxiety to keep the two halves of the concept of desire to act from flying apart would probably lead us to say that the disjunction could not be complete, and that some new clause should be added to it. We would probably feel that there must be some hitherto unnoticed feature of the normal situation which was absent in this particular case. If this really is how we would look at the matter, and if we now know that it is how we would look at it, the concept of desire to act is already palpably elastic, and that makes it hard to answer the crucial question. However, what we can say is that this elasticity does not help supporters of the thesis. For what they have to establish is that a desire to perform a particular action can be regarded as the causally sufficient condition of the realization of a disjunction of possibilities, one of which is the performance of the action, and they have to establish this against the objection that the occurrence of the so-called cause entails the occurrence of the so-called effect. So it is useless for them to rely on the elasticity of the concept of desire to act, because any addition to the disjunction would change the description of the so-called effect, and so lead to reformulation of the thesis which they have to defend against the objection. They may choose the ground on which to fight their battle but, having chosen it, they must stand and fight.

So perhaps they will maintain that, for any formulation of the disjunction, it is conceivable that a person just should not do what he wants to do. This, of course, would be to say that the connection between the description "desire to perform a certain action" and the disjunctive description is not entailment, but only presupposition. Their contention would be that, if the conceptual crisis occurred, the sincerity of the agent's statement would sometimes carry more weight than the falsity of the disjunction. This may be right. It may be that, if a person who has acquired the concept of desire to act is being sincere, he is sometimes the final arbiter in this matter. If so, that would break the entailment. But, unfortunately, it is not certain that this is so. It is, perhaps, more plausible to say that, in such a crisis, we would suspend judgment rather than allow the agent's sincerity to carry the day (imagine that you are the agent), and that would leave the entailment unbroken. However, this is very slippery ground. For it is notoriously difficult to conduct any Gedenken experiment of this kind, and this particular one is especially hard for two reasons. First, it is bedevilled by the artificiality of the supposition that any change in the disjunction amounts to a change in the concept of desire to act. Secondly, if the problem is generalized so as to include complex cases in which several desires are operating, it immediately becomes even more amorphous.

But why should supporters of the thesis not try a different line of defense? Could they not admit, for the sake of argument, that the entailment holds, and then try to whittle down the first horn of the dilemma, without destroying it completely? They would achieve this result if they could show that within the concept of desire to act there is another concept whose application does not entail the application of the disjunctive description, viz., the concept of the state which is a logically

sufficient condition of a justifiable, but not, therefore, necessarily correct statement that the desire to perform a particular
action comes up to the required threshold. They could then
claim that this state is a causally sufficient condition of the
truth of the disjunction. For it is only the application of the
outer concept—the full concept of desire to act—that, according to their tactical concession, entails the application of the
disjunctive description. Inside this concept there is a sort of
core, the concept of the state which is not a logically sufficient
condition and so can be a causally sufficient condition of the
application of the disjunctive description. This maneuver does
not destroy the first horn of the dilemma completely. But it
does reduce it to very little. For the amount that has to be
added to the core in order to produce the full concept of desire
to act is minute, since the possibility of a counterexample to
the causal statement about the core is marginal.

The minuteness of the addition that has to be made to the
core in order to produce the full concept sufficiently explains
the fact that in everyday life we scarcely ever distinguish the
two concepts which are being distinguished here for theoretical
purposes. Incidentally, when we do need something like this
distinction in everyday life, we use the distinction between
being convinced that one really wants to perform an action and
really wanting to perform it, and this might suggest that the
defense that has been sketched against the second argument
depends on treating the agent's conviction that he wants to
perform an action as a cause. But that is not so. What is being
treated as a cause is the state which justifies him in saying that
he wants to perform the action.

The success of this many-sided defense of the thesis against
the second argument might be questioned, and any doubt about
its success will affect the defense which I am now going to
develop against the first argument. For I shall now try to show
that a singular statement of a reason for an action really may
be interpretable as a causal statement with a general entailment, and I therefore need a description of the cause, or at
least the possibility of a description of the cause which will not

make the entailed general statement analytic. So in what follows, when I talk about the element of desire in the cause, I
shall be using the concept which I have been calling "the core."
If this core really is a little less than the full concept of desire
to act, the defense of the thesis which I am now going to develop
against the first argument will be minutely vitiated. If it is not
less than the full concept, the defense will be, at least on this
score, wholly adequate. If it is minutely vitiated, perhaps that is
a result which need not worry supporters of the thesis. Or perhaps they would do better at this point if they invoked the
possibility that some form of physicalism is true, and suggested
that time will reveal specific descriptions of desires to act,
whose application will not entail the application of the disjunctive descriptions.

It would be best to begin with the simple case in which
there is only one desire operating, and, when the agent is
asked why he performed the action, he mentions that desire.
Of course, his information would have to be included in a full
statement of his reason, but, since that does not contribute to
the difficulties that are being examined here, I am taking it for
granted throughout this paper that he has information that
brings his desire to bear on the project. The question is whether
his statement of his reason entails a general statement. Now it
has often been pointed out that it does not entail the general
statement that, whenever he is in a similar situation, either he
performs a similar action or else one of the other disjuncts
is verified. If it does have a general entailment, it will not
be one that states a connection between his situation and
his action, but rather one that states a connection between
his desire and his action. So the question is whether it entails the general statement that, whenever he has this desire
to the same degree, either he performs a similar action or one
of the other disjuncts is verified. Or to put this question the
other way round, if on a second occasion the same desire, in
spite of being equally strong, did not produce a similar action,
and all the other disjuncts were false, would it follow that his
statement of his reason for his action on the first occasion must

have been false? Here any action believed by him to secure the desired result counts as a similar action, provided that it does not bring in any other desires.

Now, when he looks back on his action and says that the desire explains it, it seems that he cannot be mistaken, whatever may happen on other occasions. For it seems that the desire has now proved itself strong enough to bring about verification of the disjunction, because he has acted. Naturally, he might have forgotten why he performed the action, or he might make some verbal error in his statement of his reason. But at the moment when the action is performed there does not seem to be any possibility of serious error on his part. So, if his statement of his reason is sincere (imagine that it is your statement), it seems that the falsification of the general statement on some other occasion would leave it unscathed. However, it must be remembered that this is merely because we are assuming that only one desire is at work. Given this assumption, the agent only has to say how strong that desire is before the action, and, after the action, what he says will have been verified. But how will he know that there is only one desire at work? This question instantly brings in possibilities of serious error at the moment that the action is performed, and destroys the illusion that the agent's retrospective assessment of his psychological state is immune from serious error. Admittedly, it is immune from one form of serious error: if there is only one desire at work he cannot have overestimated its strength. But there are other forms of serious error. For there may be desires of whose operation he is unconscious, and, even when he is conscious of the operation of several desires, he may make a mistaken estimate of their contributions. Of course his mistakes would not be about the objects of desires whose identities and strengths were already known, but rather about the strengths of desires whose objects and identities were already known.

So it does seem to be possible for an agent's sincere statement of his reason for an action to be mistaken, and that clears the stage for the next question, which is whether in fact it would be shown to be mistaken by the falsification of the general statement that, whenever he has the same desire to the same degree, he performs a similar action, unless one of the other disjuncts turns out to be true. But, before this question is answered, there are three points that must be made about the general strategy of this defense of the thesis against the first argument. First, I might be asked why I am working with the case in which the agent's statement of his reason is sincere and, therefore, if false, mistaken. I am working with this case, because I have to do more than establish that the falsification of the general statement would show that the agent's statement of his reason was insincere. For the agent's statement might be sincere, and so known by him to be sincere, and in such a case, if the entailment really does hold, the falsification of the general statement would show that what he said was false in spite of its sincerity, i.e., that it is mistaken.

Secondly, this situation, whatever its outcome, is not to be confused with the conceptual crisis which was mentioned earlier. That was the crisis which would occur if his statement that his desire to perform a particular action came up to the required threshold was sincere, and yet the disjunction turned out to be false. This situation is different. For what I am supposing is that the agent performs the action, so that the disjunction is true, but the desires which produced the action, according to his analysis and assessment of them, recur on another occasion and do not produce a similar action. It is no part of this supposition that on the second occasion, before the moment for action arrived, the agent would have to say that his desire to perform the action came up to the required threshold. For he could say that there had been something wrong with his analysis and assessment of his desires on the first occasion. The question in what circumstances he would say this, is a question that will be answered in a moment.

Thirdly, it would be an exaggeration to suggest that a person's statement of his reason for an action will always be intended as a complete explanation. For very often he will only adduce his main operative desire, and pass over other desires which might happen to be reinforcing it or opposing it. In such cases anyone who took up his statement, just as he made it, and exposed it to the test of other occasions, would show that he had misunderstood it. It would be a sign of a similar misunderstanding if anyone took up a singular causal statement which was not about human action and exposed it, just as it stood, to the test of other occasions. The two cases have at least this much in common: the description of the antecedent must be made more complete before the outcome on other occasions is used as a test of the singular statement.

Now what is the answer to the question? Do we ever reject singular statements of reasons for actions on the ground that the appropriate general statement turns out to be false on other occasions? The answer is that undoubtedly we do sometimes argue in this way. Indeed, we use this form of argument quite frequently in order to impugn the sincerity of someone else's statement of his reason for an action. But does this argument ever lead anyone to admit that his own statement of his reason was mistaken? I think that it does. For one does sometimes find that one omits, suppresses, or is even unconscious of a desire that contributes to producing one's action, and the consequent incompleteness of one's stated reason is revealed later on a second occasion which is similar to the first in every respect except the one that aroused that desire. Naturally, these tests by the outcome on other occasions have to be used with discrimination. It would be unfair to treat a statement of a reason as if it were more complete than it was intended to be, or than it would conventionally be taken to be in the circumstances.

However, the fact that we sometimes argue in this way is not enough to establish that singular statements of reasons carry this general entailment. Supporters of the thesis need to establish that we have to argue in this way whenever the general statement is falsified. But is this really so? This is an exceedingly difficult question to answer. For there are so many perfectly legitimate ways in which a person (imagine that it is yourself) might avoid admitting that the general statement really had been falsified. For instance, the agent has to judge that his desires on the second occasion really are the same as they were on the first occasion: but on the second occasion he may well argue that, since this time his desires do not add up to a desire to perform a similar action, they cannot be the same again. Of course, he cannot always honestly argue like this For on the second occasion he will sometimes notice that an important incentive had been present on the first occasion, although he had not realized at the time that it was present, and is now absent, and that would really force him to recant in the way that has already been explained. But often it will be perfectly reasonable for him to avoid admitting that the general statement has been falsified. For the desire to act is prospective, and so it is reasonable to prefer to measure it as a whole against the yardstick of the disjunction about the sequel, rather than to measure it by splitting it up and equating each of its components with the components of the desire to act on the earlier occasion.

This is not the only thing that makes the question about the entailment exceedingly difficult to answer. For there is also something else which makes it hard to be sure that the general statement really has been falsified, and that is the elasticity of the disjunction which was mentioned earlier. Moreover, it is not obvious that it is legitimate to require that the general statement should be true without exception. Perhaps it would be sufficient if it were satisfied in a high proportion of cases. After all, causal statements which are not about human action often achieve no more than this. If this suggestion is correct, we ought not to be considering falsification by a single instance, but, rather falsification by a group of instances, and then doubt about the size of the group would introduce still more elasticity into this conceptual network.

Incidentally, the suggestion that one counterexample might not falsify the general statement may look as if it implies that the conceptual crisis which was discussed earlier might occur fairly frequently. But there is no such implication. For the general contention is not that the disjunction might only be true on the first occasion, in spite of the fact that the agent sincerely stated that he wanted to perform the action on both occasions; but rather that, if his analysis and assessment of the component desires on both occasions were correct, then it ought to be the case, but unfortunately for him might not be the case that he wanted to perform the action on the second occasion: and the point of the suggestion is that it makes a realistic allowance for the unavoidable roughness of the agent's judgment that the components of his desire on the second occasion exactly match the components of his desire on the first occasion.

So far, I have only considered a general statement about the same agent with the same desires again. But if this general statement is entailed by a singular statement of a reason, another general statement about any agent with the same desires ought to be entailed by it. If it is, the verification of its antecedent will obviously present a new difficulty. Furthermore, if we shuffle the components of the agent's desire to act, and suggest that there is another general entailment connecting any equipollent set of components with an equally easy action, we shall run up against the special problem of mass assessment which was mentioned earlier.

So what is the answer to the question, whether a singular statement of a reason for an action carries this sort of general entailment? Since the comparison with everyday singular causal statements which are not about human action is really the crucial thing, let us put the question in the comparative form, whether a singular statement of a reason for an action is any further from carrying such a general entailment than an everyday causal statement which is not about human action. In order to make the competition fair, we must weaken the consequent of the everyday causal statement by making it disjunctive, as we have already made the consequent of the statement of the reason for the action disjunctive, and only then can we ask which of the two straightforward generalizations comes nearest to being true without exception. But this question instantly raises all the difficulties that have just been described, and those difficulties really do put a gap between singular statements of reasons and everyday causal statements which are not about

human action. However, the gap is not of the kind that would help those who use the first argument against the thesis. For what they need to show is that any suggested general entailment might be false, and yet the singular statement of the reason for the action might still be true. But what has emerged from this discussion is only that the falsification of the general statement is so uncertain that it would seldom be used against the singular statement of the reason for the action. This is certainly a difference between the assessment of the forces of desires and mechanics, but it is not a difference which serves the purpose of the first argument.

Throughout this paper I have been using a fairly sharp distinction between analytic and synthetic statements. That may be a mistake. Indeed it may be a particularly serious mistake in the study of concepts which do not belong to a science. All along, and particularly in the examination of the second argument, the sharp distinction has turned things which are by nature rather amorphous into geometrical shapes. For instance, it was particularly artificial to suggest that we might distinguish two concepts of "desire to act," the full concept and its core, somewhere between which the actual concept of "desire to act" probably lies. Can we really draw concentric circles so close together? Is it not more realistic to say that in such cases the boundary of a concept is less accurately drawn, and that causal statements about instances of the concept can end within its penumbra? If so, the concept of "desire to act" might depend on the truth of a statement about the effects of its instances without actually entailing it.

However, there are two defenses which may be offered for my use of a sharp distinction between analytic and synthetic statements. First, the second of the three arguments against which I have been defending the thesis entirely depends on such a distinction, and the other two are often associated with it. So my use of it may be regarded as a tactical concession, the point being that, even when this concession has been made, the arguments fail. Secondly, this method seems to be a useful heuristic device for investigating the difference between singular

statements of reasons for actions and everyday singular causal
statements which are not about human action. The difference
does not lie where those who use the argument locate it. They
cannot show that the entailment suggested by supporters of the
thesis does not hold. They can only argue that, if it does hold,
it is in many cases a useless logical appendage. But, on the
other side, supporters of the thesis do not need to show that it
is often used, or even that it could always be used.

PHILOSOPHY AND THE UNDERSTANDING OF HUMAN FACT

A. I. MELDEN

Philosophers not infrequently are among the first to join their academic colleagues in denying that they have any privileged access to the nature of the world. We no longer think of philosophy either as the queen of the sciences or as a substitute for science. Metaphysics has long been a term of dispraise in much of the philosophical literature; and if, as recent Oxford philosophers are now declaring with increasing frequency that, all appearances notwithstanding, they really have been doing metaphysics all along, this surely is not testimony to their interest in the study of being *qua* being or to their support for Plato's view that philosophy is the love of the wholeness of things both human and divine. Philosophy, the philosopher himself is frequently the very first to declare, is concerned not with advancing our understanding of human or any other sort of fact—for what then would be the office of the behavioral and the natural scientist?—but with something very different: the analysis of concepts, an enterprise that leaves untouched any question of the cogency of their application; for that would seem to be a matter upon which only the sciences themselves could pronounce. Philosophy so described addresses itself instead to purely conceptual matters, in an enterprise the scientist can safely leave to the philosopher and ignore as of no matter to him in his endeavor to understand and explain that sector of the world that interests him. Logical analysis is one thing, knowledge or understanding of fact is something else again, and these are as separate as the academic departments that separate

This is a revised version of a public lecture delivered at the University of California, San Diego, in December, 1963.

those who engage in these radically different sorts of activities.

This would seem to be a happy way of achieving peace between colleagues notoriously jealous of their academic privileges and domains. And there is truth to this neat compartmentalization of functions, enough indeed to justify a division of labors that is both necessary and desirable, and to lend plausibility to the invidious comparison of the mere analysis and clarification of ideas with the discovery and explanation of substantive fact. But there is a myth concealed in this view that needs to be challenged. We are familiar of course with the conceptual clarification achieved by a great scientist, not too many decades ago, of the idea of simultaneity and of the great importance for recent physics and astronomy of this essentially philosophical achievement. We should be no less alive to the possibility that ideas or concepts are no mere ghostly counterparts of hard facts, but the only means by which any relevant fact may be grasped and understood. And we should, in consequence, be prepared to recognize that the clarification of ideas or concepts may provide us not merely with the means but the light in which we may grasp with increased perspicuity and a greater sense of detail and richness of subject matter, the facts which inadequacies in our ideas and our preconceptions can only becloud and conceal. We need not here adopt the Baconian view that we need only remove our intellectual prejudices in order to allow the mind with an unerring homing instinct to arrive infallibly at a knowledge of the world. Science is not that easy, and in any case it is not scientific explanation and discovery with which I am here concerned. What I want to question is the view that philosophy, insofar as it engages in conceptual clarification, is merely engaged in a kind of intellectual sanitation in order simply to prepare the way for the cultivation by others, in ways not handicapped by confusions, of the inquiry into the facts that really interest us. For what I want to contend is that the work of the philosopher, insofar as it is successful in achieving conceptual clarification, *as such,* and not merely because of the consequential fruits of the labors of others, not only sharpens but enriches his sense of the way things are. And I shall attempt to illustrate this thesis, all too frequently obscured by the excessively modest and the mistaken concessions of philosophers, by discussing the important but related philosophical issues in which the concept of a human action plays a central role. These issues have to do, first, with the problem of the freedom of the will—is anyone responsible for anything he does?—and, second, with the not unrelated problem in ethics of whether the rightness of an action is an intrinsic or a consequential feature of it. In both of these hoary issues, what is crucial is the concept of a human action, a better philosophical understanding of which, whatever its consequences for the behavioral sciences may be, can only afford a better understanding of human fact.

But why indeed should there be any obscurity at all in connection with the concept of a human action? It is not, surely, that here we have anything recondite, something hidden from our common view in the way in which this is true of the causes of cancer or the common cold. Nothing is more familiar than a human action, a matter that concerns the man on the street fully as much as it does the philosopher in his study. Nor is it that, familiar as human actions are, our conception of such events is as inadequate or as defective as, say, the concept which most nonphysicists have of antimatter. There is nothing fragmentary or sketchy about our conception of a human action as there is in the understanding by most of us of the notion of antimatter. The events that are human actions are perfectly familiar and intelligible to us—we need only contrast the intelligence and the understanding human beings can and often do exhibit of each other in the practical situations in which they find themselves with the utter bafflement with which most of us greet the new learned talk about antimatter. But how, if this is so, can there be any need for the clarification that a philosopher can provide? If we think of such clarification as something like the removal of the mists that obscure the objects of our intellectual vision, we not only confound elucidation with discovery but we also render unintelligible our thorough familiarity with the concepts in question.

If philosophical elucidation of the concept of an action were the discovery of an object of intellection which normally is concealed from view, how indeed would it be possible for us to employ, as commonly we do, that concept in that common understanding all of us have of ourselves and each other? Nor will it do to think of philosophical elucidation as the removal of a peripheral vagueness, for this is usually unnecessary and never perfectly possible. All of our practical concepts exhibit an unavoidable open texture; but that does not impair their employment in the vast majority of cases, nor would its removal, even if it were possible, contribute to our understanding of them. The concept of baldness is notoriously vague—inescapably so—but that does not render it useless; nor would the removal of such vagueness by marking sharply the division between the *bald* and *not-bald* contribute to our understanding of those cases which, clearly and unhesitatingly, we do denominate "bald."

In order to see how the philosophical need for clarification may arise and, further, what sort of understanding it may provide, it is imperative that we turn from generalities to concrete cases. And here what needs to be emphasized is that a philosophical problem is not a conundrum devised and posed only by specialists in the way in which a problem in the calculus is one that only a person with the requisite training in mathematics can propound. Philosophical problems are the common lot of all thinking persons, and if their recognition marks the philosopher, then all of us have some right to that title. We need only turn to the problem of the freedom of the will to gain assurance on that score. Here is one way in which it can be put:

Any action is an event in nature and whether it be the action of a carburetor or that of a person at the controls of an automobile, in principle a complete causal explanation of it can be given. But if so, this seems to do violence to the sense we have that persons are sometimes responsible for what they do.

Consider a person driving his car home after having had too much to drink at a party. The drink has impaired his reflexes. His responses to the child that steps into the path of his car are slowed. He hits and kills her. Is he responsible? Surely a complete causal explanation of the event—the striking and the resulting killing of the child—is possible. Given the circumstances—the impairment of the driver's responses—the death of the child is as inevitable and as excusable as it would be if it had happened because of faulty brakes. But, you say, what determined the outcome was the excessive drink imbibed, or the decision, given the recognition of the intoxication induced, to chance it and to drive on the public road. But, each of *these* events is one for which a causal explanation is possible; and each therefore is as inextricably bound up in the web of necessity as the striking and killing of the child. A man's acceptance of a drink can be explained, if not by the same events, then at least generically in the same terms as the breaking of a windowpane, in the latter case by the dispositional property of glass—its fragility—and the activating force applied to its surface; in the former by the disposition of the driver to drink and the stimulus afforded by the sight of the proferred drink. To say that the man could have refused the drink, given the proferred drink and his disposition to accept it, is as absurd as the claim that he could have been someone else if only someone not the person, who was in fact his father, had met and married his mother, and in that way provided him with a different set of genes and dispositions. So too with the decision he made once he had accepted and imbibed the drink; he could no more have decided otherwise than he could have been someone else. And if to say that he could have done otherwise—whatever he did do—is only to say that if the conditions had been different he would have done otherwise, then each of us can do what in point of fact it is quite impossible for any of us to do. For in that sense of "could have," a fool could have been a man of genius, since if conditions had been otherwise, then he too could have been another Newton. And in that sense, too, our driver could have avoided killing the child, but in no sense that is material or relevant, since if he had been in Kalamazoo rather than in California, he would not have killed the child on the main street of San Diego. But he was in San Diego and he was just the sort of man he was, in just the sort of circumstances we have described, and he could no more have done otherwise than an exploding bomb once the fuse attached to it has been detonated.

The view that actions are causally determined—for the alternative would seem to imply some a priori restriction on the limits of scientific explanation—thus seems to rob persons of any responsibility for what they do. The problem is all the more acute if the determinism is construed as physiological. For an action, such as the driving of one's car, involves the move-ments of limbs. And the supposition that a complete physio-logical explanation of such bodily movements is possible is surely plausible. In that case, any reference to the self or person as an agent in the proceedings would appear to be wholly superfluous, and each of us is reduced to the status of hapless spectator of events transpiring in and to our bodies. But suppose that an attempt is made to rescue the person from the impotence to which this conception of what he does reduces him, this time by interjecting his desires, wishes, hopes, fears, etc. as causal factors in what takes place. In that case we are to suppose such mental events as intrusions into the physio-logical order of causes and effects and the self as manifesting itself in the proceedings, as acting, by intruding mental events into the series of physiological causes and effects. But this implies that there are causal gaps in the sequence of purely bodily processes; and there is no reason to warrant this assump-tion. In any case, even if this were true, it would hardly be as certain a matter as our common-sense convictoin that we are agents who are responsible for what we do. Indeed, it would imply that a physiological explanation must inevitably present us with lacunae through which an alien self somehow butts into the causal order. But even assuming that this does happen, the remedy is of no avail. For such mental events are themselves in need of causal explanation. And even if the causes of these events are themselves mental, that does not rescue the self from its status as a mere spectator of all that is going on and in and to it. Let the causes of the doing be mental no less than physical, we have in this account of the action an event for which the person is no more responsible than he is for the motions of the heavens. In both cases the status of the person as agent has disappeared. And if somehow we are to think of the cause of the operative mental event of desiring or wishing or whatever, as the self—not other mental events of like order—how are we to understand that idea? What is the self that it somehow produces the operative mental event? Here in the effort to render intelligible the familiar commonsense conviction that it is a person who acts, we seem faced with the resort to mysterious and unintelligible acts of transempirical production— of the cause of an event as an entity, the self, that lies outside and beyond the temporal, causal order. And this is to explain the obscure in terms of the unintelligible. But short of this desperate expedient which "saves the appearances" of responsibility by introducing the self as a productive agent in ways that defy all possible understanding, let alone further causal explanation, each of us, even if we allow mental events as operative factors in the causal production of actions, is a helpless victim of all that happens in and to us, including our sayings and our thinkings, even this that is now taking place as these words are read. And now we are threatened with bankruptcy: the obliteration of the distinction between sense and nonsense. For not only our actions, but even our sayings and our thinkings, are matters before which we remain mere spectators; and we are no more responsible for what we do than we are for what we think. Even *this* consideration and the thought that it be shared by you is a matter it would be futile to recommend as right and reasonable. If persons cannot be held responsible for what they do, then by the same line of argument they cannot be held responsible for what they think; and it would be no less futile to recommend an action as right than it would be to recommend a thought as reasonable. Where what happens is unavoidable, there what happens may be fortunate or unfortunate, but hardly right or wrong, reasonable or unreasonable. In short, an engulfing causal determinism allows no place for the rationally persuasive discourse that addresses itself either to thought or to action.

There were stoics of old who inconsistently conjoined their recommendation that we conform our wills to the course of nature, with a thoroughgoing determinism in which such willings would seem to be as inevitable as the natural events with which nature confronts us. Others, notably Spinoza, have been more uncompromising in rejecting, on the grounds of its inconsistency with the sweeping determinism supposedly essential to a scientific rationalism, the whole structure of moral discourse, just because such discourse carries with it the implicit and unwarranted belief that persons are exempt from the bonds of causal necessitation. And some, less sweeping in the intellectual reforms they advocate, merely reject as prescientific superstition the idea of moral responsibility. But all such measures are themselves inconsistent stopgaps—for surely what they themselves say cannot be construed as recommendations— if they were, they would imply just that freedom and responsibility, limited as it might be to the life of the intellect, which they are concerned to reject—and must be put down as mere natural occurrences to be treated not as reasonable and right statements of the facts—that would be to endorse and to recommend them—but as idle chatter, causally intelligible but exempt from all rational appraisal.

Now it is not enough to draw this conclusion and to point to the absurdity of the determinism from which it derives. Conceivably someone, like the skeptic of old who said that he knew nothing, and not even *that* much, might offer his determinism as the only rationally defensible doctrine and then concede that the statement of his doctrine can only be dealt with in the terms to which his determinism necessarily reduces it, namely, as a natural event like any other, no more reasonable and right than the idle flapping of a damp bed-sheet hanging out on a line on a windy day. Nor will it do to reject the thesis of determinism by turning back to the sort of move made by Epicurus of old, and more recently by Eddington, in supposing that a man will be responsible for what he does only if his doing is an event for which no cause of any sort might be cited, like the totally unpredictable Epicurean swerve of a falling atom or the in principle indeterminate position of an electron given its velocity at any given moment. That would be to render our actions, not responsible, but wholly capricious. It would be, in effect, to deny that the agent had anything to do with their occurrence, to rob the action of just that connection with the character of the agent which it does have in the deliberate *and* predictable actions of responsible men, and thus to reduce him to being a hapless spectator of the events of nature, in and beyond the limits of his own body, since all alike are events that are none of his doing.

Here, clearly, we need to reconsider the doctrine, not with a view to discovering a knock-down, drag-out argument that refutes it, but to determine what has given rise to it. And surely the trouble is not a mere matter of verbal ambiguity pertaining to some crucial terms like "cause." One could argue that, of course, in some sense of "cause" one can always cite a cause for any event in nature; but that those human events that are called "actions" involve causes in some sense other than those relevant to the production of natural occurrences like the breaking of windowpanes and even the contraction of muscles and the reflex movements of the various parts of the body. And there are indeed interesting and peculiar linguistic features that mark our use of "cause" in connection with human actions. For we speak, not of the causes of actions but of what caused agents or persons to do this or that. And among the sorts of things we cite as causes in the field of human actions—the things that cause persons to act in such-and-such ways—are reasons of peculiar sorts not encountered in the domain of physical events: reasons that are not the reasons an event took place but the reasons an agent has for doing, and which, as reasons that are relevant, good and sufficient, show the action to be right and reasonable, as distinct from the reasons we cite in physics or physiology which merely show how it is that events are brought to pass. For in the field of human actions we are concerned not merely, if at all, with the natural history of their production in the way in which this concerns us in the area of the natural sciences but with their rationale and even with their rationality; for here we are concerned, not with the causes *of* actions (this, surely, is a barbarism), but with what causes a *person* to act, and even with the causes an agent has *for* acting as he does which, if relevant, good and sufficient, show his action to be reasonable and right.

Observations of these sorts, sound indeed as they may be, do not however disclose the sources of our fatal determinism. A truly important and disturbing philosophical error, like the one with which we are here concerned and which gives those who commit it the sense that now they see things clearly enough to see through their surface look, never arises merely because of inattention to verbal ambiguities or grammatical constructions, but to troubles of a far more serious nature. For it is not that we make our philosophical mistakes because of inattention to these linguistic matters, but the other way around: we ignore and neglect the variety of linguistic idioms precisely because of the important philosophical mistake that already has been made. Once that has occurred, any commentary on the variety of linguistic forms, on the fact that in our present example "cause" is used in a wide variety of ways, must strike those who have succumbed to the mistake as a superficial consideration that does not touch upon the important insights they claim to possess. At best, therefore, attention to these linguistic forms can only prepare the ground for the further and far more important inquiry that needs to be undertaken. And this is shown by the manner in which our committed determinist will respond to the linguistic matters to which I have alluded: these, he will say, serve only to conceal from our view the truly causally effective determinants of human conduct. Of course, he will grant, we speak of causes relevant to actions in the sense in which these are the putative causes an agent has for doing what he does—causes that are the reasons *he* offers in his explanations and in his so-called self-justification—but all of these matters are mere rationalizations, matters of idle verbal show, by means of which we conceal from ourselves and each other the genuinely operative conditions of human conduct and which as operatives doom everything a so-called agent does to the senselessness of inevitable happening. The fact that a committed determinist of the thoroughgoing and extreme sort here imagined will dismiss these considerations (like the feelings all of us have that normally at least we could have done other than what in any given instance we have done) as matters of mere surface appearance, shows that the troubles lie elsewhere than in the failure to see that "cause" is a many-faceted item of our common discourse.

What has gone wrong is, rather, the insinuation of a conception of nature that is both plausible and pernicious. The conception to which I am referring is of course that of a realm of physical events associated, in the case of human beings at least, with mental occurrences—ideas, desires, emotions, sensations, etc.—which somehow are connected with each other and the physical events in the body in some sort of psycho-physical mechanism.

The view is so much a part of our intellectual folklore that it seems rash to question it. And it is surely plausible. It is not only the legacy of the past, the intellectual construction of philosopher-scientists of the seventeenth century, it is also suggested almost irresistibly by every advance in the biological sciences. That what we think and feel and want and enjoy— and so with all of the various functions of intelligence—are most intimately connected with the relevant conditions within the body, is amply confirmed by every advance in the life sciences. And that an action executed through some bodily change —the movement of limbs, vocal chords, or whatever—is indeed a change in some relevant state of this bodily mechanism, seems to be too obvious for words. If we look closely at what happens when we observe some action being performed, e.g., the waving of one's arm in greeting a friend arriving at the airport, what surely occurs is that a certain part of the body, the arm, is in motion. This is the reality of the public performance, the thing that occurs *in rerum natura,* of which all of us are equally competent witnesses. And if we are to ascribe import to this public event, to be able to say not merely that it is an arm that is in motion but that it is an arm being moved in warm response to a friend, how else can one do this except by reference to the related or connected mental events—the sight of one's friend, the warm feeling this sight produces, and the response—the movement of the arm—that ensues? For these events are occurrences which take place at a given time and place. They have their properties and they stand in relations to each other and to the bodily events with which they are connected. When they occur we take note of them by means of an inner sense. And although they have characteristics which are peculiar to them as this or that kind of mental event, they are very broadly of the same very general sort of thing as physical events, differing from the latter in their shadowy and peculiarly private status within the theatre of the mind. In any case, they are events which function as causes or effects in some sort of mechanism of the mind, which at crucial points interacts with events in the body. When these mental events produce bodily movements in the way in which the sight of a friend and the warm feeling produces the motion of the arm, then we speak of the bodily movement in the way in which we do as the action of waving one's arm in friendly greeting. To perform the action is, strictly speaking, to make the relevant bodily movement happen in causal consequence of the interior mental event. And, strictly speaking, we do not observe the action, but only the bodily movement that takes place. "Seeing the action" is only a misleading, a somewhat inaccurate way of describing the facts: what we see is the bodily movement and we infer that it has occurred because of, i.e., as the effect of, the relevant mental events. We thus have a metaphysics in which nature is neatly divided into the mental and the physical, and where actions, which as public events are physical in their nature, are distinguished from other physical occurrences, not because of the features which they have as such observable occurrences, but only extrinsically because of their relations to the mental events that are their causes or their effects.

That such a metaphysics as I have here outlined has important revisionary consequences for our most deep-seated and widespread convictions is clear enough. Given these categories of the physical and the mental, it is not surprising that those who cheerfully embrace them as exhaustive and complete must deal as they do even with the simplest of human actions, e.g., that of raising one's arm. For this, being different from the bodily movement of the arm rising in the air, must now be viewed as a hybrid concoction, a bodily or physical movement to which a dash of mental bitters has been added.

But, secondly, the ingredients cannot possibly be mixed, since only one of these, the bodily movement, is observable, and the other, the mental event, is concealed. It follows that on this view no one ever saw anyone else ever do anything at all. All that one can see is some physical or bodily movement. Strictly speaking, no one has ever witnessed a signature, a theft, a robbery, or a killing; and the procedures adopted by the courts, in order to insure that witnesses confine their remarks to what they actually see, are necessarily wide of the mark when they address themselves to human actions. In respect of these, we must depart from what we actually see and engage in inferences or conjectures about the occurrence of mental events which, inescapably, are cut off from our view.

Third, an action, insofar as it is something observable, is physical or bodily in its nature, indistinguishable from the reflex movements of the body. As such, clearly, it cannot be right or wrong, any more than it can have the properties commonly ascribed to actions. For it is not the thing that we observe that is the morally right action of an agent: as something observed it is in its nature physical or bodily and hence neither an action nor anything that *could* be described as right or wrong. It is as if, looking at the moves of chess players, we suddenly saw them simply as movements of curiously shaped material objects on a checkered surface: where in such a scene do the adjectives that describe chess moves as clever, right, ingenious, etc. have any application? So what we mistakenly call the action, i.e., the thing we observe, namely, the bodily movement, being physical, cannot be right or wrong. And moral philosophers on this ground have argued that what makes an action right is something having to do only with the character of its consequences; but of course this view is "derived" from a doctrine according to which the events that are normally termed "right" or "wrong" are not really actions at all. If there is anything that is strictly speaking an action, it must be relegated to some interior performance within the mind.

Fourth, there are those who are led by the kind of conceptual framework described to reject as intellectually indefensible the conception of responsibility inherent in the traditional criminal law. Instead, they offer us the panacea of the causal explanation and manipulation of the behavior of individuals, who have been "victimized" by the social conditions in which they have been reared, in order to achieve their socially desirable adjustment and reform. Now this may be testimony to their humanitarian purpose, but hardly to their logical acumen. It is nothing less than babel; it is speaking out of two sides of one's mouth at the same time, each side addressing the other in language it could not possibly understand. For if the conceptual model is taken seriously, there is no room for agency of any sort, since what happens, happens as it does, in accordance with discoverable causal laws relating to mental and bodily events but not in any way to persons as agents. And if so, there is not even the agency of the so-called behavioral scientist, not even the manipulation about which the would-be scientist speaks with such high-minded zeal for the good of those whose plight in courts touch his sentiments. Presumably *he* is to act with responsibility in his manipulations on the basis of reasons which, if good and sound, deprive him of any agency in the matter and any moral responsibility.

Fifth, if the witnessable event is a bodily movement, what are its necessary and sufficient causal conditions? A desire, purpose, or anything else mental? Surely not. For the necessary and sufficient condition of the movement of one's arm is a contraction of the muscle. The causal explanation of the latter lies in the transmission of a nerve impulse to the muscle tissues.

And so on it goes. There is no room for the causal agency of mental events in the explanation of the bodily movements. Or, if we are to speak of desires, hopes, expectations, etc. as causes, these must now be reinterpreted or redefined as events within the body. And if so, not only does this do violence to every ordinary view of the matter, it also entails a drastic revision of the very metaphysics with which we began: we no longer have the physical *and* the mental, but only the physical.

But supposing, finally, we do acknowledge that desires, for example, as mental events are causes that spark bodily movements into being, even this much involves a radical revision, this time in the concept of a desire. For what *is* the event that is the desire? Is it not essential to the very concept of a desire that a desire be a desire *for* something? But then how is that feature of intentionality to be secured? By supposing that the event that *is* the desire is somehow dissipated by the agent's obtaining the thing desired? Surely not. And is the connection beween wanting and doing causal and hence contingent, not conceptual? Surely to think of a desire as an event whose features as the features of the desire can be read off by examining it all by itself, cut off as it were from all that connects it with the complexity of thoughts and actions of the agent— surely this is to construe a desire as a shadowy imitation of a physical event. It is, indeed, to think of it as something vaguely like an internal itch or twitch and, in so doing, to distort our view and to blind us to the complex texture of the life of the mind and of the person in which desires, *qua* desires, play their familiar roles. In the same way, any and all of the other incidents of our lives in which decisions, hopes, expectations, choices, emotions, etc., play their roles, must appear strangely distorted if, like desires, they are to be construed as events operating in some sort of mental mechanism.

In these comments, I have been doing much more than citing objections to the metaphysical preconception that prompts our radical determinism. Nor have I been merely exhibiting the ways in which this doctrine obliges us to revise or abandon this or that cherished belief. What I have wanted to emphasize is that this overly simplified conception of nature neatly divided into two bundles, one marked "physical," the other "mental"— each containing events that operate in some sort of causal mechanism—forces us to revise in one area after another the whole character of our thinking, our very sense of what happens in the area of human conduct. For the revisionary demands placed upon our thinking by our philosophical preconceptions are insatiable. It is as if suddenly we were to find ourselves in a situation even stranger than any imagined by Kafka, in which none of the concepts we employ in rendering intelligible and manageable the familiar incidents of our lives have any place at all.

How then are we to regain our sense of fact? And how are we to resist the conceptual model from which action, agency, responsibility, and all that is intelligible and familiar in our practical experience must be banished? Of course we need to take seriously the conception of a person and the conception of agency logically essential to it. Of course we must view the self not as a hidden or invisible chamber that provides a residence for Humean contents of consciousness or as a mysterious entity hovering in some transcendent region and connected in problematic ways to a body it inhabits in some sense altogether mysterious and unknown to us. But just how are these tasks to be accomplished? It is to these matters, albeit briefly, that I wish to address myself in my concluding remarks.

Our questions are not unrelated. Indeed, they invite the further query "Whence the fascination of the philosophical preconception?" It is not enough to note its pernicious consequences—it remains, despite the troubles to which it impels us, an inviting conceptual model. Part of the reason may lie in our desire to apply to matters of human fact the categories of explanation which, conspicuously in the natural sciences, have enjoyed signal success. This was Hume's motive in his famous *Treatise*, to do for the sciences of man what Newton had done for the physical sciences. Indeed, his association of ideas is clearly the mental analogue of the force of gravitation that explains both the fall of bodies and the motion of the planets. And modern-day psychologists, moved by this dream of how things must surely be, have been led to a metaphysics of human nature in which the a priori demand for causal explanations of the required sort has operated as a bed of Procrustes to which our human facts must forcibly be fitted even at their complete expense.

But this is not the whole truth of the matter. For, in a way, what operates to render plausible the conceptual model we wish to employ in matters of human fact and thus to becloud, distort and conceal what is all too familiar to any of us is the fact that we look at things from too close to. We concentrate our gaze upon the things at the very focus of our attention; and ignore the whole context of our lives in which these events enjoy their status as actions and passions, desires, decisions, and so on with the whole gamut of the incidents of the lives of intelligent beings like ourselves.

Thus we look closely at the action of a person raising an arm; and, ignoring this incident in the life of an agent, quite naturally see only a bodily movement. It is as if we could understand and see more clearly what a person was doing when he was writing a check if we ignored all of the circumstances surrounding this transaction between persons and confined our attention to the details of a cylindrical object (we call it "a pen") leaving a deposit of ink, of a curious design, upon a rectangular piece of paper we call "a check." As if, too, we could really know better and see more clearly what a person was doing if, watching someone play chess and move a king from this position to that, we concentrated our gaze upon the details of the movement of an object of a certain shape from one place to another on a checkered board. To do this is to lapse into the "seeing" of a child that is blind to the social transaction that is the writing of a bank check, and blind to what is going on in a game of chess. The truth is that we do not see if in our seeing we are oblivious to all that surrounds and imparts to what is seen the status it has in the lives and experiences of those who only thereby are able to see well enough what is going on.

Our trouble is that in our doings, of whatever sorts these may be, we must focus our gaze. We cannot, in the course of our numerous and varied affairs, attend to all that is relevant to the things at the center of our attention. As long as we are agents familiar with the events that confront us, this is of no matter; we have learned through training and instruction to go about our business and we know our way about without too much difficulty in many or most of the situations in which we are placed. It is, however, when as philosophers we try to understand the things we see from too close to, i.e., when we ignore the practical setting in which this seeing is achieved, that we go wrong; that we suddenly feel, as it were, liberated by the apparent discovery that an action is *really* the movement of a limb. For now the focus remains clear and sharp but this time it is cut off from the background circumstances of a person trained to respond and to see. And what we as philosophers are called upon to do is to try to understand by looking at and thinking about, yet, since we are reflecting, not resorting to, our own status as beings trained to respond to and deal with the things upon which we focus our attention. It is as if the seeing and thinking were both to displace and be about, the practical lives within which alone, as lives that are lived and not merely thought about, we are able to see clearly and to think correctly.

It is this that is involved in taking the concepts of person and agency seriously: it is regarding the activities in which persons have learned to engage with the things about them and with each other as the rock-bottom context within which whatever undersanding we have is possible of what persons are, see and do. This, in Wittgenstein's terminology, is the language-game of action, agent and all of the related concepts that apply to matters of human fact. To gain a perspicuous view of this whole context within which alone they have any application is to get a fuller and a better sense of what the facts are to which we as philosophers address ourselves.

For this purpose—in order to achieve such a view of the facts that concern us, to see them in all of their variegated texture and detail—a variety of devices can be employed. Wittgenstein himself found it useful to invent severely truncated language-games, that is, imaginable systems of discourse connected with practical activities of various kinds, and to discuss highly artificial situations like games in our familiar sense— persons playing chess or whatever—in order to bring out, by means of similarities and differences, various features of our own use of crucial terms, features which we are likely to ignore because normally they lie outside the focus of our attention. Such devices are eminently useful because they present us with languages the whole content of which can be kept clearly in view, precisely because they are truncated and artificial. But these are by no means the only methods that philosophers can and do employ in order to reveal something of the complexity of our familiar concepts. They may and do employ argument, they often comment on linguistic idioms and they may even employ jokes, not frivolously, but with serious intent, in order to bring into sharp relief some important feature of some concept and of the facts to which it applies which only too easily we are apt to ignore just as soon as we begin our reflections.

I realize that in this paper I have not solved the grand problem of the freedom of the will, nor have I demonstrated the truth of the conviction, questioned by many moral philosophers, that the rightness of an action need not be a matter pertaining solely to its consequences. But the successful treatment of a philosophical problem is not like that of a problem in mathematics, by means of a proof all competent mathematicians must understand and accept. And what alone will resolve the grand problem of the freedom of the will, what alone will show whether or not, and how if at all, the rightness of an action need not wait upon its consequences, is success achieved in gaining just that perspicuous view of the facts which is achieved by showing the role of the relevant concepts in the language-game, in the practical circumstances in which alone they have any application. To do this is difficult, it is to see firmly and clearly, despite all temptation to ease our labors and depart from our difficult station, the role of crucial terms like action, decision, desire, reasons, etc.—a whole range of psychological and practical terms—in discourse employed by agents such as you and I who, as Locke once put it, are concerned and accountable. For the concepts we employ are connected with the interests we have; and we are interested, not merely in offering causal explanations of bodily movements, but in these occurrences as the actions of agents in their dealings with one another. Just as it is one thing to consider the physics of the movements of chess pieces on the board—How much force needs to be employed to move this piece from here to there?—so it is another to consider the geometrical design traced by the movements, their aesthetic qualities, and the chess moves executed through such occurrences. Only a being trained and competent to play chess—this is the practical context within which the crucial terms we employ play their role—can *see* the movement of an object on the board as this or that move in the game, or recognize it as clever or foolish, right or wrong, as this or that tactical or strategic move. Only such a being can engage in the discourse in which moves are challenged for their propriety or wisdom, and reasons, excuses, and apologies are offered as indeed they are during and after the course of play. To insist that only the language of a causal explanation of what happens is relevant and pertinent to what takes place during the course of play, where the causes are the necessary and sufficient conditions of the physical movements of the material objects on the checkered surface, may strike some as hardheaded and tough-minded, but for those of us who are sensible of what is relevant and important, it may be learned and sophisticated, but it is nonetheless folly. Similarly, to insist that we employ only that language in which causal explanations can be given of the bodily movements that take place when a person does anything, is indeed to make a mystery of agency, responsibility, and rationality and all that is relevant and pertinent to our practical lives. And to conclude that no one, not even "the poor victim of his society" who brutally orders the execution of countless Jews, is really responsible for what he does, is intellectually incoherent and morally disastrous. For to see what happens as occurrences to be dealt with in these terms is not to see anything that anyone does at all and hence neither to invite nor justify any absolution of responsibility. Agency and responsibility simply have no place at all in events understood in such categorically impoverished terms. The application of these practical concepts lies elsewhere, in the lives of social beings of the sort that you and I are, beings who are morally concerned and accountable. To elucidate these concepts, in their complex connections with those other practical concepts involved in the whole body of the discourse we apply to ourselves and to others, is to exhibit the ways in which these concepts apply to events in the lives that are lived by such beings. And inescapably, this is to grasp, with increased perspicuity and a heightened sense of its complex and multivaried texture, the human facts that interest us, the way things really are with us in the daily living of our lives.

INDEX

Alexander, Henry, 6
American College Dictionary, 188
Analysis of Mind, The, 129, 134
Aristotle, 65, 81 n.
Austin, J. L., 32, 49, 81 n., 89–91,
    104, 106 n., 178 n., 193, 202 n.
Ayer, A. J., 10, 14, 29, 31 n., 54,
    70–74, 81 n., 129, 130, 139, 149,
    157 n.

Baier, Kurt, 136, 137, 155 n.
Berkeley, Bishop G., 20, 53 n.
Brown, D. G., 83 n.

Cartwright, Richard, 186, 187, 191,
    193, 194, 202 n., 203 n.
Chisholm, R., 53 n., 67, 73, 81 n.,
    82 n.
Church, A., 62
Cohen, L. J., 62, 65, 66, 80 n., 81 n.
Concept of a Person, The, 139
Cook, J., 156 n.
Crawshay-Williams, 177 n.

Danto, A., 4, 5
Descartes, 39, 40, 47, 119

Eddington, A., 236

Epicurus, 236

Forrest, T., 5, 83 n.
*Foundations of Empirical Knowl-
    edge, The*, 129

Geddes, L., 203 n.

Hemingway, E., 120
Hintikka, J., 10, 29, 31 n., 37–39, 42,
    50, 51, 53 n., 54, 66, 67, 72–76, 79,
    80, 81 n.
Hume, D., 89, 244
Hungerland, I., 5

Individuals, 139

Kafka, F., 244
Kant, I., 20
Kennedy, J. F., 69
Kenny, A., 81 n.
Khrushchev, 69
Kirkby, R., 203 n.
Klein, F., 44
*Knowledge and Belief: An Intro-
    duction to the Logic of Two
    Notions*, 10

251

Language, Truth and Logic, 129
Lemmon, E. J., 4, 5, 80 n., 82 n.
Locke, D., 131, 132, 134, 248

Malcolm, N., 5, 42–48, 53 n., 90
Mates, B., 197–199, 203 n.
Melden, A. I., 6, 7
Moore, G. E., 178

Nowell-Smith, P., 178 n.

Pears, D., 6, 7
Philosophical Essays, 139
Philosophical Investigations, 138, 193
Plato, 8, 10, 67, 79
Prichard, H. A., 34–43, 47–51, 52 n., 53 n.
Problem of Knowledge, The, 10, 14, 139
Pythagoras, 61, 62

Quine, W. V., 76

Reid, T., 155 n., 177 n.
Rowan, R. J., 83 n.
Russell, B., 129, 134, 202 n.
Ryle, G., 58, 65

Rynin, D., 4, 5

Sachs, D., 155 n.
Schodenhauer, 38, 51
Socrates, 27
Sorensen, T., 69
Spinoza, 236
Stace, W. T., 130, 131
Strawson, P. F., 95, 100, 101, 106 n., 128 n., 139, 143
Stroll, A., 6

Taylor, R., 48, 53 n.
Theatetus, 10, 43
Tractatus Logico-Philosophicus, 150
Treatise of Human Nature, 244

Urmson, J. O., 73

Webster's Seventh New Collegiate Dictionary, 189
Wilbur, A., 155 n.
Wisdom, J., 196
Wittgenstein, L., 104–106, 134, 138, 143, 146, 147, 155 n., 156 n., 158 n., 192, 193, 202 n., 203 n., 246, 247
Woozley, A. D., 67, 81 n.
Wright, H. von, 76, 82 n.